BLUEPRINTS

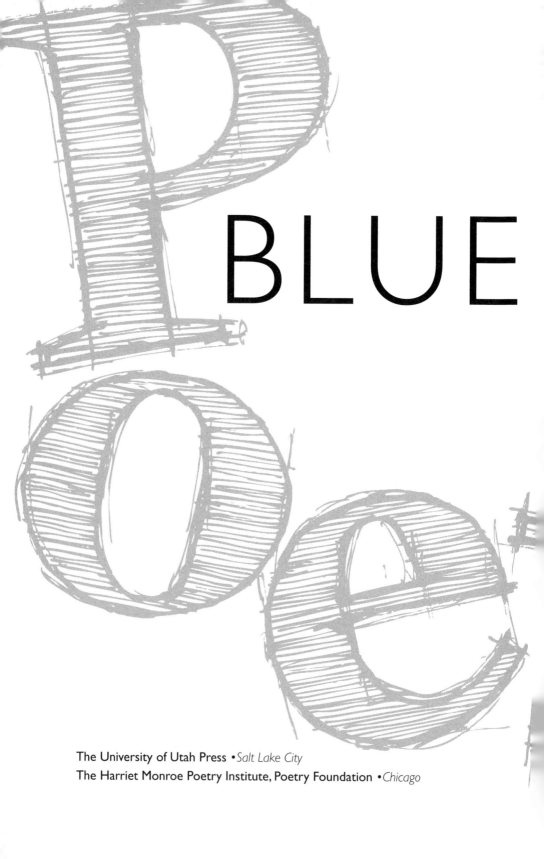

BLUE

P
o
e

The University of Utah Press •*Salt Lake City*
The Harriet Monroe Poetry Institute, Poetry Foundation •*Chicago*

PRINTS

Bringing Poetry into Communities

Edited by KATHARINE COLES

The Defiance House Man colophon is a registered
trademark of the University of Utah Press. It is based
upon a four-foot-tall, Ancient Puebloan pictograph
(late PIII) near Glen Canyon, Utah.

15 14 13 12 11   1 2 3 4 5

LIBRARY OF CONGRESS CATALOGING-IN-PUBLICATION DATA
Blueprints : bringing poetry to communities / edited by
   Katharine Coles.
      p. cm.
   Includes bibliographical references.
   ISBN 978-1-60781-147-3 (pbk. : alk. paper)
   1. Poetry—Programmed instruction. 2. Poetry—Social
aspects. 3. Poetry—tudy and teaching. I. Coles, Katharine.
   PN1031.B57 2011
    808.1—dc22   2011002347

CONTENTS

ACKNOWLEDGMENTS

The Harriet Monroe Poetry Institute would like to extend its deepest gratitude to all of the essayists and toolkit members who participated in the Poetry in Communities project, as well as the following people to who the project owes its gratitude: Glenda Cotter and her colleagues at the University of Utah Press, Rachel Berchten, Douglas B. Borwick, Stephanie Hlywak, Pamela Michael, Lily Sutton, Kathleen White, and Lily Whitsitt.

INTRODUCTION

Blueprints

Katharine Coles

When I became the inaugural director of the Harriet Monroe Poetry Institute in 2009, I was handed a pile of some two hundred questionnaires. These had been generously filled out and returned by poets, teachers, scholars, readers, and others in response to the Poetry Foundation's efforts to assess the needs of the poetry community in preparation for getting the Institute up and running. The responses came from around the country and from communities large and small, affluent and struggling.

Being a poet and therefore perhaps naturally suspicious of efforts to enumerate anything about or around the art, I approached these questionnaires at first with some hesitation. But I was struck both by the openheartedness, passion, and hope reflected in the responses and by the way certain important themes kept emerging in them. People who are already passionate about poetry—and our numbers are large and growing—feel powerfully that poetry fulfills an essential human need, that it provides a source of richness and pleasure that nobody should be without, and, therefore, that poetry should be readily and widely available to everyone.

Which, as many of our respondents rightly point out, it is not. Certainly, as they recognize, there are successful poetry programs being run across the country and around the world by committed people at every level, from the extremely local to the national to the international. Many are to some extent happy with the liveliness of their own poetry communities. But they also see—and are pained to acknowledge—that they are, almost by definition, among the fortunate few. Many of them are poets, teachers, or scholars living in academic communities; all are in some way in touch with the Poetry Foundation and its programs and are aware of and making use of other excellent programs as well, both in and beyond their own communities. They are also acutely sensitive to the fact that what programs they have access to are often precarious, depending on the commitment sometimes of a single dedicated person and funders who themselves are endangered by hard economic realities.

As our respondents observe, these excellent programs tend to exist in pockets; there are still far too many gaps in what we might, with tongues in cheeks, call poetry-related services. If they may seem difficult to fill for ordinary American poetry lovers who perceive that something vital is missing from their neighborhoods, it shouldn't surprise us that these gaps feel impossible to overcome in the far corners of the Navajo Nation or for aid workers in Somalian refugee camps. In spite of the urgency of the need many of us perceive, and in spite of the many very fine programs out there, people tend to feel that it is almost overwhelmingly difficult to get good programs up and running, especially in communities that are geographically or economically isolated or otherwise disadvantaged. People know that resources and expertise exist, but they are not sure how to gain access to them. They perceive both an absence of effective networking among poetry programmers and a lack of practical support. They understand that there is knowledge out there to share, but they do not think they have the ability to access or leverage knowledge and resources within and across communities and programs.

This is the case even though every generation of poets and poetry lovers who see gaps in poetry offerings in their communities faces essentially the same set of questions, the first being simply "How and where do I start?" Thus, these programmers also face the persistent obligation to reinvent wheels that have been invented over and over again elsewhere—whether "elsewhere" is up the block or on the other side of the country.

Our question, then, was "How can we help?" This book, we hope, provides one answer. Here, a dozen people—mostly poets themselves, all intimately involved with the arts—who have done important work bringing poetry into communities of different sizes and kinds, offer narratives and insights about their experiences. Their mandate was to identify important moments—of initiation, of crisis, of growth—in the development of their projects or organizations, then tell us how they met those moments. In particular, we asked them to tell us how their decisions arose out of the values that drove them to create and maintain their programs in the first place.

These essays make up the heart of the book and are meant to provide both inspiration and guidance. Each one connects the hard work of poetry programming with the moments of passion, revelation, and inspiration that make the work of programming worthwhile. And each has something to say about why and how poetry becomes important to communities of various kinds by connecting community members with one another, with their places, and with themselves.

The second half of the book, A Toolkit for Poetry Programmers, provides systematic, hands-on, practical advice and resources for those working to found new programs or to sustain or transform existing programs. Don't know how to become a nonprofit? The Toolkit provides websites and other resources that will help you. Don't know what a board is or how to get one going? Again, both advice and resources are here. Forgotten why you ever wanted to do this often thankless work in the first place? The Toolkit provides advice for remaining connected to your own values and inspiration, for finding your way back to those moments and experiences that first convinced you that the power of poetry exists not only for the solitary reader under the lamp but for those who come together to read it, hear it, recite it, study and write it, and discuss it together, in community.

I come to this project with my own sense of what a community, and therefore individuals, might be missing when poetry is absent. When I was an undergraduate, studying first to be an actor and a poet and then finally just to be a poet, I would speak with my parents every Sunday. And every Sunday for a long time, my mother said to me, "You know, it's not too late to be an engineer." I won't go into the reasons why for a long time—maybe all my life—it had been too late for that. She must have figured this out. When I asked her why she'd stopped suggesting a change in direction, she said, "Your father and I realized you can make a living waiting tables if you need to." (This was a compliment: waiting tables had long been acknowledged in my family as difficult, skilled work requiring more fortitude than most of us have, certainly more than I have in order to do it for a lifetime.) "And," she went on, "we've come to realize that there are still living poets."

My parents, both of them scientists, are neither naïve nor uncultured. They took me, with their season tickets, to the theater, the ballet, the opera, the symphony, even to modern dance concerts once Salt Lake City finally had a company, beginning in 1966. And I came to my love of language and reading through my family. When she wasn't running rivers or climbing high peaks, my mother usually had her nose buried in a book, and not always differential equations, though she read those for pleasure too. Her own mother had wanted to be a poet and exposed her children to the poets of her day, as my mother exposed us to all kinds of literature, permitting us to read any book in the house at any age we stumbled upon it. My parents still have poems I wrote as young as seven, when I announced my ambition to become a poet and a fireman, there being in 1966 no "firefighters"—yet.

And no living poets, as far as any of us knew. This was a different era, both from my grandmother's time and from our own. Robert Frost died in 1963, when I was three years old. No poet read at Johnson's inauguration or at Nixon's, Ford's, or Carter's, as Frost had at Kennedy's. Though my parents were academics, the explosion of poetry in the academy had yet to begin—it would be beginning, luckily for me, as I was trying to decide where to go to college—and they didn't know poets personally. I don't believe that among the scientists (or, for that matter, the English professors) they socialized with, contemporary poetry was much talked about or even read, and there weren't many (maybe not any) public readings in Salt Lake City. Obviously, if there were living poets at all, they were hardly at the center of American cultural life, at least not in the country's wide middle, Iowa City and maybe Chicago excepted. So, through junior high and much of high school, I read Dickinson, Shakespeare, Browning (both of them), Rossetti, Millay. Frost, of course. For two years, I wrote a sonnet every day, unable to imagine any other training that might prepare me for the work I wanted to do.

Then I won a literary award at my high school, and the teacher—blessings upon you, Helen Mulder—chose as the prize James Tate's newly reprinted first book, *The Lost Pilot*. A decade after it first won the Yale Younger Poets Prize, it felt brand-new to me, felt as if it spoke not *to* so much as *through* me. The poem "Flight," especially, reenacted whimsically, in poetry's one-fell-swoopedness, my own ache for escape and may have given me, a serious child, a first inkling that my desires might best be treated lightly. At the end of the poem's journey, the speaker wakes his companion, sleeping beside him in the car, to say, "Already we are in Idaho." James Tate knew nothing of me, of course, but Idaho was where my high school sweetheart lived, and "Flight" carried me in my imagination over familiar roads transformed, made new and promising. From the moment I read it, I had to stop telling people I was going to be America's only living poet, but this trade-off was well worthwhile.

Still, Tate was, as far as I knew, the only other one, and I consumed him privately, only on the page. I didn't encounter a poet in the flesh until I was in college in Seattle, where William Matthews arrived the year after I did, hired to revivify the creative writing community Theodore Roethke had made legendary in the '40s and '50s (like Frost, he died in 1963) and that Nelson Bentley and David Wagoner had heroically kept on life support. For the first time, I was in the physical presence of poets, first in classrooms and then in various campus auditoriums. I remember those early readings vividly: the sensation of them, of the presence of poetry coming at me through the body of the poet. Like James Tate, my teachers and the people they selected to read to me—as if they were giving me, personally, a hand-chosen gift—voiced not only their own lives but also mine, and in voicing my life, they made it larger, more capacious, more open to imagination and revision. Richard Hugo. Charles Wright. Stephen Dunn. Stanley Plumly. C. K. Williams. Eventually even a few women. Jane Shore, Maxine Kumin. I became the brief intimate and perpetual student of them all. They returned to me some inner voice or inflection I didn't know was there. They made me larger inside.

A few years later, after I moved back to Utah to get my PhD, my parents began to come to poetry readings. The first was my own, for the Salt Lake City Arts Council. I had chosen to read a poem called "Father," which imagines my dad in a much more glamorous life than the one he chose, the one that made me possible. I had to read it. I knew it was my best poem at the time, and I had few enough of them, but it did occur to me to wonder how my mother, who had turned down a job at NASA during the space race to stay in Salt Lake City with her family, was going to experience the poem. Afterward, she said, "You know, I always felt just the same way about him." In that moment when she was, I am sure, seeing me anew, I saw her anew as well.

For my parents, attending that first reading was their way of supporting me and my peculiar decisions—also, I guess, of satisfying their curiosity. But it wasn't long before they were going to readings for the sheer pleasure and wonder of being read to, of being spoken to in the intimate and profound way that is unique to poetry, that helps make visible the liminal territory between an individual inner life and the world outside and so tells us, even across vast time and distance, "in so many words," as Mark Strand says, "what we are going through."[1] This is the gift of poetry, the thing those of us who love it keep coming back for poem after poem, book after book, reading after reading. Many of us are content to read and listen, to let ourselves be spoken to by another and so enlarged. Others, my parents among them, find their own voices called forth by the poems and cannot resist speaking back. They have both gone on to write and publish—my mother poems, my father essays. Though they remain amateurs, so they claim, they have been drawn into that large conversation. They also now volunteer for organizations that help bring poetry to our local community.

However, as all the essayists gathered here discovered at some point, training as a poet can move a person only so far toward a life than includes poetry programming. For one thing, it ties the joy of making strictly to the writing of poetry; it provides few chances for us to learn that there are other kinds of making to which we can apply the same imaginative skills. Perhaps these are lessons we can learn only in the larger world.

While I was working on my PhD at the University of Utah, I supplemented my meager fellowship as a part-timer at the Waking Owl Bookstore, an establishment run by Patrick de Freitas, who, I suspect, embarked on the whole enterprise largely so he could be regularly read aloud to. British, tall and lanky with a little George Washington ponytail, Patrick is one of those rare people all writers love, who reads everything, poetry included, with no ambition to become a writer himself. His store held readings by poets and writers famous and infamous, widely published and just starting out. I remember him, when all the folding chairs were taken by customers, sitting on the floor, his back against a shelf of books, his eyes closed while he listened, a silly little smile (bliss, I think), on his mouth. The store gave me my own first exposure to the work of bringing literature to a community, to the details and arrangements that needed seeing to, from getting books in to getting flyers out to seeing that writers got enough wine, but not too much, before they went on. It was my job to know which poets got so nervous that they routinely threw up before reading, which ones had to eat first and which after. Arts administration, it turns out, can be surprisingly intimate work.

Eventually, I asked Patrick if I could set up a series showcasing the English department's graduate students, and though we students mostly had no books to sell, he not only assented but also attended those readings religiously. In the world of the hand-sold book, small, independent stores create their own communities around the collective love of the word. Suddenly, we fledgling poets and fiction writers had access to an already-established audience of people committed to that love, and to spreading it, who received us with a generosity of spirit I have trouble believing even now.

It was at these readings that I first met G. Barnes, who eventually brought me on as an intern and then a paid assistant in the Utah Arts Council's (UAC) Literature Program (now ably run by Guy Lebeda, official wrangler of the poet laureate of Utah). For almost three years, I traveled the state with him, bringing poetry and prose to large towns and cow towns, to colleges and art galleries and barbecues and primary and secondary schools. Susan Boskoff, now the director of the Nevada Arts Council and a member of this book's Toolkit group, was then directing the council's Performing Arts Tour; she was instrumental in its (to me visionary) move to include poets and writers on the roster along with musicians and other kinds of performers.

What I think I mean to tell you is that once you get started on this kind of work, you don't stop, at least not until it has chewed you up and spit you out, which it hasn't me, not yet (though at times, like all of us, I feel a little gnawed around the edges). After the UAC I became a professor, but all along I have stayed close to the work of bringing poetry to larger audiences, by directing reading series, serving as president of Writers at Work, creating projects as Utah's poet laureate, and now working at the Poetry Foundation. It's work that feels as important and urgent as writing poems. I think I'm like Patrick, in that I want to be read to, to encounter poems in the right conditions for receiving them, a desire that has sometimes required me to create those conditions myself. As Tree Swenson said in one of our Toolkit meetings, "I realized if I didn't do it, nobody would." But I also want to be in the presence of others receiving poetry, to be able to watch Patrick close his eyes and smile at a line.

This is the call to which all of the essayists collected here, as well as the members of the Toolkit group, responded. When they asked the question, "Who will do it?" a single answer presented itself: "I will." Because they all then went on to fashion, further, or make visible programs that are unusually resonant, the Harriet Monroe Poetry Institute asked them to tell their stories, focusing both on practical concerns and on answering the question "Why do this?"—and thus focusing on the values they work to express through their labors. They have been unusually generous and open in their responses, not only about their successes but also about their mistakes and failures, which they frankly examine here. Taken collectively, these essays, and the stories they tell, communicate both why this work matters and something about the people who undertake it—people who, to a one, have had their own powerful encounters with poetry in community and want to create similar opportunities for others.

So:

Elizabeth Alexander, Cave Canem, Brooklyn. Lee Briccetti, Poets House, New York. Sherwin Bitsui, Navajo Nation, Tohono O'odham Nation, and Nizhoni Bridges, Utah and Arizona. Alison Hawthorne Deming, University of Arizona Poetry Center, Tucson. Dana Gioia, Poetry Out Loud, Washington, DC. Robert Hass, River of Words, Berkeley. Bas Kwakman, Poetry International, Rotterdam. Thomas Lux, Poetry@Tech, Atlanta. Christopher Merrill, University of Iowa's International Writing Program, Iowa City and Somalia. Luis Rodriguez, Tia Chucha's Centro Cultural & Bookstore, Los Angeles. Anna Deavere Smith, New York. Patricia Smith, Chicago Slam, Chicago.

As I read about the struggles and experiences of these twelve people—how they sow, what they reap—I could want to be any one of them, could want to be part of their stories, each full of passion and of realization, even of revelation—each brimming with moments that propel their writers into, and sustain them through, the hard work of bringing poetry into their communities. It *is* hard work. It isn't for the timid or poor in spirit—or, indeed, for those who are looking for praise and glory. It involves the sorts of tasks creative people are notoriously irked by: chasing money, chasing space, chasing small, irritating pieces of paper or e-mails, often containing news we don't want to hear about the canceled grant or lease, the scheduled demolition, the poet with the flu who has to back out of an appearance at the last second.

And, of course, this work is not for anyone who is in it for the money. These people are way too smart for that. They do this work because by it they are continually re-impassioned and renewed by what they make. In this, as Tom Lux points out, making an organization that brings poetry to a community is in its values and satisfactions not so different from making a poem. Each is a space a stranger is invited to enter, shaped for that stranger's pleasure and enlargement. Each makes of that stranger a fellow traveler and brings him or her into community. Each requires a powerful force of imagination applied not to individual needs and desires but to collective ones.

Such making is the pure work of the heart.

The people who do it are among the toughest and most determined I know. As these essays show again and again, they are also among the most richly rewarded. When I think of the world as it looked to a Utah child in the late '60s and early '70s, a child who, with her parents, literally believed she was going to be the only living poet, and compare that world to the one we now inhabit, in which poets visit school classrooms, libraries, Indian reservations, barrio community centers, refugee camps, and local bars, and in which teenagers routinely and vigorously participate in workshops and slams and recitation contests, I understand that for young people who want to be in the presence of poetry, whether as writers or as readers and listeners, the world is transformed for the better. This new world, in which poetry has a vigorous presence, is the product of the hard work of people who said once and then over and over again, "I will." The world is lively, but it, and its work, are far from finished.

NOTE

1. Mark Strand and David Lehman, eds., *Best American Poetry 1991* (New York: Scribner, 1991).

ALIVE IN THE WOR(L)D

Why We Do What We Do

THE FLYWHEEL

On the Relationship between Poetry and Its Audience—
Poetry International

Bas Kwakman
Translated by Michele Hutchison

I.

It was the sound of a poem that made me fall in love with poetry once and for all. I wasn't in my living room, I wasn't next to a reading lamp, nor did I have a book on my lap. It wasn't even the poet himself reading out his poem, but rather his translator, standing at a lectern on stage in a small auditorium.

In 1992, I was working for a cultural organization in Rotterdam. As I prepared for a poetry evening, I placed the lectern next to the mike, focused the light, and put a carafe of water on a small table. Next, I directed the audience inside, and, when the first reader came on, I made sure that he was properly lit, that the door was closed and the audience quietly seated, and that his voice was audible from the beginning.

The poem went as follows:

Alone this summer morning on the deserted wharf,
I look towards the bar, I look toward the Indefinite,
I look and I am glad to see
The tiny black figure of an incoming steamer.

And continued

I look at the far-off steamer with great independence of mind,
And in me a flywheel slowly starts spinning.
(Translated by Richard Zenith)

Reaching this strophe, I completely forgot about the lights, the chairs, the audience. I understood little of what I was hearing but felt how deep inside me my own flywheel was set in motion, first slowly and creaking with unfamiliarity, but quite soon proudly revolving along with the waves, currents, and tempests of "Maritime Ode," by Portuguese poet Fernando Pessoa. From the first revolution onward, I was convinced that it would never stop. I was sold.

Eleven years later, I became the director of a festival that was famous around the world, because for years it had been providing a stage for the greatest voices in poetry: the Poetry International Festival in Rotterdam.

Each year, around thirty poets from all four corners of the globe are invited for a weeklong event to read from their own poetry and listen to that of others. For forty years, a broad and varied audience has attended the festival in search of emotion, enlightenment, experience, meaning, and mystification. For forty years, Rotterdam has been the crossroads of international poetry, a platform on which cultures, languages, voices, and thoughts meet.

2.

An artist invites a famous poet to come and see a work inspired by one of the latter's poems. "See," he says, "your poem is about this and that, and so I've represented it like this." "My poem isn't about that at all," the poet says, to which the artist exclaims indignantly, "Keep your hands off my poem!"

Modern poetry has a difficult relationship with the general public. Poetry seems to have an image problem. It has been a long time since poetry was a way of spreading news to the next tribe or displaying the technical and linguistic ingenuity of the versifier. Over the centuries, it has tended to distance itself from the prevailing religious, political, and/or social issues of the day and seems to accept only itself or language as a theme. The public sees language as a medium of communication, and if language no longer communicates, but confuses or disturbs, it leads to anxiety and irritation.

Nevertheless, poetry won't leave the public alone. T. S. Eliot once said that a good poem communicates before the words are understood. This comment seems to have been unconsciously embraced by the majority; the notion of the "poetic" is frequently used to indicate beautiful things that people don't understand: incomprehensible passages in Andrei Tarkovsky's films, nonlinear texts in James Joyce's prose, the apparently structureless passages in Olivier Messiaen's piano compositions, or Wassily Kandinsky's inexplicable formal experiments.

The general public follows poetry from a distance. Just when the European audience seems to get used to a modern, often difficult, often inaccessible poetry, riddled with ingenious references, metaphors, and library shelves full of interpretations, a new frontline of poets shifts the helm, overturning the audience's role once again. "No metaphor / will enter here" the poets cry.[1] The poem says what it says; things are what they are. They extinguish meaning, and the sensation of language remains. The message to the public is that "the meaning of a poem is no longer inherent to the text but constructed by the reader herself."[2]

A worldwide, linear evolution in poetry doesn't exist. In every country and in every culture, developments take their own independent course. While postmodernism raises its head in Europe, politically engaged poetry prevails in Africa and South America. When a new generation of European poets requires more engagement and political awareness from poetry, Africa's and South America's poetries become more language-focused. Every country, every culture knows a centuries-old poetic tradition that is carried along on waves and washes up on the beach and then back out.

The Poetry International Festival displays all these currents. The festival doesn't subscribe to a particular poetics and is fully autonomous in its choices. It doesn't have any political, social, or ideological obligations. All year round, the festival searches worldwide for autonomous quality in poetry from the different currents and trends and puts it together on stage for an audience. An audience that, just like poetry itself, is carried along on the waves.

We make this search in spite of all of the limitations of operating internationally: the difficult and sometimes downright surreal procedures surrounding arranging for visas, translations, and travel, not to mention difficulties in navigating cultural differences, different (and often passionately held) viewpoints on poetry and the translation of poetry, and the political and social consequences of which poetries and poets we choose to present. We do it because bringing together the world's greatest poets remains a glorious experience, one in which the true nature of poetry is revealed. United within the context of a festival, we find year after year that poetry turns out to be the true world language.

I understand now that I don't
need to understand everything.

Since 2008, the Poetry International Festival has invited the public to come in without buying tickets in advance. Audience members can pay afterward; the amount they pay is based on what they think the experience was worth. A young poetry fan who for years hadn't dared to come to the festival was encouraged to visit by this campaign. "I've always thought it would go over my head," she said on her way in. "I find poetry so difficult, and I'm worried I won't understand it." I saw her again afterward. "The problem was just in my head," she told me. "I've had a wonderful evening. I understand now that I don't need to understand everything."

3.

Fifteen minutes after the start of the evening program, a man left the auditorium. I asked him whether the program was that bad. "Oh, of course not," he said. "I come to the Poetry International Festival every year, and every year, I hope to discover poetry that will last me a whole year. Sometimes I don't, other times only at the end of the festival week. But now, on the first day, the first poet, bull's-eye! I'm going to buy all his books and plunge into them for the coming year. Marvelous. To listen to other poets now would be needlessly confusing. The festival has been more than a success for me. Thanks, and see you next year!"

The Poetry International Festival in Rotterdam lives on the power of spoken poetry. For years, the subtitle of the festival has been "The Voice of the Poet." In the 1970s and 1980s, the word *voice* mainly referred to political voice: the poet was a revolutionary and lent voice to the repressed. At that time, the political message often seemed more important than the quality of the poem.

In the 1990s, politics lost its power as a theme, and a space opened for the autonomous quality of individual poetry. The focus on the poet's voice remained, but it had a different role: a guide to the contents. Far more than a critic's or someone else's interpretation of a poem, a poet's voice is the best guide imaginable to lead a reader or listener into a poem. Not the voice that before or after the performance of a poem elaborately explains the origin and meaning of the poem, but the voice that knows how to balance tension and contemplation, that places commas in places a reader doesn't see them on paper, that draws out the meaning of blank spaces, and that brings to life the dialogues and voices of all the people, objects, events, and thoughts contained in the poem.

The audience experiences the poem directly and in all its completeness; the audience immediately understands why the poet sings, bows, bellows, hisses, whispers, quotes, or acts.

At many international festivals, a poet's performance is followed by a reading of the poem's translation. Generally, the translation is delivered in a rather flat, businesslike way because the translator doesn't want to imitate the way the poet read. With this construction, the audience can indeed fully enjoy the sound of the often unfamiliar language, but any direct association between the sound and the meaning of the word is lost. At Poetry International Festival, we project the translation behind the poet during the reading so that the words and lines appear at the same tempo as the original is spoken. Through this, the audience experiences the poem directly and in all its completeness; the audience immediately understands why the poet sings, bows, bellows, hisses, whispers, quotes, or acts. It experiences the role of every tonal change, of every hesitation, every dynamic that the poet brings to the performance.

Such an experience requires, of course, a poet who is capable of reading his poems well, which certainly isn't the case for all poets. The ideal poetry ambassador is the poet as performer, rising up from the paper and distinguishing herself for the audience within a theatrical context. "Theatre," Federico Garcia Lorca once said, "is poetry standing up."

4.

After one program, I met a couple who had been faithfully attending the Festival for years. A love of poetry had once brought them together and still connected them. For years, they'd shared and worshipped the same poets and poems and gone to all the poetry evenings together. For the first time in their lives, they were having an enormous row: he thought that evening's poetry the best he'd ever heard; she found it dreadful. I walked on, satisfied.

The Netherlands has 17 million inhabitants and around 750 living, serious poets who have each published at least one collection with a renowned publishing house. The average poetry collection in the Netherlands has a print run of between eight hundred and one thousand copies. A large number of these disappear to the publisher, the press, the critics, libraries and archives, colleagues, family members, and friends. Part of what's left disappears under the author's bed, and the rest seek out a path to readers via the bookshops. After around 150 have been sold, the surplus is remaindered.

Every self-respecting city in the Netherlands has a poet in residence, and not long ago, twenty thousand people voted for the new poet laureate.

Is no attention paid to poetry in the Netherlands, then? Nothing could be less the case. There has rarely been so much energy in Poetryland as in recent years. "Poetry" was one of the most searched-for words on the Internet in 2009. The annual Poetry Day reaches tens of thousands of people with hundreds of programs in theaters, libraries, bookshops, and schools. Every self-respecting city in the Netherlands has a poet in residence (*stadsdichter*—"official city poet"), and not long ago, twenty thousand people voted for the new poet laureate. The election dominated the media for weeks. Theaters organize poetry slams; poets perform along with musicians from the best orchestras, dance companies, and theater groups; poets are chosen as sidekicks on the most popular television chat shows.

There may be very few volumes sold, but poetry finds its way to an audience. And that audience? Its members don't want books on their laps. They are looking for an experience.

The essence of an evening at the Poetry International Festival comprises the voice of a poet, the poem, and its translation. For years, people have been coming to Rotterdam to listen to the poets. Still, these specific, concentrated, and intense cultural experiences are becoming rarer. Because the cerebral cortex at the back of the human brain, the area that governs perception, has evolved enormously in the wake of the digital revolution, a compulsion to serve all of the audience's senses has arisen among programmers. Each program maker who brings literature into the contemporary theater must reflect on the form in which he or she does this. By now, the Netherlands is acquainted with every form possible in this area. Literary performance can deliver interesting combinations—combinations with music, theater, dance, digital poetry, debates, interviews, even competitions—that can strengthen, deepen, and even rejuvenate the reception of poetry.

Unfortunately, this new and exhilarating range of possibilities tempts many program makers to pull out all the stops in order to respond to the demand for experiences. And when content loses out to form, as it inevitably does, the balance is lost. Audiences may be subject to a flood of text, image, and sound fragments cast over the reading poet from all directions, or to poets hoisted into theatrical costumes or presented in box outfits standing on soapboxes. And meanwhile, the bar stays open and nibbles are passed around.

People often think that they'll attract a young audience with this kind of circus. This is not only untrue but also an insult to that audience. Recently a young writer, tired of all the bells and whistles in Poetryland, set up the series Nur Literatur[3] in Rotterdam, in which he placed nothing more than the poet and his or her poetry on the stage. The programs are now enjoying a sizeable, young audience.

A good poem by a poet who is capable of bringing his or her work into the limelight contains all the sensations necessary for the requisite public experience. It's a challenge to the program maker just as much as to the audience to remain focused on content.

5.

A poetry teacher asked a student what he was reading. "Nothing," the student answered. "But if you only write poetry and never read it, you'll never develop," the teacher said in astonishment. "No, man," the student responded candidly, "I've only got two hours a week for poetry, and it takes me all that time to write." Despite this, the student had the ambition to become a great poet.

As I previously mentioned, the Netherlands has a population of seventeen million. A million write poetry from time to time. At least half of these aspire to careers in poetry, but only a handful end up in the circuit of poetry workshops and creative writing courses. Thanks to poets such as Lord Byron and Arthur Rimbaud, one of the most persistent fallacies in Europe is that you need to study very, very hard to become a musician, a dancer, or an actor, but you don't to become a poet—you are born one. Poetry, many think, alas cannot be learned.

> Poetry *can* be learned, mainly through reading it, reading it, discussing it, and reading it some more.

Actually, poetry *can* be learned, mainly through reading it, reading it, discussing it, and reading it some more. The earlier the better. It is extremely important to bring children into contact with existing poetry from an early age. The concentration on language that contact with poetry affords them helps them for the rest of their lives. But it's important not to go down on your knees to the children and offer them only poetry on their level. Good guidance, which doesn't explain but raises questions and different suggestions, which doesn't interpret but stimulates independent thought, is the flywheel that sets a young generation on course, as I was set on course when I heard "Maritime Ode."

Among the other audiences for international poets at Poetry International Festival is an audience of twelve-year-olds. The children listen to the poets, and a presenter guides them through the translations, interviews the poets, and translates both his or her comments and the questions and the answers of the poets. The poets don't often look forward to this confrontation because they didn't have children in mind when they were writing. Yet after it's over, I often hear, "That was the most attentive and intelligent audience I've ever had. They understand it better than anyone!"

If for adults poetry only really comes to life when they struggle with a poem or a stanza for days, weeks, or months in their beds, at their work, or at the supermarket checkout, then this is equally true for children and young adults. One critic I know once wrote that poems that lead to complete puzzlement are not interesting.[4] But it's wonderful to sniff around a poem; to turn around the words, the lines, meanings, forms, images, and mystery; to ponder the language; to give it personal interpretations; to reread it; to wait for sudden insights…

"Poetry," a poet once said, "is waiting next to the word."[5]

6.

From 2012 onward, you'll be able to find poems by every important international poet in the original language and in any other desired language. In most cases, you'll also be able to call up sound and/or video recordings of the poet reading the poem.

The above paragraph is part of a dream, which I voiced during the opening of the fortieth Poetry International Festival on June 12, 2009. This dream is close to becoming reality.

In 2003, the first Dutch poet laureate exclaimed that poetry had finally found its ideal partner in the Internet.[6] Since 2000, Poetry International has been providing English translations of the festival online. A large network of editors from more than 50 countries offers at www.poetryinternational.org a thrice-monthly digital magazine full of poetry, translations, essays, and news. The website, which has more than 4,000 visitors a day, includes 850 poets with more than 5,800 poems in their original languages, along with 4,100 English translations. After each new edition of the magazine has been published, the material from the previous issue becomes part of a large digital archive. The base of this archive comprises the sound recordings and translations of each of the 2,000 poets who have read at the festival. For the last ten years, this base has been regularly supplemented with material from the magazines. A gold mine is currently being opened up to a broad, international audience.

Alongside Poetry International, a great many other international organizations are opening up their poetry archives. Lyrikline in Berlin, the Poetry Archives in London, the Poetry Library in Edinburgh, and the Poetry Foundation in Chicago are important examples. The moment all these organizations are prepared to leapfrog the language, technical, and rights hurdles and throw open all the windows and doors of their websites, the wonderful possibility will arise of joining together to make all of this poetry and related content available to a worldwide audience—an audience that that will get to experience the emotion of the opening sounds of Walt Whitman's "Song of Myself" scratched out onto a wax cylinder by Edison himself, that loses itself in the stirring voice of Joseph Brodsky, and that feels proud when its favorite poet still stands up in Spanish, Swahili, or Chinese.

The digitalization of international poetry in word, sound, and image is no danger but a great binding force between poetry and the public. The unique possibility of being able to directly access a poem, its translation, and the poet reading out his or her work guarantees curiosity, enthusiasm, fascination, and further enquiry. A nice adjunct to all the digital activity is the simultaneous growth of the number of visitors to poetry websites and the number of festival visitors. Meanwhile, festivals such as Poetry International and the Scottish StAnza Festival have started live streaming of their events so that audiences from Sydney to Lima can watch along too. Sister festivals have sprung up, like the one held last year in Antwerp, where the local audience watched projections from the Poetry International Festival on a large screen.

My flywheel for poetry was brought into motion by a reading, by a poem that grabbed hold of me before I could process it. It brought me not just a great love of poetry but also an enormous compulsion to share it with others. I became convinced that a poet on stage, a poem on the Internet, or an inspiring teacher can set a broad public's flywheel in motion. I'm also convinced of the unbelievable enrichment this will offer us all.

NOTES

1. Hans Faverey, "Geen metafoor" ("No Metaphor"), *Gedichten* (Amsterdam: De Bezige Bij, 1968).
2. Yves T'Sjoen, *De gouddelver* (Tielt/Amsterdam: Lannoo/Atlas, 2005).

3. The young writer is Ernest van der Kwast; the name means "Only Literature" in German.
4. Piet Gerbrandy, *Een Steeneik op de rotsen* (Meulenhoff: Amsterdam, 2003).
5. Erwin Mortier, *Hollands Dagboek, NRC-Handelsblad*, August 16, 2008.
6. Gerrit Komrij, presentation on the National Library website, March 4, 2003.

•

THE SECOND THROAT

Poetry Slam

Patricia Smith

In August 1999, the tenth anniversary National Poetry Slam was held in Chicago. Depending on whom you talked to, the slam either strode back home sporting a cocky grin and a glittering lopsided crown or she limped in from a back alley, jittery and bruised, avoiding direct eye contact and reluctantly showing her age.

By the time the celebrated and vilified poetry competition reached double digits, everyone in the poetry community and many beyond it had an opinion. The slam was necessary breath, a rousing kick in the rear for an art form that wheezed dust and structure. Or it was a death knell for the genre, a brash and quirky theater complete with scorecards; unruly poetics by common, untenured folk; and "judges" who were actually prized for their lack of qualifications.

But no matter how you felt about her, the ole girl had certainly grown up. And everyone agreed that she couldn't have been born anywhere else.

My hometown is the land of blatant politicking, Vienna hot dogs at five in the morning, and the city as mean but efficient machine. It's Mayor

Daley (Richard, not Richie); nasty, gut-level blues guitar; and the sprawling specter of the housing project Cabrini-Green, the blackened windows of its abandoned units like missing teeth in an already rotted smile. Chicago is cops with their guts spilling over their belts, the riots in '68, midwestern "howdy" and Big Apple envy. It is sly and beauteous and unbridled drumbeat. The slam, ragged and mesmerizing, had the gall to tweak language and rattle convention while serving drinks on the side. It was the Windy's, in and through.

The final of the four-day National Slam was held in the 3,600-seat Chicago Theater, that gaudy State Street showplace with the megawatt marquee grin—the letters C-H-I-C-A-G-O lined up vertically and twinkling relentlessly, reminding locals that it was still among the city's dwindling downtown entertainment options and providing tourists with the perfect wish-you-were-here backdrop for their cheery digital pix. Despite its inner opulence, the theater sat on the edge of a downtown that had given up on transformation. Buy a coat dripping mink at Marshall Field's and then walk half a block to get a flimsy paper plate heaped with oily, artery-cramming soul food. Ah, yes, the slam was back home.

> The slam was necessary breath, a rousing kick in the rear for an art form that wheezed dust and structure. Or it was a death knell for the genre....

The concluding night of nationals had come a long way from its lower wattage counterpart a decade before. This time, more than 3,000 people packed the theater. A number of former competitors, having moved on to greater and more profitable glories, dotted the crowd like celebs on Oscar night. Mike Wallace of *60 Minutes* was in attendance, and even he couldn't keep a little awe from seeping into his "I've been in war zones and nothing fazes me" countenance. Cameras from FOX and CNN scanned the chattering audience. For weeks, predictably, the local media had been saturated with stories "discovering" the slam. Again.

But beneath its tendency to glitter, the night had that prideful, pieced-together feel that typifies an ongoing revolution. Those who'd been involved from the beginning linked eyes and nodded imperceptibly, rueful little smiles playing at the corners of their mouths. A paper bag wrapped around a bottle of bargain red vino made its way stealthily down one of the theater's fancy aisles. Nervous competitors mumbled their lines like mantras, repeatedly, repeatedly, repeatedly. Downtown and uptown were both sitting in the fancy seats—and though no one was gearing up for an inspiring rendition of "The Impossible Dream," no punches had been thrown. But it was Chicago, and it was still early.

Darting about the theater, his eyes meaningfully manic, Marc Kelly Smith did what he's always done so masterfully—he dropped like fuel on a fire that, up until then, everyone thought had been contained. The ex-construction worker had passed up a lucrative job with the city (all Chicago construction workers eventually wind up working for the city, and in Chicago, if you work for the city—just sayin'—you can pretty much count on lucrative) and surrendered a steady paycheck, choosing instead to wallow in the heady come-on of a very small limelight. Anyone who knows Marc knows that if it hadn't been for the slam, he would have crafted another outlet that would've allowed him to be both ringleader and ringmaster, the lion tamer and the droop-eyed clown. He'd need to conjure a safe haven for a heart that cracked all too often and easily, a rubber-walled room to store his rampaging ego when he wasn't using it, and a place—with a reliable mic, a jukebox, and snazzy lighting—where he could trade rhythmic war stories with other flawed, fallible, and occasionally narcissistic human beings.

Marc was just enough of all of us—a heartbroken souse, madly in love with lyric and leaving shards of his self-esteem on beer-slick floors. We appreciated his litany of failures and trusted him with our collective voice, trusted him to wail the stories we were afraid of. Punch-drunk, he took the falls for us and then scrambled to his feet, facing off the next flurry of fists. We lived vicariously through the sexy riveting mess of him. Behind the mic, he wore our fears proudly. The stifled halls of academia wouldn't have had a clue about how to handle him. His words flowed like barroom light through a crack in a wooden door; he needed fools like us to cheer him on, and we needed him to trumpet the syllables we wouldn't dare. No one—no one—could have done this but him. He would be vilified, underestimated, misunderstood, and attacked. He would be blamed for both his successes and his failures. His fiery poetics would be dismissed as mere snippets of theater, and the kingdom he had crafted would be pointed to as an example of what poetry can be if the unwashed, untrained, and underfunded get ahold of it.

No one else would have held on so tightly, crazed and committed enough to see the madness through to this inevitable moment of box office respectability. At the tenth final of the tenth National Poetry Slam, the undisputed daddy of the chaos slapped backs, pumped hands, charmed the media, scanned his kingdom, and tried to keep his eyes from wandering upward to behold a chandelier the size of a small country, a sight that would have undoubtedly caused reality to overwhelm him. He would not have been able to keep from bellowing over everyone and everything, "We're in the fucking Chicago Theater!"

My only part in the proceedings that evening was a short opening performance with Marc, Cin Salach, and Dean Hacker, fellow members of the team who'd snatched all the marbles at the very first national championship a decade before in San Francisco. All those lifetimes ago, we stunned everyone who encountered us, busting the boundary between stage and audience, leaving the podium and joining listeners in their seats, providing them with no way at all to turn away from stanzas that simply didn't know their rightful place. We did what we'd been doing all along in Chicago while assuming that everyone else was doing it too. But we'd been existing in a feverish bubble and, as far as the rest of the poetry world was concerned, nothing like us ever was.

Ten years from that triumph, we hurriedly huddled and managed to pull together a brief collaborative piece highlighting each of our voices. Backstage was teeming with edgy competitors, dizzy with bloodlust, thinking of slam as head-to-head, line-by-line warfare. But the four of us were proof that there was life beyond the score sheets, that the words went deeper and friendships were forged.

I was under no illusion that the majority of the audience would know any of us except for Marc or understand why we were delaying the meatier part of the show with our feisty little wordplay. The slam had grown so huge so rapidly, and each year a little of the history—the faces and voices and almost embarrassing hunger of those who nurtured the beast in its early days—fell by the wayside and was later trampled by poets stampeding toward recording contracts, television commercials, and the bright lights of Broadway.

With each passing year, I admit feeling a palpable sense of loss and a growing disconnect as new faces and ritual flood the slam landscape. Standing there in the Chicago Theater all those years later, I wanted to tell everyone how fierce and boundless and sloppy those first days were; how I lived and died for that Sunday night at the Green Mill; how I ached for Marc's addicting, godlike approval and guidance; how desperately I craved audience; and how the rush of words frightened me, spilling from my body like an expulsion of fever. But increasingly, whenever I would corner some poetry ingenue and start babbling about the wonders of yesteryear, eager to sense that same fever in her, I was indulged with a glazed but respectful gaze, not unlike the one kids give elders who are not yet completely useless but not useful in the ways they once were.

> I wanted to tell everyone how fierce
> and boundless and sloppy those first days were.

Here's what I'd tell them if I could.

At the Green Mill, there were eight open slots every Sunday. Anyone could sign up. The judges were people picked at random from the audience. They could be English professors, unemployed welders, or high school students. They didn't have to know poetry. It was our job to introduce them to it. The judges would listen to the poets in turn and judge them on a scale from one to ten, the scores based on both the content and delivery of the poems. Judges were monsters or saints, depending on the poem, the crowd, the poet, Marc Smith's sly indicators of yea or nay, the strength of the drinks, the weather. The whole thing was a statistically catastrophic crapshoot, art on a dartboard. It was the most beautiful thing I had ever seen.

The Green Mill was a long room cloaked in a maroon darkness, a cavern peppered with the twinkle of neon. Imagine the battered bar, the comfortably gruff barkeep, the overwrought grand piano at the front of the room, and Patsy Cline unfurling silk in the jukebox. Throughout the years, I heard bits and pieces of the Mill's sweet mystery: The name? A tribute to France's Moulin Rouge (Red Mill) but green so as not to be linked to the city's numerous red-light districts. By 1910, the joint had morphed into the Green Mill Gardens, an outdoor dancing and drinking spot frequented by Sophie Tucker and Al Jolson. But the stories didn't get juicy until Al Capone entered the mix. His head henchman, "Machinegun" Jack McGurn, obtained a 25 percent ownership of the club. As the story goes, he slit the throat and lopped off the tongue of comedian/singer Joe E. Lewis when the entertainer threatened to move his act to another club. The scene, and the Mill, were re-created in the film *The Joker Is Wild*, starring Frank Sinatra.

That's the true stuff. But I also I heard, over and over again, with no proof whatsoever, that Al Capone had blasted a piano player off his bench because a tune was not to his liking. I loved that story because it fit so perfectly with the spirit of the slam: entertain me, or your time in the spotlight is short.

But the mess didn't begin at the Mill. The foundation for the slam was a series at the old Get Me High Lounge, where Marc founded a poetry reading series in 1984. Wanting to avoid the owl-rimmed glasses, tweed jacket, and relentless droning of the academic stage and the drunken spittle of the typical barroom bard, Marc emphasized performance and the capture of audience. By the time he was approached by Dave Jemilo, the Green Mill's owner, two years later—to help inject a bit of sizzle into slow Sunday nights—the ex-construction worker had the blueprint. Stanzas and spirits were a potent mix. Obstinate judges and teeny cash prizes made things interesting. The word *slam* sounded brisk, relentless, and final, something that couldn't be argued with. The limelight felt great on Marc's skin. A star was born. A phenomenon found root.

Marc presided over the buzz like a blade-edged Svengali. He decided who was legit, who wore the fever like a cloak, and who were there just to beef up their social circle, drink heavily, and talk in the back of the bar while poets were onstage. He never apologized for running the world inside the threshold of the Mill. Often he was gruff and unreadable. He was stubborn. He was frequently brilliant. At the risk of being ostracized by black folks and ridiculed by white ones, I never told anyone what an astounding presence he was/is in my life. I'd never met anyone so selfishly and selflessly fueled by language and ego. I shamelessly clamored for a spot under his wing, where I wrote like a woman possessed, learned how to control any room with words, and inherited a bit of his swagger and arrogance—just enough to grow the thick skin needed to face a restless room of strangers every week.

There are two types of people in the world. The first are people who try the slam once and are absolutely horrified from the moment they take the stage. They leave skid marks running away from the experience. They forget that it's a crapshoot, that the judges' qualifications are simply (a) they are in the room, and (b) they are willing to be judges. From the time they skedaddle from the spotlight, these folks are content to watch the chaos from the sidelines. They're glad they dipped their toes in the water—it *is* a badge of honor of sorts—but they will never approach the mic again. The judging aspect of the slam proves to be more wounding than it looks. They make the common mistake of believing that a low score means that their poetry stank. They reveal much more than they thought they would. Or all those expectant eyes are just too—expecting.

The other type of person slams and discovers a surprising and mildly unsettling competitive streak. When I first hit that room, clutching my two or three poems, the local Green Mill slam champion was a woman named Lisa Buscani, a wizard who worked miracles by holding whole audiences in her hand. It was for her that I first used the word *diva*. When she finished a poem, there would be a moment of white-hot silence—audience members were so flummoxed, they didn't know whether to clap or weep. I'd never seen anyone wield that type of power over an entire room. I wanted to know if she did it by telling her own stories. I wanted to know *how* she did it.

But Lisa's not the person who introduced me to the idea of the second throat.

We all have one. Our first throat is functional, a vessel for the orderly progression of verb, adjective, and noun. It's the home of our practiced, public voices. But most people live all their lives without discovering the second throat, that raw and curving parallel pathway we use to sing the songs, tell the stories, screech the truths that any fool knows should be kept silent.

Before I knew there was a slam, before Marc Smith set my complacency ablaze, I knew there was an audience somewhere and that something inside me ached to connect to it, to open that second throat and singe the air. Even the hard syllable and inferred violence of the word *slam* reminds me of how completely and irrevocably my world was changed because of one moment, one woman, one atypical Chicago night.

It was a signature blend of Chi-town chaos, with all the elements in attendance. Alcohol? Yes. The blues? The place was drenched in them. Insanely subpar temperature outside and a bellowing wind clawing at the doorframe, begging to get in? You betcha.

In January 1988, in the fledging days of slam, forty poets came together at Blues Etc., a raucous juke joint on the city's North Side. They were there for Neutral Turf, a benefit for Guild Books, a venerable and funky literary institution and one of those places that was always in some stage of revolt.

Ten bucks got you more than three dozen word-slingers in a blues club for four hours over the course of a blistering late winter afternoon—you couldn't ask for more Chicago than that. Well, yeah, you could—that same ten bucks got you into a performance of the Johnny B. Moore Blues Band later that evening. The place was packed. In true Windiest City style, it wasn't just the place we were. It felt like the only place to be.

When I walked into that blues club on that January afternoon, I was one of those people fully prepared to get mildly (okay, not so mildly) buzzed and to laugh at funny people saying funny things onstage. I was prepared for poetry of the June-moon-spoon-spittoon variety, grade-school rhymes delivered with grown-up earnestness. *Real* poetry, I felt, was inescapably dull, necessarily inaccessible, relegated to dusty, high-up bookshelves, buried in tomes that opened with a reluctant creak. Real poetry certainly wasn't real poetry if you could understand it. Real poetry was about the universe revealed in the defiant way a flower bursts through a crack in the concrete. Real poetry mused about maddeningly cryptic quotes from deities. Real poetry was written by alcoholic white men in musty tweed jackets or their anorexic, suicidal female counterparts. I didn't know much about poetry, obviously, but I had heard somewhere that a woman poet had taken her life by sticking her head in an oven and gulping mouthfuls of gas. You had to be a real poet to do that.

> [It was] a space and time for the city's disparate creative elements to commune, connect, raise a glass or two, and discover—well, I'll be damned—that their work was crafted on a common canvas.

Neutral Turf was designed to be a space and time for the city's disparate creative elements to commune, connect, raise a glass or two, and discover—well, I'll be damned—that their work was crafted on a common canvas. An academic stepped gingerly down from his ivory tower to hear poetry penned on a scarred bar top by an edgy artist. A painfully shy high school sophomore listened to Luis Rodriguez and recognized a little of himself. People who had never picked up a poetry book or strolled into a college classroom heard Michael Anania, whose work was featured in the *Norton Anthology of Modern Poetry*; Reginald Gibbons, the editor of the prestigious lit journal *TriQuarterly*; and Lisel Mueller, who would snag a Pulitzer ten years later. There were rants, villanelles, poets reciting from memory. Marc Smith, just another stranger at the mic, wailed his fiery odes to the rafters, and possibility was static in the air.

With my jaw on the floor, I listened while boundaries blurred, lines were definitively crossed, walls crumbled. Those attending their very first poetry reading (many, like me, initially attracted by the booze, the four hours of guaranteed warmth, and the opportunity—they thought—to publicly guffaw at reams of bad rhyme) got an enviable sampling of everything the city's poetry community had to offer.

But that formidable chasm between the poets from academia and those with street cred wasn't the only one being bridged that day.

Chicago's dirty little secret is the blatant segregation lurking directly beneath its midwestern charm. Blacks, comprising more than 30 percent of the city's population, live primarily on the West and South Sides. Whites huddle on the North Side. Hispanics, southwest and northwest. The practice of herding minorities toward particular economically stifled areas of the city, fueled by fear and good ole garden-variety racial prejudice, took hold in the late 1800s. At the beginning of the next century, thousands of Delta residents streamed northward, searching for the blessing of city, and settled into those same areas, where faces and perspectives mirrored their own. That "comfort around my own kind" took root and continues today, effectively reinforcing the borders and earning Chicago—which produced the first African American president—the title of the most segregated city in America.

Any Chicago native can recite the rules. Stay out of Garfield Park and Lawndale. No black folks allowed in Cicero or Bridgeport or Berwyn, unless they're going to or coming from work. Englewood? Gangs. Wrong or right, lines drawn long ago are still etched in the minds of the city's residents, and the poetry community traveled along those same lines. North Side poets (mostly white) and South Side poets (mostly black) not only rarely mingled but also tended to sniff rather dismissively at one another. And the West Side? Poetry? Could there have been any poetry at all in those abandoned apartment buildings, rusty park swings, and block after block of taverns, storefront churches, and fly-by-night commerce?

Poets in Chicago felt possessive of their stories. Neighborhoods were starkly defined, each with its own defiant character, quirky ritual, and local folklore. Neighborhoods were kielbasa, black-eyed peas, Vienna red-hots, chitlins, or cannoli. Neighborhoods were towers of public housing, sturdy two-flats, or manicured McMansions. Just like everyone else, poets love that *boing* of instant recognition; they love being surrounded by people who have lived the same stories they have. Outside of that warm circle, there was a glaring mistrust of the "other." What will you do with my stories? How can I hand them over to be interpreted by you, a stranger, someone whose skin/history/environment/outlook is different from mine?

On that long-ago winter night, Blues Etc. was filled with folks from the West Side, the North Side, and the South Side, suppressing their doubts and spinning their tales across boundaries. The night's klutzy harmonics marked a first for Chicago's creative community—it was a ragged ballad sung by the whole city at once.

And she sat there, amid the frenetic swirl, watching as stanza after stanza stepped to the mic. Many times, she looked as if the poet on stage was a child of hers—she nodded with a mixture of patience and bemused pride at the occasional overworked rhyme, mumbled delivery, or tangled syntax. She glowed when a passage touched her and seemed about to reach out and touch those poets whose work probed deeply and reached bone. She laughed in all the right places and served up compassion when it was called for—stopping every now and again to push up slipping coke-bottle specs with her forefinger, adjust her heavy winter stockings, or graciously acknowledge an awestruck admirer.

For hours she defied the odds, front row center, rapt and nurturing during what amounted to the longest, most eclectic reading ever. And when she was finally introduced, those who hadn't recognized her dropped their jaws in amazement, and those who had known she was there all along thanked the Muse that they were among those huddled in the club on that day, at that moment. She unfolded her body slowly and stood to amble to the stage, where she turned to face those who had already spoken and those who had come to listen. They were C-minus students and ex-cons, pump jockeys, middle school teachers, drunks and bag boys, black folks from Lawndale and white folks from Schaumburg, word addicts, coke addicts, Wicker Park and Winnetka, slammers, GEDers and grad students, academics, dropouts, Baptists and Buddhists, lone wolves and prizewinners.

And *she* was Gwendolyn Brooks.

When you hear the words *Chicago poetry*, the scene-stealing poetry slam begins its low relentless roar and barges in to hog the limelight. The raucous, controversial competition—the brash Olympics of lyric—drew its first breath in the Windy, which of course makes perfect sense when one considers the blustery, sexy beast it's become. The slam is constantly rediscovered and dissected, lauded and loathed, and has gradually risen to the level of idle cocktail party fodder for those who wish to appear "in." Unfortunately, simply hearing *Chicago poetry* causes some folks' synapses to fire wrongly and insanely, and the slam *becomes* the city's creative community. Was there a community before the slam, and did one come after? Was the slam itself birthed by a larger, more ambitious community? Who knows? It's easier to succumb to that handy catchphrase overwhelming everything, much easier to slather the whole wall with that bright red paint.

> Was there a community before the slam,
> and did one come after? Was the slam itself birthed
> by a larger, more ambitious community? Who knows?

There *is* an official history of poetry slam, as well as several unofficial ones. There are exaggerations and outright lies to be had for the asking. There are painstakingly researched timelines that feature all the major players and defining moments. It's simple to find out that the first poetry slam at the Green Mill was held on July 25, 1986, that the first national competition was in the fall of 1990, who was there and how the competition caught fire from that instance. For some, the proceedings were nothing more than a unique, booze-fueled recreation; for others, like myself, the slam became necessary breath. I went on to snag the stats—four individual championships, the most in the competition's history—and became, arguably of course, one of the slam's most recognizable and successful competitors. But, as slam's defenders are fond of saying, "the points are not the point." I believe that those of us who flourished during those first heady days brought unfinished voices and bare need to the table. For many of us, those voices had their beginning in some other arena, in some other room.

For me, it was that singular moment when a regal, bespectacled colored lady stood before that ragtag cross-section of the city's poets and poetry lovers. If I hadn't seen her there, I might never have discovered that poetry held answers for me. It was that stark moment when the glasses stopped clinking, the chatter stilled, and we held a familial breath, waiting for her. It was that unforgettable moment that still, for me, typifies the breadth and strength of the Chicago poetry community. I didn't know it at the time, but the slam's boisterous brilliance was made possible because it found a city that was finally ready for it. And because, in so many ways, writers were finding a need and needing an answer.

And remember that community of black folks and rusty park swings, abandoned apartment buildings, and block after desolate block of taverns, storefront churches, and fly-by-night commerce? The poetry-starved West Side of the city? During the Great Migration of blacks from south to north, when my mother came up from Alabama and my father came up from Arkansas, they settled on the West Side. That's where I was born, where I grew up. Needless to say, when I set out for Blues Etc., intent on a little cultural entertainment, I didn't expect that anyone there would know, or understand, the stories I held close while I searched for the voice I needed to tell them. Although my public motto was "people who say they're impassioned about writing should write in as many ways as possible," I didn't hold out much hope that poetry could offer a West Side colored girl any real resolution, consolation, or guidance.

All she had were her stories and a naked need
to have them heard and understood.

Until a South Side colored girl stood up and began to speak. Gwendolyn Brooks, who I knew was from Chicago, who I knew was famous, who I knew had won a big writing award or two, who I knew from—well, photographs. Somewhere along the line, I'd memorized her poem "The Pool Players. Seven At the Golden Shovel," which I, like everyone else I knew, assumed was titled "We Real Cool." I thought of her as a comfy homegrown attraction, more as a local personality than a poet, someone who had slipped through a slit in the canon of moody alcoholic white men and their suicidal female counterparts.

In a voice that was warm, crisp, and encompassing, she told snippets of story that belonged to us both. She knew the cluttered neighborhood streets, the tenement apartments, the forgotten schools. In her I sensed the black-girl uncertainty, the gangliness, the ache of never quite belonging. I suddenly saw myself there, emboldened under the hot lights, holding the attention of a room full of people who I never thought realized my existence. Gwen Brooks didn't capture that room with histrionics or trendy wordplay. All she had were her stories and a naked need to have them heard and understood. I realized that nothing mattered as much as having a room full of strangers invest in my story in just that way—and helping them find ways to tell stories of their own.

★　★　★

So we stepped out on the huge stage of the Chicago Theater, Marc, Cin, Dean, and I, and looked out at the past and future of slam. Folks who had sweated out the particulars during those first days, who had helped Marc map out rules we could break, seemed a little overwhelmed. New blood, alternately wary and cocky, scanned the hoopla, dying to be seen. Mike Wallace was still in awe. These were *poets,* after all.

Before we began our poem, the four of us listened as our names were shouted from the audience. Chicago was claiming its own. I was a fool to think it had forgotten us.

We rooted ourselves, waited for silence, then opened our second throats.

Somewhere in the back of the theater, my muse smiled and slipped out the back door. She was wearing coke-bottle specs and stockings pulled to a roll just beneath her knees.

CONVERGING WOR[L]DS

Nizhoni Bridges and Southwest Native Communities

Sherwin Bitsui

One late winter afternoon, gray clouds clinging to surrounding sandstone cliffs, I drove to a high school nestled in the reservation community of Monument Valley, Utah, that was participating in the In-Reach literacy project. I was a visiting poet in the schools for Nizhoni Bridges, a non-profit foundation for the arts serving rural area public schools in the Arizona and Utah regions of the Navajo Nation. It was good to be home in the midst of familiar faces, to see a familiar landscape, to immerse myself in a language that I'd gotten used to hearing and speaking only on telephone calls to my parents and other family members. It was good to be back in *Dinétah (*Navajoland*)*, red earth blanketing the horizon in every direction around me, the sheer red cliffs of the buttes contrasted with the weightless blue sky unfolding into more shades of blue: clean, crisp detail everywhere. Home.

Earlier in the year, the director of Nizhoni Bridges, Phil Hall, asked Arthur Sze if he knew any Navajo poets interested in visiting reservation schools to present poetry to students. Arthur was my professor when I attended the Institute of American Indian Arts in Santa Fe. He recommended me to Phil and gave him my contact information. Phil e-mailed and invited me to give a poetry reading in the fall of that year for the annual FANDANGO! Writers Festival, another of the nonprofit organization's programs.

During a break from the festival, as evening light began glinting into the dark green waters of the San Juan River, Phil and I edged our way toward the sandy bank. I was trying to skip a few sandstone pebbles across the river's moving face when he began talking about poetry's power to harness beauty and inspire change for people facing adversity, such as what he saw on a daily basis on the Navajo Nation side of the river. I listened quietly, absorbing this moment as he listed the names of his poetic heroes: Pablo Neruda, Lawrence Ferlinghetti, and Allen Ginsberg. The names and their poems when spoken aloud echoed faintly through the slot canyon near where we were standing. I had also found these poets on *my* journey toward poetry. Poets who spoke to me during the long hours I spent baking in the hot desert sun while herding sheep for my grandparents in the rocky valley behind my paternal clan's settlement in the southern part of *Dinétah*.

History's witnesses are here. Within these wind-carved rocks are songs dappled with ancient starlight, suns, wind, and rain. Like flowing water, these stories weave through the land.

Poetry had just begun watering my mind with new patterns and designs. It now faced us from a river that was also a political border between the Navajo Nation in Utah and the rest of the United States. Phil mentioned an event in the earlier part of the twentieth century: white ranchers had forced a Navajo family, at gunpoint, back across this same river to the Navajo side because their livestock were grazing on what once had been their winter camp. This history, Phil said, is loaded with the true story of this land, its people's conflicts and resilience. History's witnesses are here. Within these wind-carved rocks are songs dappled with ancient starlight, suns, wind, and rain. Like flowing water, these stories weave through the land, leaving their traces etched on canyon walls. Elders who have never learned to read or write carry vast archives within their memories. Elders who create epic stories during wintertime at the kitchen table or on drives to the nearby border town Laundromats are poets too, if one just listens.

In Navajo thought, language is sacred.

In Navajo thought, language is sacred. Language, when performed as a ceremonial function, attempts to create harmony, enact change, and metaphorically transform time and space for those directly involved in the presence of a song/poem. Through this activity, the lineage between past, present, and future is "reconnected"—replanted, watered, grown, and harvested to counter what is considered inharmonious. Navajo philosophy does not divorce good language usage such as that found in poetry and/or prayer from alignment with a deeper cosmological/spiritual knowing. Navajo ceremonies use language to bind the universe and self and restore *hózhó* (balance, peace, harmony) to a person or a family. This spiritual restoration occurs when a medicine person recites songs/poems drawn from cultural memory—a language that brings forth healing to the participants in a particular ceremony. Thus, ours is a culture that still, according to Navajo author Irvin Morris "holds the creative use of language in high regard."

I was not privy to what Phil had witnessed "across the river" that may have sparked his intense passion for wanting to heighten poetic awareness among "the kids" in those particular communities. I agreed with his sentiment that there was a need for the youth to seize the path of story and knowledge and claim it as their own. I had been an example of such a youth. At the time I stood with Phil looking across the border between worlds, I was compiling my poetry manuscript, which later developed into my first book, *Shapeshift*. I knew from my experience growing up through the school systems, both on and off the reservation, that many Native kids inherited, by default, negative perceptions about their abilities to transcend history's bonds and continue the journey toward strengthening their communities from within. Native kids were somehow perceived as being stuck in two places at once, unwilling or unable to move toward a contemporary worldview, always in conflict with self and duty to tribe and family.

Of course, the reality is more complicated than any such stereotype. It is true that in Native America, a significant number of students enrolled in public schools will not graduate, and their nations suffer high unemployment rates. The outside perception is that college success for Native people is limited because of students' failure to develop the necessary English and reading skills that would make them more competitive in an academic atmosphere. The more complicated truth is that *Diné* culture has survived countless attempts at erasure because it is both dynamic and rooted in tradition. It continues to adapt to change and finds new ways to bring in outside influences and make them its own even while it draws strength from the legacy of ancestors and from pride in culture and history. Though some people have been subsumed by years of acculturation and assimilation into the dominant culture around them, many remain on the high desert reservation to raise families, stay connected to traditional lifestyles, maintain clanships, and work to make their communities amiable places to live. Thus, Native people are simultaneously trying to maintain a way of perceiving life in some form that might have existed prior to the invasion of nonindigenous ideologies while encountering and negotiating the newness of contemporary culture as it is transported to their isolated communities through popular media and technology. Contemporary culture continuously laps at the shores of our way of life, rooting its consciousness to our own, thus restructuring our contemporary identities alongside the accelerating language shift from indigenous paradigms of communication to standard English. All these tensions and conflicts affect Native children in a way that can render the conventional Western curriculum irrelevant at best and damaging at worst.

When I return to my community now, I can see, both around the community and within the school setting, that the majority of the local children's first language is English. Because elderly grandparents within the same household may not speak the same language as the child, traditional information is lost and gaps in knowledge open. Bilingual poems by Navajo poets such as Laura Tohe, Hershman John, Esther Belin, Orlando White, Nia Francisco, Rex Lee Jim, Venaya Yazzie, and Luci Tapahonso attempt to fill these gaps, inspiring youth to see firsthand the mixed languages of their homes represented in poetic form. Such recognition and validation are important to these kids because there are not many places beyond their communities that share their story and native language, including their classrooms.

This is especially unfortunate because even when Navajo children do write in English, poetry is inherent in their sensibilities. When Navajo students have permission to break free from the standards of English, the poetic quality and perspective remains within their creative work. This breaking free allows them to imbue their work with aspects of their unique cultural experiences, perspectives, and languages.

Cultural differences beyond linguistic differences can create tensions for Navajo students in mainstream educational settings. In most Native communities, there are cultural attitudes that favor listening to speaking. In non-Native institutions, students are encouraged to be vocal and assertive from a very young age. A Navajo child is often instructed to listen to older people and absorb the knowledge and wisdom that they may have. During my visits to classrooms, I experienced many moments when teachers seemed frustrated at how quiet the students were when asked to answer questions or read their work publicly. I've also been met with silence when I have asked students to volunteer to read their new poems to the class. I was one of those kids at one point, defaulting to silence many times when I was their age. I, too, came from a family tradition that encouraged listening over speaking. In many cases, it was apparent that the lack of response wasn't because the kids feared being examined publicly by their peers or because they were shy; they simply weren't culturally receptive to this component of western educational practice.

It seems natural for new narratives to emerge, narratives that can help illuminate a changing world.

With all the problems faced by indigenous nations undergoing incredible shifts in identity and self-definition, it seems natural for new narratives to emerge, narratives that can help illuminate a changing world.

And so, on that riverbank, Phil and I agreed: the time had come to tell our own stories. It was time for Navajos and other indigenous people, in Joy Harjo's words, to "reinvent the enemy's language" and thus restore connection between our communities and one another through story and poetry. We talked about the power of literary works by prominent Native American poets such as Joy Harjo, Luci Tapahonso, Simon Ortiz, and Sherman Alexie and agreed that their books should be included in the curriculum of all reservation schools to help young people see familiar experiences reflected in these literary works. These writers took up a pen at some point in their lives and wrote poems that spoke to history when the eye of history had long ago looked the other way, ignoring the predicaments of their nations as they stood in the path of Manifest Destiny a century and half earlier. Together, these writers and all the other Native American writers of their generations revolutionized the way Native people looked at themselves. They crossed boundaries in the imaginations of people and stirred those of us who were reflected in their storytelling to write down our own stories.

The time has come for us to tell our own stories.

It was a turning point for me when I discovered their books. While attending public school in the reservation border town of Holbrook, I was exposed to the literary works of Western writers only. I never imagined that people from cultures like mine could write books. If there were books of Native interest in public places, they were often tourist guidebooks showcasing Southwest Native arts and crafts or New Age manuals that offered semimysterious ways people could get in touch with their spirit animals. It was as if an insider's narrative of Native people did not exist in these border towns, although throughout the land Native people did daily tasks and interacted with local communities. Little did I know before my discovery of their work that there were Native authors regularly writing. These authors were nationally recognized and respected but unknown in the rural border communities I came from.

The kind of turning point I encountered was just what a program like the Nizhoni Bridges In-Reach project, which brought authors to reservation schools, was created to encourage and foster. The project allowed me to remember, firsthand, as an adult and as a poet, how powerful the tool of poetry can be when given back to a community like mine. Poetry in its essence has no boundaries and can bridge divergent worlds. Through poetry, programs such as In-Reach and others can help restore education to relevance for Native American students.

★   ★   ★

April Ignacio, community liaison for the Tohono O'odham Nation, also works to bridge divergent worlds and empower her people through education in their ancestral land. She echoes many similar concerns regarding community writing programs and their relationship to Tohono O'odham schools. According to April, "These kids struggle with identity issues. They are impoverished but still wear brand-name clothing and have the latest electronic gadgets. One has to ask, 'Who are we?' Our Nation has a 56 percent dropout rate, 76 percent unemployment rate, and 47 percent poverty rate. Many students from the Nation's schools begin dropping out in the fourth grade." She continues, "This is why it's important for communities and community programs to work together. Many of these kids completely break down; they don't know how to cope. When you read poems written by these kids, you sense the way they see themselves as Tohono O'odham." She says that she'll never forget a poem written by a young girl from her village. The young girl wrote about having a medicine man come over to her house, how he used the sacred clay and made a sign of the cross on her window to protect her. The girl also wrote about how she needed a *santo* (saint) under her bed. "We O'odham truly believe we come from the earth, and it was amazing to see this young girl acknowledge her culture and heritage in her poem. We can't lose this connection."

I, too, can't help but notice similar examples among many students from my community and other indigenous communities in regard to personal issues they have that are beyond my comprehension. There are sometimes moments after a day's workshop when I've driven back to my hotel or to my home in Tucson in disbelief over the daily realities these students face at home, and how those realities welled forth in their poems and overwhelmed any kind of ideal I might have projected on them. The phrase "they are *just* kids" doesn't apply in these communities the same way it might in other, more mainstream, places. These youth will inherit complex situations and continued crises rooted both in their respective nations' histories and in present-day dynamics.

I was asked in this essay to look at certain moments of tension or crisis that provided opportunities for transition. I realized that the realities these youth and their respective nations face daily are the *event* they must define for themselves in order for growth and transformation to occur. I continue to hold fast to the belief that creative writing workshops and organizations that bring poets into schools with Native American populations promote positive attitudes toward literacy within communities and give youth hands-on methods of translating for one another the worlds around them. I continue to hope that literary arts, if seeded within the young minds, will leaf forth in a new generation of Native people invested in the well-being of their own cultures and nations.

I continue to hope that literary arts, if seeded within the young minds, will leaf forth in a new generation of Native people invested in the well-being of their own cultures and nations.

A fellow poet who worked for ArtsReach[1] told me that he cried, on several occasions, all the way back to his home in Tucson from an elementary school on the nearby reservation where he was visiting classes. He said he was in shock over the depth of experience that some of his seven-year-old students wrote about. According to him, when he did simile exercises, many of the students compared an object of their choosing with someone in their family who had recently passed away. He also said that he would like to come back in some capacity in the future and that it was necessary to continue to bring poetry to these communities.

Like him, after a day's workshop, I sometimes just want to press hard on a gas pedal and drive off into the desert sunset to escape these circumstances that are not mine to carry as personal burdens. Given the numerous and dynamic social issues young people face in these classrooms, I can imagine collapsing under the weight of the apparently impossible odds their nations face. But because I come from a similar community, I feel responsible to those youth and their families. I cannot simply turn my back when I might be able to help students recover their balance through the medium of poetic language. I still believe that poetry can be an agent of transformation for Native students and a positive asset in reclaiming their ability to see their own possibilities. The difficulties make it all the more pressing that these youth continue to write and perform their work.

The question is this: what would it mean for the students to completely write this experience poetically? And can we as community members or even teachers embrace the difficult realities presented in their work—and do so without feeling that it simplifies or re-creates stereotypes that should, in some way, just disappear altogether if we ignore them long enough?

April, in response to the literacy programs and their presence in her nation, said, "Creative writing helps empower our kids. It gives them a way to take control of language, saying, that's me, that's the way I see things. Writing is that guiding force. As they grow older, they'll remember the Indian poet who came to them and built a relationship with them. We can't lose that connection."

Poetry can be a liberating force for all people…new gifts unfold and illuminate the world around us.

Poetry can be a liberating force for all people. Students writing bilingually or in indigenous tongues bring forth perspectives inherent in their endangered languages and offer new dimensions of thought to the world around them. They also bring forth a third place, where the edges of difference are folded back and new ways of seeing emerge; new gifts unfold and illuminate the world around us. They will offer their voices, upon which their poems might fly free from their interior lives to astonish, astound, surprise, and emerge from years of silence.

NOTE

1. ArtsReach at the Tucson Indian Center is a nonprofit organization dedicated to creating communities of literacy for Native American students and families and encouraging cultural vitality and academic success through the power of imaginative writing.

THE WORD BECOMES YOU

Anna Deavere Smith

How do communities change because of the language that is used to create or change their identities? Can art play a part, even a small one, in the way a community changes specifically, merely because all art forms are types of language that at the very least can "move people" (even if to move them out of their seats at intermission or out of the gallery before the end of the exhibition)? This is difficult to analyze, and it is presumptuous, I think, other than in very specific circumstances, for those of us who are artists to take the credit for a dynamic that occurs because of a variety of shifts in culture and in consciousness. Yet one can aspire, at least, to be *part* of community and outside it at the same time. Artists are sometimes exactly located in the inside-outside position. Many of us are just plain nomadic. Our language is a language that chronicles movement. I am told that before the end of the century, an extraordinary number of languages *will die*. Artists in such communities should announce the funerals of such languages, for they are evidence of a dramatic change in cultural identity and power shifts in the world.

There is a long tradition of creating, of using, art as a mirror of society. Such is the work that I do. I have been studying the English language as spoken in America, individual by individual, to take a close temperature of how my country has been changing.

What do the ways people speak tell us about the world in which they live?

The work that I do started from many vantage points. In part, I was seeking to answer a set of technical questions—without any credentials as linguist or psychologist—about how language, as a phenomenon of sounds being made, works. What do the ways people speak tell us about the world in which they live? What does the *manner* in which a person speaks tell us about how he or she is organized intellectually, creatively, and psychologically? By "manner" I mean the actual rhythmic and syntactical patterns.

These questions, in all honesty, started humbly, out of my quest to build my toolbox of acting techniques. Yet the original set of questions ended up leading me down a path that became immediately sociological and political. My question became this: if I were to extend my fascination with speech by looking at how individuals express themselves, could I cause the theater itself to look and function differently? By "look," I mean both *how* it looks and what those who run, work in, and go to the theater actually look *at*.

I studied acting in San Francisco, California. In the 1970s, San Francisco and the larger metropolitan area occupying the beautiful landmasses around the stunning bodies of water in the Bay Area were moving, calmly, it seemed, out of the cultural revolutions of the 1960s. It was almost as if those many bits of land were settling back peacefully after what had been an enormous quake. I left college, like many of my friends, exhilarated on the one hand by possibilities I never would have imagined as a youngster, but reeling on the other hand as if I'd been hit in the face with a two-by-four. I had no choice but to *design* another way of being. I was at a crossroads, a crossroads that I would later call a "crossroads of ambiguity." Everything I seemed to have been working toward was up for grabs. Yes, we were on our way out of the Vietnam War; yes, there was the sense that there would be a lot more equity for people of color than my parents had experienced; yes, there were possibilities for women; and yes, the way people would partner and live together was wide open, at least in San Francisco.

And so, the cultural scene there was quite like the land. Stunning pockets—quiet almost—in which people minded their own business in small fiefdoms. After the unsettled decades before, there was not really a *desire* to have it all come together. Perhaps because there would be no coming together and no language calling anyone to come together (anymore), I and others were left to find a new language. I chose to have others give me the language. I went to acting school, where great language already written would be studied, and where I would learn *how to speak* that language of others. And that language, the language of modern playwrights, though it looked like normal talk—was not normal talk at all. It was heightened speech. From that point, beginning first with the language of realism, which seemed like normal talk, we began to build the imaginations and the physical ability to speak the language of the classics, the language of poetry. We were also trained to move in that way. It was my mime teacher—*the person without words*—who said to me, "Have a rich life, and haiku will come."

San Francisco was the most diverse community I had ever lived in. I'd grown up on the East Coast, where diversity meant blacks and whites, or "Negroes" (as we were then called) and whites, or Negroes (big wall), or whites (big wall). Inside the white community where Gentiles (big wall) and Jews. Or inside the Gentiles, Polish (big wall), Italians (big wall), Catholics (big wall), Lutherans (big wall), and so forth. And inside the Negro community, educated (big wall) and un-educated or lower-middle-class poor people (big wall), light-skinned Negroes (big wall) and darker-skinned Negroes (big wall) or Baptists and Methodists or those who went to Sharp Street Methodist Church (big wall), those who went to other Methodist churches, kids who went to private school (biiiiiiiiiiiiiiiiig wall), the rest of us who went to public school, and so forth. If people were anything other than black or white, let's say Japanese or Indian, they were categorized as black or just plain "other." Luckily for me, I went to an all-girl's public high school where intellectual desire trumped many of the big walls, and where there was a space, particularly for those of us who were involved in student government, to create a community that was not divided by the walls. I really loved that. This tangible possibility perhaps inspired me on some level to do the kind of work I do today.

I set about studying everything I could about acting and about how an actor's imagination could potentially work—which meant dutifully practicing my Shakespeare monologues every single day, no matter what, to see what the Bard understood and exemplified about language and psychology.

On nights when I was finished with school and my part-time job, I would catch the last couple of scenes of whatever play was being performed at the extraordinary theater that was coupled with the conservatory in which I was enrolled. I'd sit in the second balcony and think in the back of my head, "Gee, everyone on the stage is white." Except for the two black actors who had small parts as a maid and a delivery person. I took the place of the female in that couple when she left and so was onstage as a "bit part" player of color. It occurred to me, as I walked out the stage door, to the cable car dinging in the distance and the magical lights shining down from the hills, that nearly every single person who came to that theater as audience was white (except when August Wilson's plays were staged).

Walking through the city or going around Oakland, I'd marvel again at the extraordinary diversity—Latinos from all over Central America, Asians from all over Asia. Although to see blacks you needed to go to Oakland or into a very poor area of San Francisco (the city's grid eliminated most of those people in the central neighborhoods). Nonetheless, I left my experience in San Francisco highly inspired to continue to hone my skills as an actress (and as a teacher) and to try to think about ways to open the theater to more than one kind of person.

Occasionally an artist such as August Wilson succeeded in calling blacks who would not normally go to white institutions to come out of churches, homes, and known communities to listen intently to his words. Theaters such as the ones that honored August Wilson had sometimes staged primarily those works scripted by white, Western (for the most part) males. I thought, naïvely, that if one were to put more kinds of people *on* the stage, more kinds of people would come. This was naïve because that assumption does not dig deeply enough into the economics of who goes to the theater nor does it dig deeply enough into why people go to theater at all. That has something to do with identity. We live in a time when people find their identities by joining camps. We are not segregated in the same sense that my parents understand segregation, but we still live within those assumptions of segregation. We are dominated by our preferences, and the market takes advantage of that.

So. Where are the spaces where one can deliberately try to mix that up? It is not as dangerous to mix things up now as it was, for example, to integrate schools in Arkansas or to do what Rosa Parks did. But one is working against the grain. (As a side note, it is the case that people cross race to enjoy parts of the market; however, these crossings are not opening real doors for everyone who crosses.) White children may buy Jay Z's music or Diddy's clothes, but they may *not,* when old enough, make a case for diversity in their corporations. Jay Z's music, though played on the yacht of someone who owns a corporation, may *not* induce that titan to shake up the way education works in this country: who gets educated and who actually gets turned on to the sheer joy of learning. Deep, deep, deep inside our culture we profoundly desire to remain separate from those we perceive as different.

The way in is language, I thought.
And if you don't speak the language, especially
if you don't speak the specific language of a community,
the most important issue is listening.

The way in is language, I thought. And if you don't speak the language, especially if you don't speak the specific language of a community, the most important issue is listening. There is listening, and then there is *talking as* (the foundation of acting). My grandfather once said, "If you say a word often enough, it becomes you." And so I have been going to communities, tape-recording people, and saying their words over and over. I'm putting myself in people's words the way you might think of walking in someone else's shoes. But our identities are accounted for through stories as well as actions. So I also collect stories with the idea of juxtaposing contrasting stories to illuminate some truth. The communities I have visited while collecting stories range from riot-torn Los Angeles and riot-torn Brooklyn to the cool hallways and wood-paneled rooms of the Yale–New Haven Hospital. My work starts with listening. My ongoing project, On the Road: A Search for American Character, seeks to absorb America. I've heard that Walt Whitman wanted to absorb America and have it absorb *him.* Having been born and bred in a divided community—racially divided Baltimore, Maryland—I have sought to ease the gaps in my own cultural understanding by diving into America, community by community.

I developed a form of theater based on interviews of diverse groups of people with opposing or varying points of view, often about controversial issues. Initially this theater was meant to be performed by casts of actors, but for financial reasons I developed it into a one-woman-show format. I initially act the plays myself, playing as many as (in one case) fifty-three parts and as few as two parts. It is my intention that once the plays are published, casts of actors will perform the plays, playing people who are quite unlike themselves physically in terms of gender and in terms of race.

One of these plays is *Fires in the Mirror*. It is about a divided neighborhood in Crown Heights, Brooklyn, where blacks and Hasidic (Lubavitch) Jews lived side-by-side yet had very little to do with each other. Civil unrest broke out in that neighborhood one hot August in the 1990s. The grand rebbe, who was the leader of the Lubavitch community there, was going through the streets one night in an entourage of cars. One of the cars ran a red light, hit a sidewalk, and killed Gavin Cato, a young black boy. Later that night, a group of black youths stopped Yankel Rosenbaum, a Hasidic scholar from Australia, on the street and stabbed him to death. The streets then rocked. I went to Crown Heights, where I tape-recorded more than fifty interviews, and used them to create *Fires in the Mirror*, in which I played twenty-six parts: blacks and Jews, women and men, all with varying points of view about what had occurred. The play made the national press and my career as a documentarian using theater was begun.

Perhaps what allowed me to think I might embody that story was my experience at Western High School in Baltimore. When I met the people who should have seemed excruciatingly different from me, the Lubavitch rabbis, their children and their wives, I found something extremely familiar. Sitting in the kitchens and at the long dining room tables of the Lubavitch, I saw beyond the hats and yarmulkes of the men and the wigs of the women. I saw all the way back to the kitchens of my Jewish friends at Western, who had cut holes in the big walls between us by inviting me home to meet their families, including grandparents who were often unassimilated. I went back to a time twenty years earlier, when cultural walls had fallen, if only briefly, and possibility was tangible.

Here is an excerpt from *Fires in the Mirror*.

Roslyn Malamud
The Coup

Do you know what happened in August here?
You see when you read the newspapers.
I mean my son filmed what was going on,
but when you read the newspapers....

(Resonding to a question.) Of course I was here!
I couldn't leave my house.
I only would go out early during the day.
The police were barricading here.
You see,
I wish
I could just like
go on television.
I wanna scream to the whole world.
They said
that the Blacks were rioting against the Jews in Crown Heights
and that the Jews were fighting back.
Do you know that the Blacks who came here to riot were not my
neighbors?
I don't love my neighbors.
I don't know my Black neighbors.
There's one lady on President Street—
Claire—
I adore her.
She's my girlfriend's next-door neighbor.
I've had a manicure
done in her house and we sit and kibbitz
and stuff
but I don't know them.
I told you we don't mingle socially
because of the difference
of food
and religion
and what have you here.
But
the people in this community
want exactly
what I want out of life.
They want to live
in nice homes.
They all go to work.
They couldn't possibly
have houses here

if they didn't
generally—They have
two,
um,
incomes
that come in.
They want to send their kids to college.
They wanna live a nice quiet life.
They wanna shop for their groceries and cook their meals
    and go to
their Sunday picnics!
They just want to have decent homes and decent lives!
The people who came to riot here
were brought here
by this famous
Reverend Al Sharpton,
which I'd like to know who ordained him?
He brought in a bunch of kids
who didn't have jobs in
the summertime.
I wish you could see the *New York Times*,
unfortunately it was on page twenty,
I mean, they interviewed
one of the Black girls on Utica Avenue.
She said,
"The guys will make you pregnant
at night
and in the morning not know who you are."
(*Almost whispering.*)
And if you're sitting on a front stoop and it's very, very hot
and you have no money
and you have nothing to do with your time
and someone says, "Come on, you wanna riot?"
You know how kids are.
The fault lies with the police department.
The police department did nothing to stop them.
I was sitting here in the front of the house
when bottles were being thrown

and the sergeant tells five hundred policemen
with clubs and helmets and guns
to duck.
And I said to him,
"You're telling them to duck?
What should I do?
I don't have a club or a gun."
Had they put it—
stopped it on the first night
this kid who came from Australia...
(She sucks her teeth.)
You know,
his parents were Holocaust survivors, he didn't have to die.
He worked,
did a lot of research in Holocaust studies.
He didn't have to die.
What happened on Utica Avenue
was an accident.
JEWISH PEOPLE
DO NOT DRIVE VANS INTO SEVEN-YEAR-OLD BOYS.
YOU WANT TO KNOW SOMETHING? BLACK PEOPLE
    DO NOT DRIVE
VANS INTO SEVEN-YEAR-OLD BOYS.
HISPANIC PEOPLE DON'T DRIVE VANS INTO SEVEN-
    YEAR-OLD BOYS.
IT'S JUST NOT DONE.
PEOPLE LIKE JEFFREY DAHMER MAYBE THEY DO IT.
BUT AVERAGE CITIZENS DO NOT GO OUT AND TRY
    TO KILL
(Sounds like a laugh but it's just a sound.)
SEVEN-YEAR-OLD BOYS.
It was an accident!
But it was allowed to fester and to steam and all that.
When you come here do you see anything that's going on,
    riots?
No.
But Al Sharpton and the likes of him like *Dowerty,*

who by the way has been in prison
and all of a sudden he became Reverend *Dowerty*—
they once did an exposé on him—
but
these guys live off of this,
you understand?
People are not gonna give them money,
contribute to their causes
unless they're out there rabble-rousing.
My Black neighbors?
I mean I spoke to them.
They were hiding in their houses just like I was.
We were scared.
I was scared!
I was really frightened.
I had five hundred policemen standing in front of my house
every day
I had mounted police,
but I couldn't leave my block,
because when it got dark I couldn't come back in.
I couldn't meet anyone for dinner.
Thank God, I told you my children were all out of town.
My son was in Russia.
The coup
was exactly the same day as the riot
and I was very upset about it.
He was in Russia running a summer camp
and I was very concerned when I had heard about that.
I hadn't heard from him
that night the riot started.
When I did hear from him I told him to stay in Russia,
    he'd be safer
there than here.
And he was.

—Mrs. Roslyn Malamud, interviewed by Anna Deavere Smith
  in Crown Heights, Brooklyn, 1991

After all I have said about the possibility that was reawakened in me when I wrote and performed *Fires in the Mirror*, I will give here a word of caution. The play, in terms of mirroring community and bringing community together, was enormously successful. But did I change any opinions or beliefs at the epicenters? Did I change opinions or behaviors of any Lubavitch? Did I change opinions or behaviors of black activists? Unlikely. On opening night, Roz Malamud, quoted above, came to see the play. She was very excited by it. When the reviews came out she called me at my home to congratulate me and to invite me to her home for "a nice kosher meal." A year after the play opened, I was invited to perform the play in a theater quite near Crown Heights. Blacks and Jews from the community attended, including black leaders and key rabbis. The brother of Yankel Rosenbaum, Norman Rosenbaum, who is depicted in the play, attended. The accomplishment there is that blacks and Jews sat side by side in the theater. However, I would never say that I changed any minds—I am not certain of and cannot account for change at all. When *60 Minutes* took me back into the neighborhood to do a profile on my work, Roz Malamud, who had privately called me from time to time to invite me to come to her home (for her grandson's bris, for example), said of me on national television, "What does she know? She's not from here." So, it seems, Roz and I have to agree to disagree. But at least we are talking. And maybe that's something.

Did my speaking the language night after night, inside darkened theaters around this country, and in Australia and London, change anything? To answer this question, one would have to chronicle the behavior of audiences, once dispersed back into communities and their workplaces. Did it change their voting, their purchasing, their imagining, their relationships?

Likewise in Los Angeles, when I performed *Twilight: Los Angeles*, about the Los Angeles riots and the hostilities between communities and those who policed the communities, I succeeded in bringing communities into the theater. I broke box office records. But did I *change* anything? The process itself broke holes in big walls—my own walls included. One of my muses was a gang member—Twilight Bey was his name. I interviewed over three hundred people: a gang member on the one hand, a patrician, southern aristocrat who was editor of the *Los Angeles Times* on the other. One of the police officers who had beaten Rodney King met with me. I met with jurors from both trials, including a juror from the jury that voted not to send the police officers credited with causing the riots, causing the deaths, to jail. I began to feel like a friend of Rodney King's aunt. My assistant and I sat in her shop one day with the rain pounding outside. At one point, she burst into tears as she tried to share with us her frustrations with the "system." The recording of that interview has for at least five minutes only the sound of the rain and her tears. That was a moment of bonding for my assistant and me as well. Early in our journey around the wide area of Los Angeles, it brought home to us the gravity of what we were trying to capture. I lived in the embers of that riot, in fragments of the community of Los Angeles: Beverly Hills on the one hand, South Central L.A. on the other. (Later, when I went into neighborhoods in South Central to be photographed for profiles on my work, the magazines that were doing the stories sent police escorts with me.) In the midst of collecting the interviews, the many stories, the many recordings, I got a call from some graduate students at UCLA, all Korean American women. They had heard what I was doing and expressed their concern that in regard to the Korean American community whose businesses and homes had been burned down by the mostly black and Latino rioters, they were certain I would "get the story wrong." This blunt assessment, before they had even met me, was hard for me to take. However, the sentence that began "We think you are going to get it wrong" ended with a surprising "so we want to help you." And indeed they did. They took me to their communities. They introduced me to people who would never have spoken to me otherwise. They translated for me, and they sat with me as I listened to Korean Americans talk about how

The sentence that began "We think you are going to get it wrong" ended with a surprising "so we want to help you."

their communities had been ravaged. One man I interviewed had been shot point-blank in the head at a stoplight. They sat with me in his home, and we listened quietly as his horrible story unwound.

One such story follows. I still perform this excerpt from *Twilight: Los Angeles* whenever I can. The language is so beautiful and it comes from an interviewee who was constantly apologizing for her English. Mrs. Young-Soon Han was a widow and a liquor store owner. Her store was burned to

the ground during the uprising, the riot, the social explosion—as the civil
unrest in Los Angeles was variously called.

Mrs. Young-Soon Han
Former Liquor Store Owner
Swallowing the Bitterness

When I was in Korea,
I used to watch many luxurious Hollywood lifestyle movies.
I never saw any poor man,
any black
maybe one housemaid?
Until last year
I believed America is the best.
I still believe it.
I don't deny that now.
Because I'm victim.
But
as
the year ends in ninety-two,
and we were still in turmoil,
and having all the financial problems,
and mental problems,
then a couple months ago,
I really realized that
Korean immigrants were left out
from this
society and we were nothing.
What is our right?
Is it because we are Korean?
Is it because we have no politicians?
Is it because we don't
speak good English?
Why?
Why do we have to be left out?
(*She is hitting her hand on the coffee table.*)
We are not qualified to have medical treatment!
We are not qualified to get uh

food stamps!
(*She hits the table once.*)
Not GR!
(*Hits the table once.*)
No welfare!
(*Hits the table once.*)
Anything!
Many Afro-Americans
(*Two quick hits.*)
who never worked
(*One hit.*)
they get
at least minimum amount
(*One hit.*)
of money
(*One hit.*)
to survive!
(*One hit.*)
We don't get any!
(*Large hit with full hand spread.*)
Because we have a *car!*
(*One hit.*)
and we have a *house!*
(*Pause six seconds.*)
And we are *high tax payers!*
(*One hit.*)
(*Pause fourteen seconds.*)
Where do I finda [*sic*] justice?
Okay, black people
Probably,
believe they won
by the trial?
Even some complains only half, right
justice was there?
But I watched the television
that Sunday morning
Early morning as they started
I started watch it all day.

They were having party, and then they celebrated *(Pronounced*
   CeLEbreted.)
all of South Central,
all the churches,
they finally found that justice exists
in this society.
Then where is the victims' rights?
They got their rights
by destroying *innocent Korean merchants (Louder.)*
They have a lot of respect, *(Softer.)*
as I do
for Dr. Martin King?
He is the only model for black community.
I don't care Jesse Jackson.
But,
he was the model
of non-violence
Non-violence?
They like to have hiseh [*sic*] spirits.
What about last year?
They destroyed innocent people!
(Five second pause.)
And I wonder if that is really justice,
(And a very soft uh after justice like justicah, but very quick.)
to get their rights
in this way.
(Thirteen second pause.)
I waseh swallowing the bitternesseh.
Sitting here alone, and watching them.
They became all hilarious.
(Three second pause.)
And uh,
in a way I was happy for them,
and I felt glad for them,
at least they got something back, you know.
Just let's forget Korean victims or other victims
who are destroyed by them.
They have fought

for their rights
(*One hit simultaneous with the word rights.*)
over two centuries
(*One hit simultaneous with centuries.*)
and I have a lot of sympathy and understanding for them.
Because of their effort, and sacrificing,
other minorities like And Hispanic
or Asians
maybe we have to suffer more
by mainstream,
you know?
That's why I understand.
And then
I like to be part of their
joyment.
But.
That's why I had mixed feeling
as soon as I heard the verdict.
I wish I could
live together
with eh [*sic*] Blacks
but after the riots
there were too much differences
The fire is still there
how do you call it
(*She says a Korean word asking for translation. In Korean, she says
      "igniting fire."*)
igni
igniting fire
It canuh
burst out any time.

Suffice it to say, "I was swallowing the bitterness"—spoken by a woman who was apologizing for her English, at least to me as an actress speaking those words on stage—seems to stand as elegantly as any sanctioned bit of poetry I have spoken.

And I needed guides in every community. I could not have met the celebrities I interviewed (Eddie Olmos, Charlton Heston, Anjelica Huston) without the help of Gordon Davidson, who ran the theater, and his connections. I could never have met the police officers and politicians I met without the help of my friend Stanley Sheinbaum, who had been police commissioner. I could never have met the black activists whom I met if it had not been for Twilight Bey, the gang member for whom the show was named. Yet Twilight *never came to see the show.* Years later, I heard from him. He called to ask me to help him write a book. That book collaboration never took off, but we reunited, and I learned something very important. In terms of the kind of theater I do, Twilight sees himself as audience, as someone who is coming *for* me. He did not see me or my work as being *there* for him. Yet ultimately, when he thought he did need me, he called out. And maybe that's enough. Maybe it's enough for us to make introductions out in what seems to be the wildernesses around us, *just in case.* Perhaps that's enough, and we should not expect, as the missionaries did, to *convert* people. Perhaps it is a way to initiate conversations of the sort we'd like to bring into the dominant cultural circles. Does change call for conversion—or is it enough to declare that spaces exist in order to foster further conversation down the line? Those who measure would like to quantify what art can do. But art has never been quantifiable, and, sadly, some of the most widely known works of art became so without the artists themselves living to see that happen. Twilight subsequently, saw the movie based on the show. But movies, you see, are automatically more accessible.

My work has extended beyond my own work in the theater. I now seek to create spaces for community among artists, scholars, and activists. I developed and directed the Institute on the Arts and Civic Dialogue at Harvard in the late 1990s. The project was funded by the Ford Foundation, after I had been their first artist-in-residence. While in residence, I had a number of conversations with program officers at Ford about the lack of a place in society where true conversation can take place, where real content can be explored, where truly difficult things can be said. I sought out and brought together artists from all disciplines, as well as scholars. The aspiration was to seed art as expression and as a tease for increased conversation, contemplation, and activism.

The work at Harvard was experimental. Three years were not enough; however, that effort became the seed for further thinking and design, and I want to discuss one of the offshoots of that project here.

I brought together many artists over three summers at Harvard and produced many events. I also created what I called "the core audience."

Members of this core promised to come to everything we did in the first summer; we started with over a hundred people in the core. I had wanted only thirty-five and was astonished that so many responded. About sixty-five of them religiously followed and participated in our events over the three summers. By the second and third summers, I met first with the core audience. To me, if we think of the theater as a place with three walls (the stage), the core audience was the fourth wall of a room in which we would look at the pressing issues of the world upside down, specifically to get another point of view than the one being presented by the media.

I now direct an organization called Anna Deavere Smith Works. It is dedicated to creating a global community of artists doing work about the world's most pressing problems. These artists are necessarily nomads. I have most recently brought together nine artists from around the world, and one scholar, in a symposium in which we looked at how boundaries and borders can be places of limitation but also of possibility. The fellows included a Zimbabwean-born choreographer now living in the United States; a South African playwright now living in Canada; a Vietnamese visual artist who was raised in the United States and has now returned to Vietnam; a photographer who has been taking photographs along the U.S.–Mexico border, predominantly of the border patrol; an American Muslim author; a cellist and composer who believes that music can inspire compassion and world peace; an Algerian French rapper, who just won a censorship case against Nicolas Sarkozy, the president of France; and an Argentinean painter, now living in Berkeley, who creates art in communities where massacres have occurred. The scholar was an extremely accomplished American historian. We were joined by a rabbi, other scholars, and a renowned Iranian filmmaker and visual artist.

What was clear from our convening is that so many people are "from" somewhere "else." There is, on the one hand, the trend toward diaspora. On the other, there is the trend toward going back "home." This means to me that the notion of community becomes one of mobility—being mobile, going to and fro, and trying to make a difference while "visiting" or while "returning." I long ago began to think of the predicament of "belonging." When one belongs to a certain group or place, one necessarily becomes a camp member, a tribe member in a kind of "safe house" of identity. My desire has been, and is, to create the places in between those safe houses, a crossroads of ambiguity where new works and new relationships evolve.

I have lived in this crossroad for the greater part of my life and created my best work there. I think again of Roz Malamud saying in my presence on *60 Minutes*, "What does she know? She's *not from here*." But what is the "here"? We are all from somewhere, but we may be changing the *here* constantly. The moment when the young Korean American graduate students began a sentence with "We think you are going to get it wrong" and ended with "so we want to help you." It seems to me that at this point, artistically, there is no possibility of community without collaboration.

Collaborations that link artists with agents of social change could be extraordinarily provocative. There was an era in which collaboration proliferated. I have been enormously affected by reading the journals of the Free Southern Theater. This group of actors and writers and thinkers went to the American South during the 1960s—probably the South's bitterest moment post–Civil War. They performed plays in community centers, and when the community centers were threatened with bombings because of the activist nature of the plays, they performed in open fields under the stars. Their cause? Their provocation? Getting the vote for African Americans. Did they cause a change? Yes, but against the background of a huge movement, a movement that included many kinds of change agents—among them artists. The big haunting questions about art and change, or change of any kind, are: What are you willing to lose? and What are you willing to sacrifice? Change does not come for free.

My suggestion is that we find ways of sparking unlikely collaborations—collaborations that will enrich the public sphere, inspiring and encouraging all kinds of people to come out of their safe houses. In those spaces, with singular people who dare to leave the safe house of identity, intellectual or artistic discipline, or political encampment, we might create some movement. We live in a world where some people don't even carry their wallets or change in their pockets anymore. It's too bothersome. It's a big-bill world, at least in the United States. There are people begging for change on our streets and on streets all over the world. Art cannot supply all of the change. However, because so many artists are nomadic, on the move, outside of safe houses, we have a chance to join up where change is on the verge. Our companionship with those who understand policy, or the deeper things that ail us as humans, could at least put some holes into the larger and more ominous walls.

section•two

COMMUNITY AND BACK

Poetry in Dialogue

TIA CHUCHA COMES HOME

*Poetry, Community, and a Crazy Aunt—Tia Chucha's
Centro Cultural & Bookstore*

Luis Rodriguez

*I secretly admired Tia Chucha.
She was always quick with a story,
another "Pepito" joke or a hand-written lyric
she'd produced regardless of the occasion.
She was a despot of desire,
uncontainable as a splash of water
on a varnished table.
I wanted to remove the layers
of unnatural seeing,
the way Tia Chucha beheld
the world, with first eyes,*

like an infant who can discern
the elixir within milk.
I wanted to be one of the prizes
She stuffed into her rumpled bag.

—excerpt from the poem "Tia Chucha,"
by Luis Rodriguez

Tia Chucha was the name of my aunt, "the crazy relative of the family," who impacted me in ways I didn't know until years later when I decided to do a crazy thing and dedicate myself to poetry.

Tia Chucha loved to write poems and songs, play guitar, and even create her own perfumes and colognes that "smelled something like rotting fish on a hot day at the tuna cannery." Like most eccentric people, she was gossiped about, laughed at, and asked to leave whenever she visited for more than a week. But I harbored a respect for her ability to be unique, interesting, bold, and even somewhat off her rocker.

Unlike other relatives who tried hard to fit into the molds of family, church, or society, my aunt definitely danced to a different drummer. She never married because she didn't want a man to tell her what to do. Her art was her church. She once tried to teach me guitar but got so swept up with the fingering and notation that she forgot I was her student, and she played and sang through the rest of the lesson time. Even though as a kid I was shy and unobtrusive, in time her spirit fired up my own creative furnaces, pervading many of my decisions as an artist, an activist, a human being.

This is why I helped establish Tia Chucha's Centro Cultural & Bookstore—to honor imaginative possibilities and to help people find the courage not to be corralled, pushed aside, or dismissed. Our values are embodied in our tagline: Where Art and Minds Meet—For a Change. We organized ourselves around the idea that the arts, particularly the language arts, help regenerate communities, families, our stories, our futures— that even a weak economy has new life in the arts.

We understood that the first move from chaos isn't order—it's creativity.

BECOMING A POET

To appreciate what we do at Tia Chucha's Centro Cultural & Bookstore, allow me to tell our story.

It started when I was a drug addict, gang member, and lost soul in a poor East L.A.–area barrio during my youth. This changed when I became active in the Chicano Movement of the late 1960s and early 1970s. A leading aspect of this movement was the arts—along with social change, there were murals (East L.A. eventually had more public art than any other community in the country), music, theater, cafés, and poetry.

The art forms included lowriding (cars, bikes, and motorcycles), Chicano R&B and rock (over the years with bands such as Thee Midniters, El Chicano, Tierra, Los Lobos, Ozomotli, and Quetzal), murals and paintings (Willie Herron, Judy Baca, Alma Lopez, Gronk, East Los Streetscapers, Barbara Carrasco, John Valadez, and Gilbert "Magu" Lujan to name a few), theater and film (through ASCO, Jesús Treviño, Culture Clash, Josefina Lopez, Las Ramonas), and poetry and prose by writers such as Marisela Norte, Gloria Alvarez, Roberto Rodriguez, Victor M. Valle, Helena Viramontez, and Manazar. Through all these art forms, but especially the last, I began to swim the sea of two languages—and I learned how these could be part of their highest manifestations in poetry.

I began to swim in the sea of two languages— and how these could be part of their highest manifestations in poetry.

As difficult as it was, I quit all the drugs and violence; I was arrested for the last time at eighteen, and while in the county jail awaiting trial for fighting with police officers, I decided to begin my first heroin withdrawal. At the same time, the community wrote letters on my behalf, some people showed up in court, and a judge decided to give me a break—I was released with time served. The community and judge recognized that I mattered. By then I had already been involved in rallies, walkouts, demonstrations, study groups, poetry workshops. Now I had to remove myself totally from the "crazy life," which I did by working seven years in industry—as a paper mill worker, a foundry smelter, a millwright apprentice, a carpenter, a truck driver, a maintenance mechanic. I spent four years in a steel mill. At age twenty I also began my first family, which eventually brought two babies into the world. I was "maturing" out of the intensity and violence, which is how most gangbangers do it, although it is often a long hard road—two steps forward, one step back.

After three years, my first family broke up. I felt lost for a time until in my mid-twenties I made a destiny-altering decision to quit my industrial work and become a reporter/photographer at a weekly newspaper in East L.A. I walked into the newspaper's offices and asked for a writing job. The editors said sure, but I also had to answer the phones, sweep the floors, and take out the trash. I accepted, although the pay was several hundred dollars a week less than in the steel mill.

I also signed up for writing and speech classes at East Los Angeles Community College. And I later earned a certificate from Summer Program for Minority Journalists at the University of California, Berkeley, which opened the door to my first daily newspaper job in San Bernardino, California.

In 1980, I began poetry workshops in the barrio and in prisons through the L.A. Latino Writers Association. In 1982, I served as the director of LALWA and editor of the literary arts magazine *ChismeArte* (Gossip Art). I also freelanced for magazines and helped with community radio programming. And I turned up at local poetry readings on the east side, eventually ending up in the bigger Westside venues such as Beyond Baroque. In 1985, when I moved to Chicago to edit and write, I also attended poetry events in the burgeoning scene there. Later I worked as a typesetter and on weekends as a writer/reporter at an all-news radio station.

> I decided to create my own press,
> publish my own book, and suffer the damages later.

All along, I was working on writing poems. By 1989—at age thirty-five—I decided to publish my first book of poetry. After sending my manuscript to various publishers and contests, at a cost of a few hundred dollars, the rejection notes piled up, my self-esteem fell to pieces, I had no book, and I almost gave up on poetry altogether. But like many artists, especially the "crazy" ones, I couldn't stop. So I decided to create my own press, publish my own book, and suffer the damages later.

Something my aunt would have done.

At the time, I worked for the publications department of the Archdiocese of Chicago. With the help of our book designer, a Menominee-German artist named Jane Brunette, I put together a beautifuly designed book of thirteen poems—of the hundreds I'd written, these were the ones I deemed publishable. I obtained funds from city and state individual grants. My friend Gamaliel Ramirez, a Puerto Rican artist, provided the cover art. I called the book *Poems Across the Pavement*.

When it came time to name the press, I didn't hesitate. I named it for my favorite aunt. Unfortunately, Tia Chucha had passed away not long before, so she never knew how important she was in my life. Yet, somehow, I sense my aunt has been with me ever since.

At the time, Chicago was engendering slam poetry and other performance-oriented expressions—poetry bands, poetry and dance, poetry theater, poetry fish fries, and more. I worked with such luminaries of the scene as Patricia Smith, Michael Warr, David Hernandez, Tony Fitzpatrick, Lisa Buscani, Carlos Cumpian, Cin Salach, and Marvin Tate. My book became a local hit—I sold it out of the trunk of my car. Soon other poets approached me about publishing their works. Eventually, the press published all of the above authors as well as local poets Rohan B. Preston, Jean Howard, Dwight Okita, Sterling Plumpp, and John Sheehan, among others. And when poets from outside Chicago began to send their manuscripts, we published the likes of Kyoko Mori, Diane Glancy, Nick Carbo, Ricardo Sanchez, Melvin Dixon, and Virgil Suarez.

In 1991, the Guild Complex, a nonprofit literary arts institution run by Michael Warr, took over Tia Chucha Press, providing me with an editorial board that included Reginald Gibbons, Julie Parson-Nesbitt, and Quraysh Ali Lansana—and opportunities for larger grants. Before long, we began to receive two hundred manuscripts a year. With 100 percent consensus from the editorial board, we published A. Van Jordan, Terrance Hayes, Anne-Marie Cusac, and Angela Shannon. We also produced a CD called *A Snake in the Heart: Poems and Music by Chicago Spoken Word Performers*, with the artwork of poet-artist-actor Tony Fitzpatrick (whose work has graced a number of our books over the years). Eventually we had a chapbook series for Chicago poets.

In time, our authors, often after moving on to bigger publishers, won National Poetry Slams, Whiting Writers Awards, Lila Wallace–Reader's Digest Writing Awards, Lannan Fellowships, Illinois Arts Council fellowships, Chicago Abroad grants, National Endowment for the Arts fellowships, and nominations for the Pulitzer Prize and the National Book Award. Tia Chucha Press and the Guild Complex became instrumental in the Chicago Poetry Festivals—called Neutral Turf—where some three thousand people came to readings along Lake Michigan. With city funds, we sent slam poetry winners to places such as Accra, Ghana; Prague, Czechoslovakia; and Osaka, Japan. My community work at the time also involved poetry workshops in prisons, juvenile lockups, schools, and shelters for homeless people. I helped create Youth Struggling for Survival (YSS) for gang and nongang youth and, later, the Humboldt Park Teen Reach program. I wanted to expand my work with poetry to include communities kept outside the margins of literary funding and expression, which is highly marginalized in the larger culture as it is. I wanted to remember where I had come from—and to give back to those still caught in the street life's steely grasp. I traveled around the country spreading the gospel of poetry—and then over the years to Canada, Mexico, El Salvador, Guatemala, Nicaragua, Honduras, Venezuela, Peru, Puerto Rico, Japan, England, France, the Netherlands, Austria, Italy, Bosnia-Herzegovina, and across Germany.

I married my third wife, Trini Cardenas, in 1988 (we've had two sons since then). But ten years later, Ramiro, my oldest son from my first marriage, was sentenced to twenty-eight years in state prison for three counts of attempted murder. I had written the 1993 best-selling memoir *Always Running: La Vida Loca: Gang Days in L.A.* to help Ramiro avoid just such a situation, but though I had helped many gang youth get out of the madness, I could not help my son. I also had a daughter and four grandchildren to worry about. We had many friends in Chicago but no family. Trini had a large, active, and healthy family in the northeast San Fernando Valley, so in 2000, we decided to go back to Los Angeles.

POETRY AND THE CITY OF ANGELS

Over the years, I published more poetry books at other presses, as well as children's books, a short story collection, a novel, and a nonfiction book on creating community in violent times. I had paying gigs all over and a few fellowships and awards. It was time for me to give back on another level.

For years, the Northeast Valley was known as the "Mexican" side of the valley. When we arrived, it had a population of some 450,000—about the size of Oakland—mostly Mexican and Central American people. Yet the area lacked a bookstore, an art gallery, a movie house, or decent cultural space. Trini was disappointed that not much had changed since she left her Northeast Valley home twenty-five years earlier. After buying a decent home in the city of San Fernando, I didn't need to get a sports car or a swimming pool. Instead, with the extra money that came my way, I invested in Tia Chucha's Café Cultural, a café, bookstore, workshop center, art gallery, and performance space in Sylmar, California.

Trini, my brother-in-law Enrique Sanchez, and I built a full coffee bar with an espresso machine, roaster, grinder, deli cases, refrigerator, ice-making machine, sinks, wood cabinets, and stock shelving. We had portable wood shelves for books, a small gallery space, and a Mayan-motif look . throughout the store. Trini picked out amazing, warm, earth-tone colors. We obtained our first inventory of books. And we hired a manager and a young café employee.

That was in December 2001. The Liberty Hill Foundation provided a three-year social entrepreneur grant to supplement what I put into the place. We even had a Navajo elder (Trini had been adopted by Anthony Lee and his family on the rez a few years before), local friends, and Chicago friends from YSS in attendance during a community blessing.

We were ready to rock this world.

A DREAM OF COMMUNITY EMPOWERMENT

One of the first things we did was set up a weekly open mic. Poets read, spoken word artists performed, people sang, and guitarists played. To accommodate the Spanish-speaking community, we held a weekly *Noches Bohemias* for Spanish-language performers. I showed up during the first years to read my work and encourage others. Other L.A.-area poets included Poets of the Round Table, In Lak Ech (a Chicana women's poetry group), and Street Poets. Multigenre groups such as the Chicano hip-hop group El Vuh, the Spanish-language rock band Noxtiel, the punk-Aztec-traditional Mexican group Hijos de la Tierra, and the Peruvian music–based band Raices started up at Tia Chucha's, along with theater outfits such as Tres Chingasos and Teatro Chucheros. We soon had our own resident *Mexika* (so-called Aztec) *danza* group called Temachtia Quetzalcoatl. Authors such as Sandra Cisneros, Ruben Martinez, Victor Villasenor, Adrienne Rich, Denise Chavez, and Wanda Coleman graced our stage. The music ranged from traditional Mexican to indigenous, rock, hip-hop, blues, and R&B. One of my favorite '60s bands, Charles Wright and the Watts 103rd Street Rhythm Band ("Express Yourself"), played there as well.

In 2003, singer Angelica Loa Perez and rapper Victor Mendoza joined me in starting a nonprofit sister organization to the café and bookstore. We called this Tia Chucha's Centro Cultural and soon incorporated all the workshops of the café and most of the events. By the mid-2000s, Tia Chucha's had served thousands of kids, teens, parents, and seniors—mostly for free. We hired more staff, mainly young bilingual activists. With the addition of the nonprofit, we obtained grants from the L.A. Department of Cultural Affairs, the California Arts Council, the L.A. County Arts Commission, and foundations such as the Solidago Foundation, the Attias Family Foundation, the Middleton Foundation, the Center for Cultural Innovation, the Not Just Us Foundation, and the Panta Rhea Foundation.

Although we expanded into all the arts, poetry was still at the heart of our programming. I worked to get Tia Chucha Press back from Chicago's Guild Complex by 2005, and in the following years we published the work of ariel robello, Patricia Spears Jones, Linda Jackson, Alfred Arteaga, Susan D. Anderson, Richard Vargas, Luivette Resto, Linda Rodriguez, and Chiwan Choi—and created additional anthologies. When Tia Chucha Press poet Elizabeth Alexander was selected in 2009 as the poet at the inauguration of forty-fourth U.S. president, Barack Obama, we reprinted her 1996 book, *Body of Life*.

On top of this, we started a recording company called Dos Manos, which produced CDs, and we began the first outdoor literacy and performance festival in the San Fernando Valley—Celebrating Words: Written, Performed, and Sung—and an annual benefit at Hollywood's John Anson Ford Amphitheater. Eventually, we set up a youth empowerment project called Young Warriors, founded by two teenaged community leaders, Mayra Zaragoza and Brian Dessaint.

CRISIS AND LOSS

The first major crisis involved the tripling of our rent in late 2006. Although we had brought badly needed life into the strip mall where we were located, the landlords wanted to replace us with a high-end laundry service. Our five-year lease ended, and the rent was increased. We fought, but money talks in the commercial rental business. We were doing well but not well enough to pay triple rent.

I admit this tore at my resolve. The tens of thousands of dollars I'd invested to create Tia Chucha's were now going down the drain. We received our notice to vacate in early 2007. Other possible locations were pulled out from under us. Although there was nothing like Tia Chucha's for miles around and despite our immense community support, we had nowhere to go for remedies—not the city, not the county, not the state, not any major funding source.

I was on the verge of quitting when I decided one Friday to go to Tia Chucha's open mic. I sat in the back, depressed. Poet after poet rose to read. An eight-year-old girl read from her journal. A Mexican waiter at an Italian restaurant did a hearty recital of Spanish-language poetry standards. People sang, including a woman who sold tamales on weekends. That's when I realized I couldn't let this go. Despite the trouble, the losses, the money burned up, I had to keep Tia Chucha's going.

In two months, we found a smaller place, hidden away in horse country, only ten minutes from the old spot. The community was Lake View Terrace, surrounded by ranches and open land. Community members brought their tools and hard work to tear down the old place and to help paint and build out the new one. Soon our programming continued, but we couldn't set up another coffee bar. We had to place our expensive coffee bar equipment in storage.

Unfortunately, business at the new space was bad. People had a hard time finding the place. There was no walk-in traffic. Our workshops and events were largely curtailed. But we soldiered on. A few events drew large audiences—hip-hop, comedy nights, musical performances, and open mics continued to bring people in. We received strong media attention, including articles in the *Los Angeles Times*, the *L.A. Daily News*, *La Opinion*, *L.A. Weekly*, *People (en Español)* as well as local and national TV and radio broadcasts. Celebrating Words and our annual benefit at the Ford Amphitheater brought in more acts, funding, and audiences—between five hundred to one thousand people.

But for the most part, we lost momentum.

Then the private storage space we used for our coffee bar equipment, bookshelves, books, CDs, and other important items was broken into—not once but twice. Vandals destroyed our neon sign and painted over shelves and boxes. They tore up books and CDs. Worse, they stole our most expensive café items. Even though we had insurance, the company refused to adequately compensate us.

We lost our precious coffee bar.

The Northeast Valley is a working-class area with large swaths of poor people. There are gangs, housing projects, and crime. The economy was worsening. Again, I could have given up—but didn't. Instead, I worked on obtaining a new space back in Sylmar. We found a newly constructed, six-unit structure at a strip mall near Mission Community College, flanked by Interstate 210 and a major thoroughfare. The rental market was suffering by then—it was the autumn of 2008, when the stock market fell faster than at any time since the Great Depression. For months, I saw that none of the units had been leased. A supermarket in front of the structure was boarded up. Units alongside the market included a few vacancies.

It took a while, but we finally persuaded the landlord to lease us a corner space in the new structure. He wanted top dollar per square foot, which explained why nobody was leasing. I got the landlord to go to half of what he was asking by convincing him to give us part of the rent back every month as a tax write-off. We took a five-year lease that included an option to continue the same rent agreement if we wanted another five years—we didn't need to be caught as we had been with the first lease. The great thing was access to a large parking lot. We could hold events there.

On the day of our grand opening in March of 2009, we set up a stage for bands, poets, dancers, actors, and speakers. There were food stands, including one featuring a restaurant in the strip mall that specialized in Mexican and Salvadoran dishes. As many as seven hundred people came, and the *L.A. Daily News* did a major piece.

We folded the café-bookstore business into the nonprofit. We are now a full-fledged, community-based 501(c)(3). Today, more people than ever attend our workshops, performances, open mics, and festivals. We've had major media coverage, including NBC's *Nightly News with Brian Williams*, KABC-TV's *Vista L.A.*, CNN's *What Matters*, and CNN's *Leaders with Heart*. In addition to city, county, state, and federal funds, we now have grants from the California Community Foundation, the Thrill Hill Foundation, the Annenberg Foundation, the Weingart Foundation, and the James Irvine Foundation—and donations and other services from notables such as John Densmore of the Doors, Cheech Marin, Dave Marsh, Lou Adler, and Richard Foos of the Shout! Factory. In April of 2009, Bruce

Springsteen invited Tia Chucha's to set up a table with donation buckets at one of his sold-out concerts at the L.A. Sports Arena. During the concert, Bruce mentioned Tia Chucha's and asked people to donate. Later that evening, Trini and I made our way backstage to personally thank Mr. Springsteen.

WHAT WE LEARNED

Poetry, like all art, comes from within people, within families, within community. Literacy rises from the hunger people have for knowledge, ideas, stories. We found an abundance of art, song, music, poetry, and more already existing within the neglected northeast San Fernando Valley.

> Poetry, like all art, comes from within people, within families, within community.

I knew that companies like Barnes and Noble had been asked to set up shop here. We heard they wouldn't touch this area. What they failed to recognize was that poor people, even with little material means, have an abundance of imagination and talents. Our resident artist, Juan Pueblo, a Mexican sculptor, painter, guitarist, and poet, found us one day when he noticed our lights while walking down the main drag. He now facilitates an array of arts and music workshops and leads community members in painting walls and murals at Tia Chucha's and in the community. The man who emcees our open mic is a construction worker originally from Guatemala. Our indigenous cosmology classes have enrolled many Mexican and Central American indigenous people—including those whose first language is Nahuatl or Mayan.

And our bookstore, though bookselling is a rough business for anyone, has grown. One local mechanic, who had read almost no books until we opened our doors, in one year read more than thirty books. Middle school and high school students, including a group that came twice from the San Francisco Bay area, make field trips to the store.

We've also now established programming and events for the significant numbers of African Americans, Asians, and European Americans who live in the Northeast Valley and elsewhere. Since 2007, our board of directors has expanded from a working board of three people to ten members. Besides Chicanos and Central Americans, the board has included a Filipina, two African Americans, and three European Americans.

We're very active in creating policy that reflects what we've learned about community and the arts. For example, I got involved with forty other gang intervention specialists, peace advocates, and researchers in helping write a comprehensive, community-based gang intervention policy that included the arts. In February of 2008, the L.A. City Council adopted this plan as part of its gang violence and youth development programs. Now I'm working with arts advocates, artists, cultural spaces, and public art leaders in trying to establish a comprehensive neighborhood arts policy that can protect cultural spaces, independent bookstores, literacy organizations, public art projects, and similar groups from the vagaries of the marketplace, rent hikes, urban removals, and lack of funds. In Los Angeles, the so-called Entertainment Capital of the World, where most arts bucks are being concentrated in downtown, Hollywood, or the Westside, our aim has been to set policy that would help sustain living community arts in all neighborhoods—including places such as South Central L.A., East L.A., and the Northeast Valley, where bookstores and cultural spaces are almost nonexistent.

With the economic downturn, though we have seen the arts being cut in schools, cultural spaces and independent bookstores being pushed out, and murals being allowed to deteriorate, Tia Chucha's is putting forth the revolutionary concept that arts-based initiatives are the most vital ways of reviving the economy, gathering and building community, helping abandoned and suppressed youth, and imagining better and more equitable ways of organizing, surviving, and living. As proof of this—all the other units in the block of rental units we're at are now leased to local businesses. And Fresh and Easy, a global food market chain, has taken over the formerly shuttered building across the way.

Still, at the heart of what we do is poetry.

And by way of poetic justice, I must add that my son Ramiro, because of "good time" and overcrowded prisons, was finally released from the Illinois Department of Corrections in the summer of 2010 after thirteen-and-a-half years. He quit gangs and drugs in prison. And we've grown close—no matter the distance or razor wire, I never abandoned him. He's now part of the Tia Chucha family, looking into creating a similar center in the Mexican communities of Chicago.

The worst aspect of poverty is the spiritual poverty that accompanies it. When we provide places for people to imagine, to dialogue, to express, to share, and to create, we uplift the spirit needed to also help remove the real constraints of economic and social realities. This is truly substantive soul work. Tia Chucha's has succeeded because we have always responded to obstacles by becoming more imaginative and encompassing. We have refused to give up on the arts. We've tapped into the creative capacity already existing in communities, even in the most neglected areas.

At the heart of what we do is poetry.

There was a fourteen-year-old Chicana who wanted to commit suicide. She lived in a broken home. She had no friends at school and no one to turn to. One day, this young woman walked the Sylmar streets thinking of ways to kill herself. But as she strolled, she heard *Mexika* drumming, something that, despite her heritage, she did not know about. She went toward the sound and found our *danza* group practicing in front of our space. The teenager showed up every Monday as the group worked on routines and ceremonies. One day she decided to practice with the others. In time, she learned the cosmology, rituals, steps, and some of the language.

About a year later, I sat in a circle with *danza* members at Tia Chucha's. I asked people to express what they thought of the group and its learning process. This young woman finally told her story—nobody had known about her original intent until then. She finished, with tears in her eyes, saying, "I want to thank you all for helping me, for teaching me about my culture and roots. Now, I don't want to die anymore."

All that we do, all that we went through, is worth it if it turns one young person away from death. That's the power of poetry, of the arts, of community—of places like Tia Chucha's Centro Cultural & Bookstore.

WE WERE HERE, AND WE ARE HERE

The Cave Canem Poetry Workshop

Elizabeth Alexander

I became a poet in the woodshed, outside of much community, certainly outside of a community of African American peers. I came of age as a poet at an odd time in the culture, in the wake of the women's movement, as "identity politics" was starting to be named, celebrated, and then, swiftly, derided. I'd belonged to some small women's writing groups, and I was part of rich communities of black people in the heady work of academia in the 1980s.

Black poets of my generation were doing their work in diaspora. Those older than I was—Rita Dove, Yusef Komunyakaa, and others—seemed to be working on their own and were often the only ones in their teaching and poetry-writing worlds. My own path to poetry was first lit by an avuncular pen pal, the poet Michael Harper, whom I began writing after hearing him read his work when I was in college. When I would chitter-chatter away to him in letters and my own postcards, he'd kindly write me back on his signature plain ecru Brown University postcards, replying to my incessant questions about his indelible poems. "I notice that your line 'Black human history: apple tree' echoes Langston Hughes's 'night coming tenderly, black like me' in rhythm and rhyme. Did you intend that?" was one smarty-pants question written before I realized that ancestral echoes in poetry usually make their way in of their own accord. I would meditate for hours on the koans Harper would send my way. "Sometimes you need to get sick," he told me once; though I'm still not sure I totally understand all the possibilities of that utterance, I knew I was lucky that Michael Harper took me for a serious young person.

> I realized that ancestral echoes in poetry
> usually make their way in of their own accord.

I only ever had one poetry teacher and that was Derek Walcott at Boston University in the master's program in creative writing. Walcott was suspicious of anything that might be called "black identity" as well as of whether said community was necessary for the nurturance of poems. He taught me that a poet's writing community consists of masters dead and a few living and that our sacred obligation was to the poems, one by one. His own famous friendships with Joseph Brodsky and Seamus Heaney were on display for those of us studying poetry in the Boston area in the '80s; Walcott was generous about inviting students out to coffee and pubs and letting us be eavesdroppers and hangers-on to his soulful, robust friendship with these men. They were all writing out of distinct senses of place and approaches to the English language, with Hardy, Yeats, Frost, Lowell, and Bishop in their shared "rattle bag," to borrow the name of Heaney's anthology that came out around that time. I beheld their friendship and felt lucky to be nearby, quietly, quietly listening. I also learned from my year in Walcott's world that you can't kill poets, which is to say we come up between cracks in cement in wild and unexpected colors, untended, nurtured on tough soil. Story after story testified to sheer tenacity coupled with the sheer good fortune of being able to do the work. We exist despite. No one can stop a poet who truly needs to be a poet—for a while, yes, but not forever. Poets are the ones who make poems because they have to.

Something shifted for me in the wake of the death of the painter Romare Bearden. His work had been deeply meaningful to me my whole life, and I had written poems in response to that work while studying with Walcott. I made a pilgrimage from Philadelphia to the service at the Cathedral of St. John the Divine. A grand service it was—I remember the vibrant Bearden works lining the walls of the cathedral, the Alvin Ailey dancer who offered a solo, the pianist Jackie McLean, the eulogies by Ralph Ellison and by my own beloved teacher and Bearden's great friend, Derek Walcott. Afterward I went out to eat with Derek and a large group of black visual and literary artists. I was the youngest at the table, the proverbial jug with big ears listening to the fabulous grown-ups tell stories and carry on, watching them drink their liquor and put hot sauce on their food.

Everyone at the table was brilliant and black.

I knew that at the center of that vision were two pillars: unending discipline and the fertile soil of black history and creativity as source and sustenance.

Everyone at the table was brilliant and black and had made a commitment to a life in the arts. Everyone understood the one-foot-in-front-of-the-other aspects of making creative work, the discipline, the joy, the privilege, the struggle. That table of vibrant black people telling stories and eating food and sharing precious bits of black cultural history that would be otherwise lost was a dream come true for me. I had never been in such company with as clear a taste of my own life to come, a life I was committed to and would build. I wanted that world to be my home; I knew I must build and cultivate that home. And I knew that at the center of that vision were two pillars: unending discipline and the fertile soil of black history and creativity as source and sustenance. I also understood that I did not need rhetoric or declaration of anything about "blackness" as such from Derek because he made as much sense at that table as he did at the tables of Frost and Heaney and Lowell and Brodsky.

I became a poet before Internet communities, still doing it as Sylvia Plath compellingly chronicled the process of becoming a working poet in her journals: the meticulous typing and retyping on the Underwood; the carbon paper fingerprint smudges; the SASEs and trips to the post office; the occasional, encouraging scribbled replies from editors. Making the poems, sending them out, getting rejected, paying no mind, sending them out again. All this I did with no one to talk to, no peers, black or white, really. I wasn't friendless in my poetry workshop. But I was comrade-less, kindred spirit-less. I don't think that had to do with being the only black person in the workshop, actually. Rather, I think it is rare good fortune to find close poet friends. And I would not trade my solitary year of studying poetry because it cultivated artistic practice that can survive any snowstorm.

Still, there is something lost when one experiences one's becoming-a-poet not quite as an autodidact but certainly without the succor of community, the networks of community, the sense of belonging to a peer community. There have certainly been black writers' collectives over the years, from the salon held in Georgia Douglas Johnson's house in Washington, DC, in the 1920s to the ateliers of the Harlem Renaissance to the Umbra group of New York City in the early 1960s, chronicled so beautifully by Lorenzo Thomas, to OBASI in Chicago beginning later in the '60s to the funky young geniuses of the Dark Room Collective in the late '80s and early '90s in Cambridge, Massachusetts, to the Harlem Writers Guild and the Wintergreen Women of Virginia, which continue to this day. This was what Cave Canem became for me—and more. Over the time since its founding, Cave Canem has sustained itself and quietly grown stronger and more perennial. Its distinction is in its edification; is has become an institution devoted to the nurturance of black poets.

Over fifteen years ago, Toi Derricotte and Cornelius Eady had had one too many conversations with other African American poets who were weary from being "the only one" in poetry workshops. Inevitably, the black poets kept finding, when their poems were up for discussion, that conversation too often turned to racial misunderstandings or got bogged down in the call to explain cultural references unknown to their white fellow poets. Sometimes those exchanges were explosive. Lost were the poems themselves. What was in short supply was that which poets seek in workshop: feedback to make the poems stronger. So their premise was simple and elegant: it was time to create a community devoted to black poets.

Derricotte and Eady decided to hold a weeklong summer workshop retreat, with African American faculty and African American poets. They made this decision while traveling in Italy, with a serendipitous visit to

Pompeii and the House of the Tragic Poet. Subsequent worries about how to fund the workshop were allayed when Sarah Micklem, Eady's wife, said, "Why don't we do it for free?" They recruited teachers (myself included) who went in June of 1996 to the Mount St. Alphonsus monastery in Esopus, New York, along the Hudson River. We were all happy to trade a paycheck for the opportunity to work in what turned out to be one of the most vital American creative communities of the past two decades.

When people are trying to build community, they need to know something that can be difficult to articulate. They need to feel and know the time is right. And I think what we also knew at Cave Canem is that sometimes simply bringing people together in a light-handedly organized space is how you can find out what the organization ought to be. In other words, the work itself and the being together is how to define what the organization is and can be. We didn't do a whole lot of long-range planning in those early days. We simply created the conditions for people to write poems and also the "safe space" in which black poets could see what was possible. Who we are emerged from that simple purpose and from the fact of gathering. It is a particular form of genius that understands that without a community in which to make sense, the work might as well be floating in outer space. Toi and Cornelius possessed that genius.

Sometimes simply bringing people together
in a light-handedly organized space is how you find out
what the organization ought to be.

Observers of the poetry scene regularly say that Cave Canem is supporting the finest American poetry that is being written today. What began as a "safe space" for black poets to make their art turned into a vibrant community in the hundreds. Through the Cave Canem Poetry Prize, the organization publishes some of the most exciting first books being written today—Natasha Trethewey's *Domestic Work* was the choice for the inaugural book prize, and she went on to win the Pulitzer Prize just two books later. Other winners of the Cave Canem Poetry Prize would be on many lists of the finest American poetry debuts in the last ten years: Major Jackson, Lyrae Van Clief-Stefanon, Kyle Dargan, and Ronaldo Wilson, among others. The

Cave Canem Legacy series organizers archived conversations with the black poets of the generation broadly interpreted as "elder," or, better, "foundational": Derek Walcott, Lucille Clifton, Michael Harper, Yusef Komunyakaa, Ntozake Shange, Sonia Sanchez, and others. From these conversations, we now have a body of extensive interviews that is a tremendous research resource to present and future scholars and those interested in American poetry and African American culture. The Legacy series also says, indisputably, "We were here, and we are here." These publications are part of the way that Cave Canem has consciously archived itself and, in so doing, archived a piece of American literary history that might otherwise be insufficiently remembered.

Cave Canem has consciously made room for highly divergent spokes of black aesthetics and identity. The community's ethos is, to borrow Lucille Clifton's words, to live not in "either/or" but in "and/but." Derricotte and Eady have insistently modeled "safe space" for all. The space made for the apparent differences among us makes space for the differences within us, each of us, as we move through the journeys of our lives and our works. All of the prismatic faces of blackness show themselves at different times and in different degrees. So the work itself evolves, one hopes, and gives us radiant, multivocal black poetry in the new millennium.

If there are any secrets to the organization's success, they are these:

1. Do it for free. Though it is crucial that poets be paid for their labor and that overworked people of color shouldn't be expected to do more for free, sometimes doing it for free means you move with the energy of the right idea with the faith that you can work out the details later.

Sometimes doing it for free means you move with the energy of the right idea with the faith that you can work out the details later.

2. To quote Haki Madhubuti, "Run towards fear." By this I mean that a community that faces its divergences and interprets multivocality as a power source rather than Babel can build on that energy and

move toward and through issues that otherwise divide us. On the Cave Canem Listserv debates, divergence and even drama occur every day, in addition to what happens in and out of workshop. There have been times when we have needed to remind one another of our civil obligations to one another, but we have been courageous, I think, about having hard conversations and respecting our differences.

Cave Canem supports black poets. Period.

3. Stay focused. Cave Canem supports black poets. Period. Success usually makes people want to do more. But Cave Canem is not branching out to include fiction writers or poets of other backgrounds, though, importantly, there have been all kinds of rich partnerships of various kinds, and Cave Canem has inspired and supported vital groups such as Kundiman. But what Cave Canem does is plain and clear; under that simple rubric are multitudes.

4. Let the baby grow up. This is the lesson for the next decade: the organization has come of age, and its members number in the hundreds, working all around the globe. The genie is out of the bottle; the magic is out of the box. There is no controlling these people nor the work that they do. They will do their own work and define "community" and "black poetry" in many different ways. They will argue with one another. 'Tis wise to let that evolution and rub happen—then the children will come home for Thanksgiving.

5. Finally, poems come first, and poems are what last. For a week in the workshop, there is no purpose other than making them.

The experience of working outside of community sharpens the utility of community. Though Cave Canem was not a part of my formative years as a poet, it is a sustaining force in my life as a poet somewhere in midstride. For teachers and poets already published, it is truly energizing to know that there is a community that we belong to and that is paying attention to our work and example. Brilliance, brilliance in the ocean of black poetry!

ABOUT RIVER OF WORDS

Robert Hass

In classrooms all over the United States, at 4-H and Girl Scout meetings, youth detention centers, natural history museums, and in some English language classrooms overseas, children in the late fall and early spring write poems and make works of art about the natural world and the places where they live. A thirteen-year-old from Baton Rouge might make a painting of a red alligator and, with a touch of wit, entitle it *I Got the Blues.*[1]

Or a six-year-old from Northern California might be writing a poem of inner and outer weathers and call it "Sad Sun."[2]

> *Oh sun. Oh sun.*
> *Oh sun. How does*
> *it feels to be*
> *blocked by the*
> *dark dark clouds?*
> *Oh child*
> *it doesn't really*
> *feel bad at all*
> *not at all not at*
> *all not at all.*

I Got the Blues by Gerald Allen, age 13.

A sixteen-year-old from at Atlanta might be thinking about a poem in which she describes the architecture of fish to a young architect. She might call it "Letter to an Architect."[3] It would arrive in the office of River of Words typed neatly—one of thousands of poems that come into the office every spring. And one of the poets who are screening the poems might interrupt the others to read the beginning of this poem out loud because of its young author's breathtaking poise.

> *Not even you could keep me from*
> *mentioning the fish, their beauty of*

> *scaled brevity, their clipped-swishing*
> *tail funneling in everything animal.*
> *Wintertime when I saw them, their*
> *pursed old ladies' mouths, gaping under*
> *pooled clarity to share some gulled-up gossip.*
> *Their bones, pure equilateral, poked stripes*
> *at base and height, bereft of architects' errors*
> *or human compensation. I remembered then*
> *your last letter; you wrote you couldn't*
> *cut another mitre, solder another joint, peel*
> *another bit of glue from between your fingertips.*
> *I'm going to crack soon, you said.*
> *There must be some way to perfection*
> *in this grasping for centimeters . . .*

Or because this one,[4] from a thirteen-year-old American boy attending an international school, is so alert, the work of a young man emerging from childhood and taking his bearings in the world.

> *Floodplain,*
> *Bangladesh,*
> *Totally flat*
> *Except for the Chittagong Hills,*
> *Deforestation but lots of grass,*
> *Hill after hill with the Ganges River swimming by*
> *Like the stream of blood in your body.*
> *Near the split delta,*
> *Sons go fetch water in buckets,*
> *The delta in the south*
> *The life force for villagers.*
> *And so goes the Ganges River.*

Or this one,[5] which needs no unfamiliar landscape to look at and gave us a sense of how playful and insouciant and already sophisticated some of these young people are: a fourteen-year-old girl writing seven haiku on goldfish (which, she notes, were inspired by two goldfish—Stan and Oliver—by Matisse, and by Wallace Stevens). One of them reads

Tell me, what do you
think amuses a fish? No,
no, I've tried juggling.

All of this work comes from River of Words (ROW), an organization devoted to encouraging environmental awareness through the arts and the arts through environmental awareness in schools and after-school programs. ROW publishes annual books of children's poetry and art in inexpensive paperback editions designed for the classroom; it has also published larger, handsome books from commercial publishers representing many years' worth of work from children all over the world who participate in the ROW program. It maintains a gallery in Berkeley, California, and it sponsors workshops for teachers on how to use the arts to teach observation and imagination and hands-on, outdoor environmental education. To that end, it publishes a teacher's manual and a booklet about how schools and natural history museums can form partnerships with libraries, nonprofits, water districts, and watershed education programs to promote local environmental literacy. In the last two years, ROW has been developing a program for urban environmental education, One Square Block, in which children are encouraged to map and understand the flow of life through one particular patch of urban space, attending to its architecture, energy flows, flora and fauna, and range of human doings. ROW and its regional coordinators encourage interdisciplinary education by compiling regional bibliographies for teachers and students of age-appropriate literary and scientific writing about the places where they live—from literary classics to the biographies of explorers and scientists to field guides.

The mechanism at the center of this work and the one that has spread it through schools and youth programs in the United States and abroad is a contest. Every year, ROW makes awards to schoolchildren from kindergarten through twelfth grade for art and poetry they make on the theme of the watershed in which they live. The awards are given in four categories: K–2, grades 3–6, grades 7–9, and grades 10–12, one each for poetry and art. The poetry contest is for work in English, American Sign Language, and Spanish and bilingual entries only, though the Friends of the Loire River in France has initiated its own ROW program, *Fleuves de Mots*. The work of each year's winners—eight children from the United States and one child from abroad, an annual international winner in either poetry or art—is published in an annual anthology along with the poetry and art of about fifty finalists.

The awards are announced each spring at a public event at the San Francisco Public Library, and each winner receives a free trip to Washington, DC, together with one parent, for a ceremony at the Library of Congress where the children read their poetry and their art is put on display. Usually there are other activities as well: visits to their congresspersons, a tour of the treasures of the Library, a visit to the White House or the Smithsonian or the Space and Technology Museum, a boat ride on the Anacostia River, or a cleanup along the banks of the river together with children from the Washington, DC, schools. At the Washington ceremony, cosponsored by the Library of Congress's literacy and reading outreach program, the Center for the Book, an award is also made to a teacher of the year, one teacher who has done especially effective, inspiring, and imaginative work in combining arts and environmental education in the classroom.

ROW came into being in 1995, and it is mostly the creation of its director, the Bay Area writer Pamela Michael, who shaped the contest, edits the collections of the children's work and the teacher's guide, and writes most of the other educational materials ROW makes available to educators. She recruited the board that oversees ROW in its status as an educational nonprofit, and she runs the office and the art gallery and, with the board, works at the always precarious task of fund-raising to keep the organization and its work afloat. To do this work, she has a staff of two, one person to manage the daily flow of work in the office and one to work at liaison and outreach with teachers and with the Library of Congress's regional Centers for the Book, which serve as regional coordinators of the ROW program, as do other organizations. In Georgia, ROW is a program of the state's Department of Natural Resources, which employs its own coordinator/educator who takes it into most classrooms and most watersheds in the state. In Iowa, it is a program made available by the Department of Water Resources, and it is made available to communities by a department staff assigned, mostly, to talk to communities about water-quality issues.

Hundreds of classrooms, perhaps a thousand in the United States, participate in the annual ROW contest. Keeping up contact with the hard-pressed teachers whose work the organization tries to encourage and reward is an important part of the work in the main office. The office is in the industrial section of Berkeley, in an old mattress factory now called the Sawtooth Building. It is a warren of artists' studios, dance and exercise studios, small press publishers, and arts nonprofits, all jammed into a building constructed from a pattern of evenly placed skylights so that its roofline does indeed look like the teeth of a saw. It sits just down the street from a plant of Bayer, a pharmaceutical company that manufactures aspirin, a fact not lost on the people who run nonprofits. Both of ROW's staff members are on reduced hours and wages while the organization tries to weather the latest economic contraction.

★   ★   ★

My adventure with ROW, as an accidental cofounder of a nonprofit now in the middle of its second decade, began on a winter night twenty years ago after a poetry reading at a Manhattan club. A group of poets was piling into cabs to go someplace for a drink. Standing on the curb, I expressed hesitation. It was late. I had a meeting to go to in the morning at the Museum of Natural History. A young woman wearing a couple of nose rings and an eyebrow ring—it was the period when facial metal and Goth eye makeup still had a certain rawness—asked me what the meeting was about. "Spotted owls," I said. She said, amused and surprised, "You're a fuzzy-wuzzy!" I asked what a fuzzy-wuzzy was. "You know, those people who save cute animals." She thought about it. "And whales," she added. "Whales are not cute?" I asked while I sorted out my reactions. "Whales are too big to be cute. They're beautiful," someone else said, taking an interest in the conversation. I didn't go for a drink. I walked back to my hotel brooding about the fact that, depending on how you measure it, we are thirty to fifty to a hundred years into a severe environmental crisis, when the rates of extinctions among the animals and plant life of the earth are accelerating alarmingly, and that young American poets, arguably among the best, or at least most expensively, educated humans on the earth, didn't get it. They weren't themselves alarmed, and they didn't know the difference between a stuffed animal and an indicator species.

My immediate response to this moment was to resolve to find a way to teach different kinds of courses at the university where I earn my living. Over time, that led me to reflect on the fact that the kinds of writing that it would be useful to read and to teach in such courses, because they did not fit into the traditional literary genres—fiction, poetry, drama—tended not to get taught in universities or high schools. I was thinking about Thoreau's *Walden,* which does get taught, usually under the rubric of the nineteenth-century American "renaissance," and also of the essays of John Muir and Mary Austin and Wallace Stegner and Stegner's book about John Wesley Powell's exploration of the Colorado River (which is really about the conception of nature and the natural sciences that educated Easterners took with them into the West when they were exploring it). I was also thinking of the prose of Gary Snyder and Wendell Berry's essays on the culture of agriculture. I thought about Rachel Carson's work—the trilogy of books that popularized marine science in the 1950s and 1960s and *Silent Spring*, the book about pesticides that singlehandedly turned the conservation movement into the environmental movement. And Aldo Leopold's *Sand County Almanac,* probably, in the world where people work on conservation, on the way we use and treat land in the United States, the most influential piece of literary work in the second half of the twentieth century and one that is hardly read at all in literature courses in American high schools and universities.

I also thought about E. O. Wilson's intellectual autobiography, *Naturalist*, and his more speculative books about ecology and environmentalism, *Biophilia* and *Consilience.* And of some of the writers in my generation who were working in and around the natural history tradition: Terry Williams and Barry Lopez, and Richard Nelson, the Alaskan anthropologist who had been paid by the U.S. Air Force to spend a couple of seasons hunting with old Eskimos who were not raised using Gore-Tex and high-powered rifles and snowmobiles, so that he could cull survival techniques in the high Arctic for the Air Force's downed pilots. He wrote two books out of that experience: *Hunters of the Northern Forest* and *Hunters of the Northern Ice.* And then a book about bringing that experience into his own life: *The Island Within.* There was the work of Peter Matthiessen, not only his early *Wildlife in America* but also *The Snow Leopard*, his already classic book about rare animals and the coming extinctions, and *Men's Lives*, about the fishermen of the Atlantic coast, and his Florida novels. There was the desert writing of Edward Abbey and, I was sure, a whole tradition of regional natural history writing that I was only vaguely aware of. I had grown up on modernism and the Beat generation and the European experimental writing of the postwar years. There were names associated with pastel book jackets I had browsed past in bookstores: Walt Whitman's friend John Burroughs; John Hay, who wrote about Cape Cod; and a Midwestern naturalist named Edwin Teale, whose books I remembered seeing on my grandparents' bookshelves. I had associated them with the provincial byways of literature and had passed them by.

So my own education in these traditions was random, spotty. I knew that some part of my project was self-education. I was not alone in this. A whole generation of courses in American environmental literature has sprung up in the last ten years, born, I am sure, from the same perception and the same sense of urgency. And there is even a professional organization of writers, teachers, and scholars, the Association for the Study of Literature and the Environment (ASLE), who gather each year to talk about this new work. They were thinking, are thinking, that our ways of thinking about the planet and its life need to be part of formal education in the humanities and not just in the sciences. Our disciplines—with the traditional chasm between humanities and the sciences that C. P. Snow described in *Two Cultures*—did not fit the world we had made and were confronted by, and it was time to do something about it.

Around this time and in this state of mind, I came to the peculiar and temporary job of poet laureate of the United States. The poet laureate's position is an annual appointment at the Library of Congress, and it entails three responsibilities: to give a poetry reading at the Library, to give a lecture, and to curate and host an evening literary series in the Madison Building on Capitol Hill in the fall, winter, and spring seasons. In addition to those responsibilities, there were opportunities. One of them, I discovered, was to host some kind of symposium on a literary subject. There was a small budget usually available for that purpose (which came from the laureate endowment, not from taxpayer's money, a distinction I discovered was important to many taxpayers when I found myself taking questions on C-SPAN). I thought immediately, because I was the first person west of the Mississippi to hold the laureate post, that I should do something to reflect the literary traditions of the West, and I proposed the prospect of a symposium of writers in the natural history and environmental tradition. I returned the following week to find that there was no budget available for a conference, but I had already gotten to like the idea and asked Prosser Gifford, the Library's director of cultural programs and, I knew, an avid sailor with an interest in marine ecology, if I could go ahead with it if I found the money myself.

This would have been September 1995. It was an interesting time in Washington, DC. During the midterm elections the previous fall, the Republican Party had seized control of the U.S. Senate for the first time in forty years by taking forty-nine new seats in the House of Representatives and eight in the Senate. Newt Gingrich, a college professor from Georgia, was the new speaker of the House of Representatives, and he had proposed a legislative agenda he called the Contract With America, which proposed to pass a legislative program that included a number of items on the conservative and libertarian agendas, including a balanced budget, term limits, a stricter death penalty, more prison construction, a reduction in the capital gains tax, a prohibition against welfare payments to mothers under the age of eighteen, abolition of the $500-per-child tax credit, a prohibition against U.S. soldiers' serving under U.N. command in peace-keeping operations, a prohibition against U.S. payments to the U.N. for peacekeeping operations, a "loser pays" tort reform to discourage consumer lawsuits against corporations, and a reduction in environmental regulation across the board. One of the new congressmen with a particular animus against federal environmental regulation was a Texan from that state's twenty-second congressional district named Tom Delay, a born-again Christian who had made his fortune in his family's pest control business. In September 1995, it was said that the K Street lobbyists were in the offices of the forty-nine freshman representatives drafting the new environmental regulations. There was a lot of legislation to take apart, much of it passed during the administration of a Republican president, Richard Nixon: the Clean Air Act, the Clean Water Act, the Wilderness Act, the Environmental Protection Act, the Endangered Species Act, and the Wild and Scenic Rivers Act among them.

It was also the first time in forty years that the budget of the Library of Congress was overseen by a House committee with a Republican majority. I was to hear that someone in the Department of Commerce, seeing an opportunity, had proposed to the new reformers of the government bureaucracy that it would be more rational and more efficient to house the U.S. Copyright Office in the Department of Commerce, where international trade and intellectual property issues were negotiated, than to house it through some quirk of history in a library. I don't know exactly how much money was at stake in 1995, but in the year 2000, for example, the Copyright Office collected for the Library of Congress $15.6 million dollars in registration fees and $217 million in royalties. So it was a time, if you had the interests of the Library of Congress, that amazing institution, at heart, when you would have been inclined to tread gingerly. And it had come to seem to me a very good time to have a large party on Capitol Hill celebrating the environmental tradition in American writing.

When I returned to the Library (I was commuting from Berkeley and generating a serious carbon footprint in order to introduce the literary readings at the Library every other week), I was told that I was perfectly welcome to develop a symposium on the subject of my choice if I could come up with the funds. This is the more-than-you want-to-know part of the story. But I've been asked by the Poetry Foundation to write about how a practical intervention on behalf of cultural literacy came about, and this part is the story of how that happened. I had spent my adult life raising a family, teaching literature, writing poetry, and in my spare time translating poetry or studying languages to translate poetry or writing about poetry. I didn't have any experience in fund-raising, and I knew I didn't have an appetite for it. And I had no gift for organization.

My first thought was that, if a symposium of writers could be managed—let's say eight to ten writers over a three-day weekend of readings and panel discussions—they would have to be willing to volunteer their time if their travel expenses could be paid. So I called a few friends to ask if they liked the idea well enough to volunteer. I think the first person I called was the poet Gary Snyder, who did like the idea, and we talked at length about what might be the shape of it. Gary called his friend Wendell Berry, who also liked the idea, though Wendell is also a farmer and doesn't like to travel. And someone—Gary, I think—called Peter Matthiessen, who also thought it was a good idea. I called two casual friends whose work I admired, Barry Lopez and Terry Tempest Williams, both of whom had some experience with the activist environmental community, and they said they would sign on if they could. They suggested I contact the editor of *Orion*, a new literary magazine dedicated to writing in the natural history tradition. The editor of the magazine was a young man named Laurie Lane-Zucker. The magazine, he explained to me, was housed in an organization devoted to environmental education through the arts and through hands-on learning. It was housed in the Orion Institute, and its founder was a New York investment banker named Marion Gilliam. *Orion* magazine had just instituted a program to send cadres of environmental writers to American university campuses. Laurie thought there might be a way in which they could send a troop of writers to Washington, and he suggested that I might meet with his boss.

Poets laureate travel, if they choose. Invitations come in. A meeting of the regional arts councils in the state of Nebraska was being convened by the governor to survey the condition of arts funding in the new political environment for public radio stations and museums and theaters and dance companies and orchestras. (Some of the freshmen in the new Congress had also announced their intention of abolishing the National Endowment for the Arts and the National Endowment for the Humanities.) They were looking for a guest speaker, and an invitation arrived at the poet laureate's office. I was finding that my job was to be an unofficial (or semi-official) spokesperson for the American arts. (After the talk, I was made an admiral in the Great Navy of the State of Nebraska.) Another conference on the same subject was convened by Governor Christine Whitman in New Jersey, and that took me near enough to New York to arrange a meeting with Marion Gilliam. In the meantime, I received a phone call from Charles Halpern, who introduced himself as the director of the Nathan Cummings Foundation. The Nathan Cummings Foundation, I was to discover, was a philanthropy set up by the family that marketed Sara Lee cheesecakes and other frozen desserts; it was dedicated to Jewish culture, social justice, health issues, and ecological innovation. Charles Halpern said that he'd heard that I might need help with a project. To this day, I don't know who called him, but I know that a number of people had been out prospecting. I described the project to him and mentioned—for a budget—how much money I had hoped to get and had not gotten from the Library. He said he thought the gathering was a very good idea and that the foundation could probably do a little better than the amount I had mentioned and he'd get back to me.

So, when I met with Marion Gilliam and Laurie Lane-Zucker for tea in a beautifully furnished apartment on the Upper East Side on an early October afternoon, brownstones and fallen sycamore leaves and the crisp smell of the litter of leaves in Central Park funneling down the avenues, the conference was basically paid for. Marion and Laurie listened to my story and talked about the aims of the Orion Institute and the troop of barnstorming environmental writers they had organized and said they thought they could bring them to Washington, that we could assemble a list of writers to invite together, that it would be desirable to have money to get the word out to grassroots environmental educators around the country, and that they could perhaps—they would get back to me after they talked to their board—match the money from Nathan Cummings. I left, of course, with the radically mistaken notion that this business of fund-raising was actually quite easy. And though I was mistaken, I was getting my first glimpse at something fundamental about American society that I had been more or less entirely unaware of. There is a powerful philanthropic community in the United States and, as I was to see over the course of the next two years, while visiting schools for high school dropouts, literacy programs for adults, environmental education initiatives in schools, inner-city arts programs, Appalachian folk arts programs, the music education programs of regional symphony orchestras, watershed protection organizations, biodiversity initiatives (a salmon festival in the Northwest, an Everglades restoration conference in Florida), and storytelling workshops at battered women's centers in New Jersey, an enormous amount of the country's work in the fields of social justice, literacy, environmental sustainability, and the arts was undertaken by small nonprofit organizations funded in whole or in part by philanthropy.

An enormous amount of the country's work in the fields of social justice, literacy, environmental sustainability, and the arts was undertaken by small nonprofit organizations funded in whole or in part by philanthropy.

Back in Berkeley, my friend Joyce Jenkins, the editor of *Poetry Flash*, an invaluable local monthly that served as a community literary calendar and review of poetry events and new books for the Bay Area, called to suggest that I get together with her friend, the activist Annice Jacoby, and with some folks from another nonprofit, an environmental one that was small, notoriously effective, and based in Berkeley. International Rivers was founded in the late 1980s by an English hydrologist and engineer, Philip Williams. He had, as a young man, worked for international engineering and construction firms on several large dam projects, and he had seen the accelerating degradation of the world's river systems that the dams were bringing about, the levels of graft often involved in their construction, the quite unreal financial and hydrological analyses of the projects that went to the World Bank in order to obtain financing, and the millions of people (think the Narmada Dam in India, Three Gorges in China) displaced from their indigenous cultural and economic lives by the floodwaters. In response he had created International Rivers, a small crew of activists, hydrologists, and financial analysts, to provide real-world support to local peoples whose lives were threatened by big dam projects. International Rivers, I came to see when I read about it, had situated itself at exactly the place in the world where issues of social justice and environmental health were most deeply intertwined.

The university had given me a small grant of a couple of thousand dollars—as a reward, I suppose, for the honor accrued to them by my appointment as poet laureate. (My children, a month into the job, had begun to call me the poet laundromat). I used it to hire a graduate student at the university to help me with the correspondence that was piling up and to keep track of my schedule. Natalie Gerber was from New Jersey, new to California; before coming to graduate school, she had worked for the Geraldine R. Dodge Foundation, helping to organize their huge, biannual poetry festivals in Waterloo, New Jersey, events that drew thousands of people and, through the inventive PBS films that had been made at the festivals and broadcast nationally, a television audience in the millions. I didn't know this about Natalie at the time, or I had not taken it in. I had mainly noticed that she was cheerful and intelligent. I asked her to come with me to the meeting with *Poetry Flash* and International Rivers.

The original object of the meeting had been to get help with fundraising, but with the funds in place, there were other concerns. One was how, if the thing was actually going to happen, to get the environmental community involved. And the other—more troubling—was that after a couple of months in Washington, certain things had become obvious to me. One was that the main industry there was lobbying. Another was that, as a result, the local media, in fact the local culture, was profoundly cynical. I was riding weekly from San Francisco to Washington, DC, in the economy sections of airplanes filled with guys—mostly guys—dressed in dark blue suits, black shoes (gleaming), white shirts and red power ties, hair slicked back and laptops on their tray tables, pounding away at arguments for why the refrigeration industry should still be allowed to emit the chlorofluorocarbons that were eating a hole in the ozone, why the protection of wetlands and vernal pool protection were obstructions to a construction industry of exquisite environmental sensitivity, and why unnecessary worries about maritime environments had been solved by practically fail-safe, deep-well drilling technologies in the Gulf of Mexico. Gary Snyder and I had come up with a name for the conference. We were going to call it Watershed and give it a subtitle: A Celebration of the Environmental Tradition in American Writing. And having talked a bit to the *Washington Post* beat writer for local arts and cultural events, to a few people at the local PBS affiliate, and to people in the large, well-financed environmental organizations, I had a sense that, even if we managed to bring off such an event, it would very likely make hardly a blip on the screen of local attention.

As it happened, that was exactly the case. Natalie Gerber turned out to be a wonderfully gifted organizer. She and Laurie Lane-Zucker organized Watershed over the course of five months. It went on for five days from Wednesday to Sunday. A remarkable array of American writers read their work and talked to quite large audiences about the traditions of writing they worked in and the prospects for the world and for social and environmental change. There was a large audience from Washington, and there were—I think the count was—more than 800 activists from watershed organizations around the country present and participating. It was, as an event on its own terms, an enormous success. And the morning after Peter Matthiessen read to one thousand people in a beautiful church across from the Folger Library right in the middle of the Capitol Hill neighborhood about the fate of some of the oldest species of wild creatures on the earth— tigers and cranes share habitat that is rapidly shrinking—the cover story on the arts section of the *Washington Post* was a feature about four DC lobbyists who meet every year on the occasion of the anniversary of the sinking of the *Titanic* to smoke cigars and drink fine cognac. The Library of Congress newsletter featured a long article on the art of book restoration and the Library's expert on rare glues. (The Library was still nervous about its budget. It had opened all its facilities to us, something it hates to do on weekends, but had asked us not to hold any press conferences at the Library; for that purpose, we had to hire a room at the Washington Press Club.) The PBS *NewsHour*, under novelist and journalist Jim Lehrer and a young associate producer from California, Jeffrey Brown, did a five-minute piece for the arts section at the back of the news with Terry Williams and Gary Snyder and Barry Lopez, and the Washington affiliate of PBS did several interviews with writers over the course of the week. And it was over. There was quite a lot of regional coverage in papers around the country—this was the spring of 1996; the Internet was not quite yet a news medium—Natalie Gerber made a folder of clippings, and that was it.

So, by the time of the meeting at International Rivers five months before, I had already begun to think about how to make something a little more durable out of the ideas that motivated Watershed. The office, crammed with maps, scientific journals, the reports of international commissions, hydropower trade journals, images of the breathtaking sweep of the huge dams and of the improvised shanty villages of dam-displaced peoples, and posters with impudent and encouraging slogans, was situated above a Brazilian pizzeria and across the street from an auto parts store. I was introduced to Owen Lammers, the director of International Rivers (IR), and to Pamela Michael, who was working as a consultant on development. They were willing to help with Watershed because they thought it was a good idea and because Pam had had the idea to hold an environmental poetry contest for children as a way of promoting IR's tenth anniversary. Although IR worked only on projects overseas, staffers knew people in the community working on water issues, and it was they—with Natalie Gerber and Laurie Lane-Zucker—who turned out the almost one thousand watershed activists in Washington. When I spoke about my concern that the gathering, even if we brought it off, would disappear in the pond with hardly a ripple, Pamela Michael mentioned her idea for the poetry contest, and I suggested that perhaps it could focus on children learning about and writing about their watersheds. And that was how River of Words came into being.

This was another moment in my education. We came very quickly to the idea of a poetry contest on the theme of watersheds and then to an art and poetry contest. Perhaps we were thinking some of the conference speakers and readers could be connected to classrooms by television or radio; perhaps there ought to be a Watershed website. (That may have been the first time I heard the word *website,* or registered it when I heard it.) But how to get to the children or the teachers or the schools in five months, four and a half? The event had to happen around Earth Day in April. Joyce Jenkins was there, her collaborator Mark Baldridge, Pam's and Joyce's mutual friend Annice Jacoby, Natalie, Owen Lammers, several members of the International Rivers staff, and Amy Thomas, who owned three local bookstores that sold what was then an eccentric mix of new and used books, magazines, and used records and tapes and CDs. Amy suggested that we put a poster describing Watershed (and what a watershed is) and announcing the conference in the children's sections of bookstores. How could that be done? I asked. The scene felt to me like something out of a pre–World War II movie about bush pilots, perhaps with John Wayne. How are we gonna get that baby across the Strait of Malacca in this weather? With duct tape and baling wire, if we have to, the big, lumbering pilot would say.

Amy Thomas said she would call the president of the American Booksellers Association to see what he could do. At the next meeting a week later, she reported that he had agreed to arrange to have a poster sent to every independent bookstore in the country. (In the fall of 1995, that still included most American bookstores plus the several Borders stores that still counted themselves as independents.) He had suggested calling the president of Bantam Books to see if Bantam might, as a public relations gesture, pay for the printing and the mailings—to bookstores and to libraries and to museums of natural history, especially junior museums, and the education programs of state parks. And so Amy had called Bantam Books, and they had agreed. This was all astonishing to me. It was as if I were looking at some classical sculpture, an Aphrodite or the Winged Victory, and thought to myself that it would look a little better if the arm were raised a little, and, as I had the thought, the arm moved. Meanwhile, Pamela Michael had been told that International Rivers would give her time to organize the contest and that they would serve as cosponsors with the poet laureate's office and undertake the cost of it. And, she said, wouldn't it be good to have at least four age categories and give prizes for art and poetry in each category. And, if we could, bring the winners to Washington, with their parents and teachers, for the Watershed days, to have the children read their poetry and display their art at the library?

It was as if I were looking at some classical sculpture, an Aphrodite or the Winged Victory, and thought to myself that it would look a little better if the arm were raised a little, and, as I had the thought, the arm moved.

So that was how ROW took its shape—as a literature and art contest designed to take the Watershed literary gathering into classrooms. The more Pamela and I and Owen Lammers talked about it, the more birds it seemed to be saving with one stone. In 1995, there was some science being taught in American schools and, I was to learn, some very gifted teachers, but the teaching of natural history—local, place-based teaching about the energy cycles of the places where the children lived, whether in urban New York or St. Louis or suburban California or rural Iowa or Nebraska—was not, still is not, an automatic part of the curriculum. The poster that Pam created with Bantam Books began with the question "What Is Your Ecological Address?" and a large image of a blue raindrop. It defined a watershed—the path taken by water when it flows through the place where you live—and gave the details of the contest in lively language. As soon as we saw the poster, we realized that we didn't want the contest to be a one-off, that art, poetry, local nature literacy, and a basic understanding of the concept of a watershed could be in American classrooms as a regular part of the rhythm of those classrooms every year. International Rivers had an additional interest. All its work occurred overseas. Its campaigns were not focused on North American rivers, so this seemed to Owen and to IR's founder, Phil Williams, a way to be doing something about environmental education in this country that was simple and direct. Owen and Phil went to the International Rivers board with a proposal to make River of Words a permanent project in the IR office.

Around that time, I discovered the Library of Congress's Center for the Book. It is an office created by Daniel Boorstin, the eminent historian who was the librarian of Congress from 1975 to 1987. Boorstin was interested in the history of the book, the history of literacy, and the promotion of literacy and reading. He was a student of Thomas Jefferson and wrote eloquently about the connection between literacy and a democratic society. From the day it opened its door in 1977, the director of the Center was John Cole, an American historian who had also done graduate work in library science and who has written extensively about the history of the Library of Congress. I went to the Center in the first place looking for studies of literacy. I was trying to understand who reads in America, who used to read, who could read, and how many of the people who *can* read read literature, read the poetry and fiction I was supposed to be a spokesperson for. One of the things I had come to realize was that there are many opinions about the current state of literary reading and that a good deal of them had to do with a perception that there used to be many more and better readers of literature in some previous era—the golden age of the paperback book in the 1950s or the heyday of modernism in the 1920s, when Hemingway and Fitzgerald and Cather and Frost wrote bestsellers; or the mid-Victorian era, when Longfellow published "Hiawatha"; or earlier in Regency England when Wordsworth and Coleridge wrote *Lyrical Ballads* and Lord Byron was the fashion all over Europe (though at the time, about 1 percent of English males had any higher education and only about 40 percent of males and 20 percent of females could read at all). Drs. Cole and Boorstin had held a number of scholarly symposia on the history of American literacy, and I went to the Center to borrow the studies that were published afterward.

What I saw when I got in the door of this bright set of rooms in the labyrinth of the Madison Building's sixth floor was a cheerful space full of bookcases (containing the books I was looking for, published by the Library's publishing arm) and some desks and lots of posters—fresh posters that were advertisements for the Center's various Young Readers programs and posters of the kind I remembered from my children's classrooms: state maps with the homes or birthplaces of American writers highlighted on them. Here was Nebraska with its deep snows and deep green fields and summers full of fireflies and lightning storms coming south across the plains from the Dakotas. And here was the home territory of Willa Cather, near Red Cloud where the family settled in 1887, where *My Antonia* and *The Bohemian Girl* and *The Song of the Lark* had been imagined. And here, near Wayne, was where John Neihardt grew up, and here was Bancroft where, as a young man, he came to know the Omaha reservation and its people, which led to his collaboration with Black Elk on *Black Elk Speaks.* And here at Mirage Flats, Mari Sandoz was born in 1896. I had read her Great Plains books as a child from my parents' bookshelves—they were Book of the Month Club subscribers in the 1950s—and *Old Jules*, her account of her father's years homesteading on the prairie (to which I later added Wallace Stegner's *Wolf-willow,* about homesteading in Saskatchewan, for my understanding of that way of life and those years). And there was Wright Morris, born in Central City in 1919. Morris had become a San Francisco writer, a writer's writer in that city, but the book of his I had most admired was *A Ceremony at Lone Tree,* and that was the book sitting in my imagination beside *My Antonia* and *Old Jules* the first time I drove across Nebraska in a green, steamy August.

The poster—and there were others—was exactly what I had in mind when I began thinking about environmental stewardship and local literacy. And it was exactly the kind of artifact that I would have thought old-fashioned and corny a few years before. I was interested in the avant-garde writers on both coasts, in the new work coming from Europe and Latin America and Asia. This stuff (except Cather, of course, who is great) was the stuff on the Local Authors shelf in the used bookstores I browsed, about which I was supremely uninterested. Now, looking at it, I thought that if it added Loren Eiseley and a few scientists and naturalists who had written about the flora and fauna of the Plains, it was just what I had in mind. Eiseley was born in Lincoln in 1906. It was his study of the fossil collection at a university museum that set him on the path that led to *The Immense Journey*, that classic book about the wonder of life and its evolution. The books of a place, I was thinking, were a legacy, an inheritance. Young people, if they were going to become stewards of the places where they live, and have the inspiration of the writers who have made sense of life in those places, needed to know those books. Not only those books, of course. We live in a large world, increasingly connected, and the nature of that connection gets revealed in the formal inventions in writings that come from everywhere. The talented young with their radar needed to know that, too. And they needed to be given the literature of their place.

John Cole has devised a number of programs for the Center: Letters About Literature, a contest that invites children to write short essays about books that matter to them and to win grants for their school or community libraries; a new Young Readers Center for Washington, DC, children and for the thousands of visiting children who troop through the library; a collaboration with an organization called Read It Loud! (founded by Wally Amos, of Famous Amos Cookies, a passionate and inventive literacy advocate), which encourages parents to read aloud to their children; in collaboration with the White House, the National Book Festival, which has a strong children's literature component. When I spoke to John about our still nascent River of Words project, he was interested. It would make sense, he thought, if the program brought children to Washington and the Library for the Watershed conference, for the Center for the Book to host the children and their parents and teachers. Dan Boorstin had been a fan and a scholar of Thomas Jefferson's *Notes on the State of Virginia*, one of the first regional classics of our literature, and John thought Dr. Boorstin would like the idea. In the event, Prosser Gifford, the director of special programs, and James Billington, the eminent Russian historian and current librarian, also welcomed us.

Just before this conversation, I had been at the Dodge Poetry Festival in New Jersey. It was created and produced by James Haba, a poet and professor with unusual focus, imagination, and entrepreneurial flair, for the Geraldine R. Dodge Foundation. I had described our project to Jim one day—while crowds of students in the hundreds wandered the grounds of the Waterloo site, eating cotton candy and sipping lemonade as if they were at a county fair while they queued for a reading by Allen Ginsberg or Stanley Kunitz or waited in line to take their turn on a stage where high school students were doing a marathon reading of the poems of Langston Hughes—and he suggested that I talk to the director of the foundation, Scott McVay, a marine biologist by training, who had a passion for environmental education. Scott had already undertaken a number of initiatives to facilitate environmental education in the New Jersey schools, including small grants for "green teams" of teachers at public schools who could meet to talk about involving the students in keeping the school clean, encouraging efficient energy use, and aligning curricula across the disciplines to reinforce learning in natural history and the arts and social sciences. When I described the proposed Watershed event to him and the children's art and poetry part of it, River of Words was what interested him, and he suggested that we apply to the foundation for a grant. I mentioned this to Pamela Michael at International Rivers, and when she and Owen Lammers and I talked about it, we decided to apply for a grant for International Rivers to launch the program and grow it. The proposal got written and by January, when the planning for Watershed was in its most hectic phase—airfares and lodgings and the topics of panels and publicity and appropriate rooms in the Library and around Capitol Hill for the various events—we received news that we had received a grant for $75,000 and an indication that further funding would be a possibility. Implicit in this suggestion, people who had had experience hastened to explain to me, was the idea that we might expect Dodge to fund us for up to five years while we developed the program. Foundations encouraged promising initiatives; they did not fund them for life.

Pamela Michael, who had gone from a career in public radio to one in development, had been figuring out how to get the word out about the festival and the contest. I would drop in to the Berkeley office occasionally, in between teaching, my twice-monthly commute to Washington for the Library literary series, and various speaking engagements. The office was always humming and had an air of anarchic cheerfulness, though I came to understand that it was remarkably efficient—or at least was always getting work done. Lori Pottinger, the editor of *World Rivers Review*, was writing a handbook for river activists in Africa. The English-language term for watershed in Africa is *catchment*. Lori was working on a guidebook to catchments. The focus of a campaign in China was investigating the financing of Three Gorges Dam. The China campaigner would stop me to quiz me about what Berkeley faculty I knew in the business school and the economics department who might sit on the boards of investment banks. (Poets who teach in universities tend not to know their colleagues in the business school, and I was no exception.) Another campaign involved support for the grassroots movement to stop the Narmada Dam in India—or at least to see that the million people it would displace would be adequately compensated. Arundhati Roy, the Indian novelist, had written an eloquent and scathing polemic against the Narmada and the hydropower development policies that had displaced millions of Indians; the office was in touch with her and monitoring the response to acts of civil disobedience by villagers along the river. Pamela, meanwhile, was using the nascent Internet to contact schools, teachers, state parks, natural history museums. She and volunteers in the office had called the arts councils of every state in the Union to tell them about the contest. They had contacted an extensive list of grassroots environmental organizations and sent them posters, contest materials, and invitations to participate. She had also contacted the Academy of American Poets, which, under director Bill Wadsworth, was in the midst of launching another program to heighten awareness of the country's literary heritage and lively literary culture. The Academy had agreed to put a letter about River of Words in the packet that every governor's office in the country was sending out to its local arts organizations and schools announcing the first National Poetry Month.

It was fascinating to me to see people who actually do things in the world doing things.

It was fascinating to me to see people who actually do things in the world doing things. Pam—with the help of the International Rivers staff and a committee that included Joyce Jenkins, the editor of *Poetry Flash*; Mark Baldridge, who ran a public relations firm in town; Malcolm Margolin, the publisher of Heyday Books, a house specializing in environmental and regional writing; Amy Thomas, the owner of local bookstores; and Aleta

George, an environmental journalist—had from late October until the contest deadline established for the middle of February to publicize the contest, devise it, call airlines to see if one of them might contribute airline tickets for the children and their families (and consider printing the children's poetry and art in their magazines), find hotels, plan an itinerary for the winners, and arrange transportation, all the while keeping her eye on the main goals—to treat poetry and the visual arts as natural and powerful means of expression that should be celebrated and that children should be learning in school, to encourage interdisciplinary environmental education and the teachers in our schools who are trying to do it, and to let all children know they live inside watersheds. By the time the contest deadline came, Pam had generated more than two thousand entries from children in more than thirty states.

In Washington, at a meeting someone had arranged with local environmentalists, I met Robert Boone. Robert, who is a descendant of Daniel Boone, worked inside the federal bureaucracy and kept sane by taking up canoeing on the Anacostia River. The presidential yacht is berthed on the Potomac. The Anacostia is the other river in Washington, and it flows through the poorest neighborhoods in the city. A victim, like most American rivers in the 1950s, of Army Corps of Engineers policies directed toward making rivers disappear or behave like rational canals, it had been recently the scene of an extremely encouraging project in river restoration. Bruce Babbitt was Bill Clinton's secretary of the Interior at the time and, though Clinton and his environmentalist vice president, Al Gore, were remarkably quiet on the subject of the environment throughout their administration, Babbitt was vocal and had gone so far as to say that dam decommissioning and river restoration were going to be the civil rights movement of the twenty-first century. Like most American rivers, the Anacostia had a conjoint sewer–storm drain system built for a much smaller population than the city's infrastructure had now to support. This meant that, whenever there was a substantial spring or summer rainstorm, raw sewage from the city's sewer system poured into the Anacostia and—in a Dickensian touch—flowed through the poorest, mostly African American, neighborhoods in the city. And, rain or shine, the banks of the river were, like the banks of most American rivers, littered with detritus, mostly plastics, and the riverbanks in the middle of the city, even in its parks, had become unofficial dumps: there were tires half-submerged in the shallows, the remnants of abandoned sofas, all the forlorn disjecta of our consumer culture entering the decomposition phase of the carbon cycle. But the river was beautiful in great stretches, despite the defacements, and the Army Corps restoration project—thick with nesting water birds when we paddled into it in the early spring, the river surface fluid and shiny with the reflection of trees just leafing out—showed what it could be again.

Robert Boone had created the Anacostia Watershed Society to create a constituency for new storm drains (a congressional committee oversees the city's infrastructure), the restoration of the river and its flora and fauna, and improved access to the river for recreational use. Pamela Michael was anxious to see—and so was I—that the children of Washington participated in the contest and that some of them were invited to the ceremony. One friend went to work making contacts with the private schools where the children of the Washington elite were educated, and another arranged for me to meet with Kenneth Carroll, the local director of WritersCorps, which was teaching poetry in the city's public schools. Robert Boone arranged for the Anacostia Watershed Society (AWS) to give an annual prize to a DC child for the best poem or painting from the city about the city's watershed, and he arranged with Pamela Michael to take the children, their parents, and some of the visiting writers canoeing on the Anacostia while they were in Washington and to spend one morning during the weekend picking up garbage on the riverbank. On the morning of the actual cleanup, a cool sunny spring morning, the visiting writers—Terry Tempest Williams and Barry Lopez among them—in boots and gloves, the children in boots and gloves, I knew that it wasn't an entirely symbolic action. The AWS was going to continue to recruit people to keep the riverbanks clear of junk, but the morning did feel like a serviceable metaphor to me. It connected Robert Boone's idea that every river in America ought to be swimmable and fishable, biologically as well as chemically and physically alive, and that people should have access to these rivers, to my flickering notion that a healthy culture would be teaching its children to respect the places where they live. It would nurture the creativity in their history—their literary and artistic and scientific traditions—and in the kids who are their future.

I did have reservations about River of Words at the outset. I wasn't crazy about the idea of a contest, but I didn't see how else, any more than I do in the adult culture, to get people to pay attention. But my deeper reservation had to do with dictating a subject to poets, even young poets, particularly this subject. Much instruction in the arts has had to do with giving beginners set topics to get going, but proposing the subject of nature to children seemed a little complicated to me. Modern poetry—in one way of counting—began at the end of the eighteenth century in England with Romanticism; that is, with poets disaffected with the artificiality and injustice of the world, who laid claim to nature by way of a fresh start. By the end of the nineteenth century, the association of poetry with nature poetry had become a cliché. Modernism—the poetry that started with Charles Baudelaire's poems about Paris and Walt Whitman's poems about New York—was in many ways a rebellion against that idea of poetry. Not that I didn't think we need a poetry of the natural world and our relation to it. It seems to me evident that we do, and what perhaps separates us from the poets of the early part of the century is that the natural world that sits in the background of their poetry as an idea of durability and permanence doesn't seem so durable or permanent to us. But I was concerned that an invitation to write about their natural surroundings would say to kids (1) that was what poetry was supposed to be about and (2) that they were being invited to have only positive, benign, and environmentally sound ideas about nature. Poetry is the opposite of propaganda. To teach children to make art and poetry, they need to be taught to surprise themselves, not to please the grown-ups.

One of the first poems that came into the office for the first contest was by a child at an elementary school in the Anacostia district of Washington. It must have come out of a WritersCorps class, and the class must have been prefaced with the idea that a watershed was the region made out of the paths through which raindrops flow in a given place. The poem went like this:[6]

> If I were a raindrop I would not like to fall on the back
> Of a large black dog
> Because he could turn his head around
> And eat you with his red tongue.
> And I would not like to fall on the top of a fence
> Because you could fall off the left side and break your arm
> Or fall off the right side and break your leg.
> I would like to splash straight into the gutter
> And flow home.

My Precious Water, I Kiss You, by Parkpoom Poompana, age 15.

This poem stilled my worry that we were going to elicit only propaganda from the kids and reminded me that they were going to tell us what "the environment" is and that for this child, as for the rest of us, the first thing it is about is safety.

The other thing that dissolved my hesitation that first year, besides the children's work, was the children themselves. They were quite various in their ages and cultures and ethnicities, and they were, mostly, remarkably poised, vivid, alive beings, if a little shy. It seemed to me a very good thing that they visit the Library—which was Jefferson's idea—he thought a functioning democracy needed access to books—and wander among the museums and monuments of the capital. The last thing I would have been thinking about, when we began trying to invite writers and scientists to Washington, was that, because he was good at drawing, a child from Florida who was born in a U.N. camp in Thailand for Cambodian refugees would be walking up the quite imposing steps of the Jefferson Library, just across the street from the Capitol, with its checkered history and resplendent dome, to see his painting[7] displayed inside.

★   ★   ★

I need to tell the rest of the story more briefly. River of Words existed for
its first five years as a program of International Rivers funded by IR and by
annual grants from the Geraldine R. Dodge Foundation. Development
work and grant writing were done by Pamela Michael, with help from the
development office at IR, and the board that oversaw the program was IR's
board. In those relatively flush years in the American economy, other money
came in for the program: for several years, the foundation of the actor
Robin Williams and his wife, Marsha, paid the children's expenses in Wash-
ington; and in some years, airlines—American and Southwest—picked up
their fares. The program itself grew rapidly. The Center for the Book has
state Centers for the Book, and those state centers became the coordinators,
in many states, for the local ROW program. The Rhode Island Institute,
which received funds from financial penalties imposed on polluters, spon-
sored the program in Rhode Island and connected it to the annual River
Festival in Providence, which celebrates the restoration downtown of the
Providence River. In Georgia, ROW became the education program of the
state's Department of Natural Resources, and a wonderful woman named
Petey Rogers spread the program through the classrooms of Georgia by
dressing up like a large, round raindrop and making up songs about clear
rivers and healthy coasts and the water cycle. In fact, ROW grew much
faster than anyone had anticipated. And the poems and paintings came in
each spring by the thousands. Pamela Michael wrote and edited a curricu-
lum guide for the program and a booklet on how teachers and schools
could partner with community environmental programs. Each year she
edited a book of the children's art and poetry and made it available to class-
rooms. Teachers were sending in examples of their environmental and arts
curricula for us to share with other teachers, and the River of Words cur-
riculum became one of the early instances of what was to become a move-
ment toward place-based education.

   As a result, ROW became a freestanding nonprofit. It had literally
outgrown its small space in the International Rivers office—and it was
complicated to position an educational program inside an activist organi-
zation. Much of what was passing for environmental education in the
schools, I discovered, was what the environmental community called "gre-
enwashing," expensive public relations materials from oil companies, pes-

ticide manufacturers, and chemical companies, designed to teach the children what a wonderful and responsible job these companies were doing for the fruited plain, the purple mountains' majesty, and for charismatic fauna such as whales and polar bears. ROW did not want to seem to be the environmental movement's equivalent, and International Rivers was a no-holds-barred advocacy organization. It had been enormously generous—and farseeing—in supporting the program, but ROW needed to stand on its own. We applied for our own nonprofit status and spun off into an uncertain future. Once we became a separate entity, I was to learn, we needed a board. Pamela Michael became director of River of Words. I became a board member, and several International Rivers board members joined me, together with members of the committee that had helped put the program together, among them Amy Thomas and Malcolm Margolin.

At the age of fifty-six, I learned how to read a financial statement.

I had during these years left the poet laureate's office and joined the board of International Rivers, so I had some notion of what a board did, and my education in the way that this part of the world is put together—by the volunteer work of citizens committed to social and cultural change—continued. At the age of fifty-six, I learned how to read a financial statement. It wasn't a skill I brought to the board, but I needed to be able to follow the conversation. The timing of this setting out wasn't particularly fortuitous. The Dodge Foundation grants had come to an end. We had lost the overhead—rent, computers, office furniture, telephones, health insurance, accounting and auditing functions—provided by IR, and at that moment the dot.com bubble burst and the California and national economies spun into recession. But that first board meeting—of friends and acquaintances who were sacrificing their time to sign onto this work—was very moving to me. Malcolm Margolin was the director of a press. Amy Thomas, a businessperson, owned and managed three very popular Berkeley bookstores. One of our board members was a homemaker raising three children, another was an attorney, another was the director of an environmental fund. They were there, having set kids to homework, because they liked the idea of growing the literary and artistic gifts of children or of getting a love for the natural world and a notion of environmental stewardship into classrooms.

Nonprofits are the entrepreneurial sector
of that part of the culture that is trying to make
the world in some measurable way better.

The difference between nonprofit organizations and for-profit businesses, it dawned on me very soon, was that businesses do their work to make money and nonprofits have to make money in order to do their work. A board needs to be responsible for overseeing finances—getting the money to do the work and seeing that the money gets spent responsibly—helping to shape the mission and strategic goals of the organization, being a sounding board for management and staff, implementing the goals of the organization, and reviewing the work of the staff. I found myself thinking that citizen volunteers are doing this work all the time all over the United States. I think this country is not unique in growing nonprofit organizations, but it may be unique in the sheer number of them and in the vitality of the role they play in our culture—groups that work on domestic violence, music education, wetland restoration, legal help against job or gender discrimination, the cultivation of spirituality or a taste for astronomy, the protection of habitat for ducks or deer or whales, famine relief, children's health, women's rights, immigration reform, medical research, new ideas in technology and education. Nonprofits are the entrepreneurial sector of that part of the culture that is trying to make the world in some measurable way better in ways other than by launching a new business or a new product. Start-up companies go to investment banks for capital. The sources of capital for nonprofits are four: individual donors, corporations, government, and larger foundations that are themselves nonprofits. The large nonprofits—the Rockefeller Brothers Fund or the Ford Foundation or, for that matter, the Poetry Foundation—came into being as family fortunes looking for ways to make a difference. The small nonprofits are ideas for making a difference looking for capital. Some individuals with the means undertake philanthropy as a social obligation and in many cases as an interest and a vocation. Lots of other people tithe themselves and write small checks every year to organizations that work on the causes they care about. Some corporations spend some money to establish community goodwill. And some government agencies help to grow the nonprofit sector because it is, like new businesses, a seedbed of social experiment.

All of this was no doubt obvious to most of the members of our board, among whom were long-term social activists, but it was quite new to me, and I was reading the meaning of what we were doing the way I'd once tried to teach myself Chinese characters, by looking at them a long time and parsing their parts. ROW needed to replace the five-year sustaining grant we'd received from the Geraldine R. Dodge Foundation, and we found it in another Berkeley nonprofit, the Center for Ecoliteracy, begun by a Bay Area businessman and environmental activist Peter Buckley. That gave us breathing space to write other grants. Meanwhile, the program was flourishing. We were coming to know more teachers, Pamela Michael was working with other teachers on producing teaching materials, we were able to put together a first marketable coffee table–type book of the children's dazzling art and poetry—we had been publishing inexpensively formatted annual collections of the kids' work and distributing them free to class-rooms from the beginning—and we were even beginning to see poems and paintings influenced by or responding to the poems and paintings we had published a few years earlier. The ceremony at the Library in Washington each spring had become a quite sweet event, and, as long as we were able to raise enough money every year, always a precarious matter, we seemed to be accomplishing our goals. Work was coming in from children all over the world. Sheaves of paintings and drawings appeared from a refugee camp in Afghanistan because an art teacher and a ten-year-old Hazara boy there had seen a mention of ROW in the children's magazine *Ranger Rick*. The EPA had taken to using the children's art to illustrate some of the reports it sends biannually to Congress. I had gone out to Shanghai and Pamela Michael and Terry Tempest Williams to Bangkok to talk to educators in overseas English-language schools about the arts and the vital role they can play in environmental awareness, and we had begun to get entries from American schools all over the world.

We also got to know children all over the country. This child who had written an extraordinary poem at the age of eleven had just gotten into Harvard to study English, and that young man who seemed destined for an artist's career was beginning pre-dental school at the University of Florida. We got to see in the flow of annual submissions the evidence of the work of very remarkable teachers who consistently, year after year, sent us inspired work from their classes. In very short order, Pamela Michael realized that we really needed to make an annual award for exceptional teachers, which we did. The teachers often spoke at the annual cere-mony—upstairs in the Madison Building, the Capitol dome gleaming across the street in the spring air—and we were also able to put the teach-ers' accounts of their conceptions of teaching on the website to share with other teachers all over the country. There has been other work—a part-nership with the California Coastal Commission to establish a special ROW award for marine ecosystems (named for Edward Ricketts, Califor-nia's pioneering marine biologist and the model for Doc in Steinbeck's *Cannery Row*) and a recent initiative to work on curricula for urban envi-ronmental education, a program called One Square Block, which asks children to map single blocks in their neighborhoods and learn their infra-structures, social history, architecture, daily life. We have, at the moment, a staff of three to do this work. Pamela Michael serves as both executive director and director of development, not to mention founding spirit and writer, editor, and idea person. Louisa Michaels manages the office, com-plicated because there is a very large scale art and poetry contest to admin-ister every year, bookkeeping to be attended to, contracts, transportation to ceremonies in San Francisco and Washington, teacher training and idea-sharing sessions to be scheduled, and an art gallery of the children's draw-ings—it's called Young at Art—to be managed. Susan Sarratt handles the contest database, the website, and the contacts with the state coordinators, the teachers, and the students. A precarious machine ROW has been—and, as I write, in this damaged economy, just barely surviving, though its programs are thriving and doing more kinds of useful work than any of us had anticipated.

★　★　★

Watching ROW develop, it became clear to me over time what I thought the work was about—apart from encouraging and celebrating the achieve-ments of particular students and teachers every year and in that way mirror-ing these achievements back to their communities. When I was asked to articulate it a couple of years ago, I found it came down to a few thoughts.

The first had to do with children and art, the second with children and stewardship, and the third with the idea of watershed. Here's what I wrote:

I. CHILDREN AND ART

In her wonderful book, *Children's Art,* Miriam Lindstrom observes that very young children, when they are making paintings, often don't remember afterwards which of the paintings is theirs. "The picture," she writes, "seems to be only a byproduct of the main interest, the act of painting.

> Expressing their feeling-thought about some happening lived or imagined is one of the main uses of art work to children of four or five, but this procedure of "acting-out" a dramatic event is still beyond many of the two- and three-year-old ones. For them, feeling and thinking seem to be directly related to the physical activity going on rather than to mental activity concerned with concepts to be expressed. Their incidental chatter to themselves and each other is not so important as their own performance of an act of skill. They enjoy the "power of being the cause."[8]

I have loved that last sentence ever since I first read it. And I think that what it says is as true of adult artists as it is of two- and three-year olds. A national survey some years ago asked American schoolchildren if they were "mainly happy or mainly worried." I was interested and dismayed to read that more of them, fourth graders, I think, reported that they were worried rather than happy. This might be a developmental fact, that their responses came from the onset of a sense of responsibility that is also a sense of self, and in that way not a bad sign. Nevertheless, when the survey asked them what they were worried about, the principal answers were AIDS and pollution, subjects about which they could not have known very much, that their alert young antennae must have picked up from the culture at large. There are practical steps, of course, that children and adults can take to feel less powerless about the condition of the world, but in this way, especially with the young, I think art is a mighty power, and it is important that they learn it, and are encouraged to learn it, early. The words of a poet again, this time Gerard Manley Hopkins:

Each mortal thing does one thing and the same:
Deals out that being indoors each one dwells;
Selves—goes itself; myself it speaks and spells
Crying what I do is me; for that I came.

2. CHILDREN AND STEWARDSHIP

"No important change in ethics was ever accomplished without an internal change in our intellectual emphasis, loyalties, affections, and convictions. The proof that conservation has not yet touched the foundations of conduct lies in the fact that philosophy and religion have not yet heard of it," Aldo Leopold writes in *Sand County Almanac.* A little later in the book, he comes out in a slightly different way. "It is inconceivable to me that an ethical relation to land can exist without love, respect, and admiration for land, and a high regard for its value." And by "land," he says, he means not just soil but "a fountain of energy flowing through the circuit of soils, plants, and animals."[9]

One of our basic ideas lies here. We are not apt to be very effective caretakers of anything that we don't come to know and understand, and we are not apt to come to know and understand anything that hasn't awakened our curiosity or fascination. It's clear enough, at the beginning of the twenty-first century, that the fates of almost all the species of plants and animals, the biota of the earth, forests and grasslands, tundra and glacial bays, mangrove swamps and deserts, have come into the hands of human beings. And so an education in ecological citizenship has become an international necessity, especially in the developed countries that use so many of the world's resources. And it's pretty clear, or it ought to be, that the beginnings of that education lie in the natural energy, curiosity, and alertness of children and in the passion to pass on a world that commits people to the vocation of teaching.

> The children who watch plants grow
> know very well that they are growing, too.

I think human beings only gradually evolved, for reasons of efficiency, our present tendency to sort out song-making and image-making from the learning of a cultural lore about the earth and the water and the stars. Our children are educated in a system that tends to divide art and music (when they are taught at all) and writing on the one hand, and natural history and social history and science on the other, into distinctly different disciplines and different parts of the day. But they are all activities that begin in observation and imagination, and stewardship of the earth is going to require both. The energy of art is an aspect of the energy that flows through a place. The children who watch plants grow know very well that they are growing, too. And an expression of the energy and rhythm of that experience is also a kind of knowing. Children can be quizzed on the life cycle of salmon; they are apt to know it better and feel it more deeply if they have also danced it or caught the rhythm of it in words or color and movement.

We think these poems are, among other things, evidence of this power in children and of the remarkable work being done by teachers in many of our educational institutions, even though the culture has not yet really taken on the task of education in stewardship, has in fact been in denial about the need.

3. THE IDEA OF A WATERSHED

In his immensely useful essay "Coming into the Watershed," from *A Place in Space*, Gary Snyder gives us, with a characteristic elegance of mind, the definition:

> A watershed is a marvelous thing to consider: this process of rain falling, streams flowing, and oceans evaporating causes every molecule on earth to make the complete trip once every two million years. The surface is carved into watersheds, a kind of familial branching, a chart of relationship, and a definition of place. The watershed is the first and last nations whose boundaries, though subtly shifting, are unarguable. Races of birds, subspecies of trees, and types of hats or rain gear often go by the watershed.... [W]e who live in terms of centuries rather than millions of years must hold the watershed and its communities together, so our children might enjoy the clear water and fresh life of this landscape we have chosen.

He goes on to speak of his own watershed in California:

The water cycle includes our springs and wells, our Sierra snow-pack, our irrigation canals, our car wash, and the spring salmon run. It's the spring peeper in the pond and the acorn woodpecker chattering in a snag. The watershed is beyond the dichotomies of orderly/disorderly, for its forms are free, but somehow inevitable. The life that comes to flourish within it constitutes the first kind of community.[10]

This is the reason why the focus of River of Words was, from the start, watersheds. The place to begin, we felt, was not a generalized stewardship of the earth or an intellectual grasp on the energy flows of an ecosystem or lists of endangered species or, for that matter, the technological achievements of our beginning science of restoration, but helping children develop a feel for the places where they live. Asking them to think in terms of watersheds is a way of connecting what they already know from their vivid, lively, daily experience of their weather and their place to the idea of the bioregion and human and biotic community they are part of. It is also a way of recommending to teachers, though we've found over ten years that the teachers were way ahead of us, even though the schools and the schools of education and the educational reforms of politicians have done not very much to encourage them—that a good way to do art, writing, natural history, and social history in the classroom is to root it in local, hands-on experience and observation. One of our early posters for the art and poetry contest read, "Do you know your ecological address?" That was the idea and the poems that follow are some of the answers to that question.

★   ★   ★

The curious thing to me about this statement, as I read it now, is that I didn't speak directly about the power of poetry. I suppose that's because this power has always been self-evident to me. Self-evident also that poetry is a somewhat wild and unpredictable force. The thing I liked least about the poet laureate's position was the presumption that I would be required to promote poetry in general and think up ways to tell people that it is good for them, partly because it is an at least tenable idea that if poetry is good for some people, it may be bad for some people, or that, if good poetry is good for people, bad poetry is bad for them. "We have fed our hearts on fantasy," Yeats wrote—and I think he had the rhetoric of Irish nationalism in mind—"The heart's grown brutal from the fare...." So I often found that, while I found it easy to talk about literacy, education, the power of American literature, the power and reach of literature in the world, and about the environment and environmental literature, the subject of poetry left me mute. Poems were another matter. It was always a pleasure and an interest to talk about poems in particular—the amazement of this rhythm or the leap of mind in that metaphor. For several years during that time, I found myself in the position of having to write a short essay about a poem every week, and I liked doing it. But when I was asked, as poets laureate are incessantly asked, about the good of poetry or the social role of poetry or—depending on what city one was in—the popularity or unpopularity of poetry, my mind seemed to go on strike.

Yet a line of Frost's was often in my head. "The land was ours before we were the land's." I've always read that with my experience of the stunning small accuracies of haiku and of the traditions of literati painting in mind. When Basho was writing his poems in the early seventeenth century, people had been living on the Japanese mainland for at least ten thousand years and had had a tradition of written poetry in Japanese since the early eighth century, so Basho was writing his poems in relation to at least nine hundred years of a literary tradition of close observation of the land.

Though he lived in New England, in the frontier town of Farmington for at least forty years, Edward Taylor, who died in the early eighteenth century and may be the best of our early American poets, wrote poems in which the rare bird or plant he names is English, not North American. So, even in New England, the marriage of natural place and the English language and the powers of imagination and observation are no more than three hundred years old. In my part of the world, it is younger than that by almost one hundred and fifty years. As Whitman saw and as Dickinson taught us with her adaptations of the hymn form, the work required was not just a matter of putting the inherited forms of English poetry to work on the American landscape—they needed to be acclimated to one another. That work seems to have been begun in New England in the early years of the nineteenth century, roughly contemporaneous with the work Audubon and our landscape painters and our botanical and geological explorers were doing. They were learning to see the land and to find a language for what they were seeing. There is every reason—in the world we have made, in the intensively worked and transformed landscapes of every region of our country and its remnant farmscapes and preserved wildernesses—to set our children to the task of studying that tradition and putting their hands to it.

The poems of the children, as they come into the offices of River of Words, are annual evidence of the deep freshness and surprise that they are capable of. As I talked to citizen's groups about literacy, studying the ways in which the lack of it and of a rambunctious democracy of spoken language in our streets stunted people's lives—not just their job opportunities, but their lives—it became evident to me that a taste for poetry, an interest in the liveliness and eloquence and impudence and sometimes the sorrowing or wondering depths of the mind as it emerges in the rhythms of our language, must be at the core of any effort to give our country and our children the gift and task of literacy. It seemed clear that, as you could tell that a wetland thicket was healthy if the little warbler called a yellowthroat showed up every spring, or tell a healthy temperate rain forest by the low calls of spotted owls, you could gauge the health of a culture by whether or not it cultivated a taste for poetry. ROW has been one initiative among many to put the adventure of writing, reading, and reciting poetry back at the center of our common culture. I think it has served poetry and our common life in this place where its context has not been purely literary, that it can teach our children that much of our literature has been about seeing and being in this place.

NOTES

1. *I Got the Blues.* Gerald Allen, age 13, 2002 River of Words finalist. Broadmoor Middle Magnet School, Baton Rouge, Louisiana. Teacher: Alan Morton.
2. "Sad Sun." Nicholas Sanz-Gould, age 6, 1996 River of Words Grand Prize. Argonne Elementary School, San Francisco, California. Teacher: Susan Sibbet.
3. "Letter to an Architect." Rebecca Givens, 1998 River of Words Grand Prize. Chamblee High School, Atlanta, Georgia. Teacher: Diane Lynn Farmer.
4. "Watershed Life." Jeff Hwang, age 13, 1998 River of Words International Prize. American International School, Dhaka, Bangladesh. Teacher: Amy Shawver.
5. "Seven Haiku on Goldfish and Why." Maddy Johnson, age 14, 2006 River of Words Grand Prize. Submitted independently.
6. In the crush of that first year of River of Words, the original of this poem and the name of the young author disappeared. This is the poem as I remember it,

and Pamela Michael, director of ROW, has said somewhat reassuringly that this is also how she remembers it.

7. *My Precious Water, I Kiss You.* Parkpoom Poompana, age 15, 1996 River of Words Grand Prize. Fort Myers High School, Fort Myers, Florida. Teacher: Irene Linn.

8. Miriam Lindstrom, *Children's Art: A Study of Normal Development in Children's Modes of Visualization* (Berkeley: University of California Press, 1957), 8.

9. Aldo Leopold, *A Sand County Almanac, and Sketches Here and There* (New York: Oxford University Press, 1949), 214–15.

10. Gary Snyder, *A Place in Space: Ethics, Aesthetics, and Watersheds* (Washington, DC: Counterpoint, 1995), 229–30.

BIBLIOGRAPHY

Elizabeth, Lynne, and Suzanne Young, eds. *Works of Heart: Building Village Through the Arts.* Oakland, CA: New Village Press, 2005.

Michael, Pamela, ed. *River of Words: Images and Poems in Praise of Water.* Introduction by Robert Hass. Berkeley, CA: Heyday Press, 2003.

Michael, Pamela, ed. *River of Words: Young Poets and Artists on the Nature of Things.* Introduction by Robert Hass. Minneapolis, MN: Milkweed Editions, 2008.

Stone, Michael K., and Zenobia Barlow, eds. *Ecological Literacy: Educating Our Children for a Sustainable World.* San Francisco: Sierra Club Books, 2005.

THE POEM IS A BRIDGE

Poetry@Tech

Thomas Lux

I don't know who put the @ symbol instead of the word *at* between Poetry and Tech, but I guess it's appropriate, given the age we live in and given that Tech is the Georgia Institute of Technology, a very well-known university not well known for poetry.

★   ★   ★

It began like this. In the late 1990s, Henry and Margaret Bourne decided to endow a chair in poetry at Georgia Tech "to ensure," as Dr. Brown said, "that Georgia Tech students will always have an opportunity for first-rate instruction in the great poetry of the world." He considers it "especially important that, in the highly specialized and technical areas of engineering, science, and management, students' aptitudes are nurtured and supported as a foundation for lifelong learning." Dr. Bourne was an electrical engineering professor at Georgia Tech for many years, was the provost for a while, and served as an interim president in the late 1960s. A Yellow Jacket, through and through. And he loves poetry.

At about the same time, unbeknownst to the Bournes, another man, Bruce McEver, also decided to endow a chair in poetry at Tech. He is a Georgia Tech alum, Navy ROTC, a born and bred Atlantan, CEO of Berkshire Capital, and a poet who has published a full-length collection and a few chapbooks and whose work has been printed in several literary magazines. His reasons were essentially the same as Henry and Margaret Bourne's: Georgia Tech is a great university, I want to give something back to it, and poetry—both the reading and writing of it—should be part of the curriculum, an option for students at any great university. I know Bruce McEver. He took a poetry writing class of mine at the 92nd Street Y in New York City in the early 1990s. Two endowed chairs in poetry: this was new to Georgia Tech. The university didn't quite know what to do with them.

Sometime in the spring of 2000, I was invited, for one semester only, to inaugurate what came to be called the McEver Visiting Chair in Writing and help get something started. Very happily teaching for 25 plus years at Sarah Lawrence College and directing the MFA program in poetry there for many of those years, I'd taken visiting jobs before when they came up—Houston, Michigan, Iowa, UC Irvine—but I'd never lived in the South—so why not?

The next thing that happened—and the most important thing that ever happened for Poetry@Tech, without whom Poetry@Tech would not exist—happened in a classroom at the Cranbrook School, near Detroit, at a now defunct writers conference, in the summer of 2000. I was on the faculty. We were going around the room introducing ourselves at the beginning of our first poetry workshop and, when her turn came, a woman named Ginger Murchison said she lived in Atlanta. I said, "I could use your help in January." She said, "Sure."

Part of the deal was this: Georgia Tech paid for my housing (I still had to pay rent in New York), and there was some money set aside for poetry readings. As part of the appointment, I asked to teach a workshop, free and open to anybody in the community, as well as teach at Tech.

As soon as Ginger Murchison got back to Atlanta (she wasn't paid a dime at this point), she went to work: scouting venues, talking to people at Tech and to poets in the local poetry community whom she knew. She even prevented a proctor's room in a dormitory from being my housing!

Back in New York, I wrote a mission statement—about three single-spaced pages. Later, someone told me mission statements are supposed to be one or two sentences. Here's part of a paragraph:

> "I see nothing antithetical to a major university known the world over for its engineering/computational science/business, and other related subjects of study also making available to its students writing, literature, and the arts in general. The making of art (let's use poetry as an example!) is a task that requires a kind of engineering, a kind of architecture, and very real and complex technical skills. Good poems, historically, are *made*; they don't just flow down the arm of the dreamy poet to the page. Good poems are the result of planning, rigor, attention, intuition, trial and error, discipline, and the luck that sometimes comes when all of the previous are applied. A flawless architectural design, an elegant chemical equation, a good poem is supposed to *seem* simple, spontaneous, fluid. To achieve his or her goals, that precision, that truth, the engineer, the chemist, the poet usually must work diligently, must sweat blood."

I wrote a mission statement—about three single-spaced pages. Later, someone told me mission statements are supposed to be one or two sentences.

When representing Georgia Tech at a function on or off campus, I most often compare the making of a poem to the making of a bridge, which falls under the category of civil engineering. A bridge and a poem. They both make important connections, they have all sorts of things going on inside them that make them stand, they allow us to span the deepest of chasms, and the best of them are even beautiful!

When I actually got to Atlanta very early in January 2001 (I started teaching the day after I arrived), Ginger was already arranging the community class and various venues for readings. We wanted to have them all off campus, and we both knew many of the people we wanted to invite to read.

Our first reader at our first reading was a young spoken word artist named Ayodele (M. Ayodele Heath). I like to think of him as an emblem of Poetry@Tech's reason for being. Several years earlier, he had been a presidential scholar at Georgia Tech. That's a big deal, very prestigious, very competitive, full ride. But he dropped out. Because he fell in love. With poetry! There wasn't much going on regarding poetry at Tech then. Ayodele had to go elsewhere to find his art. A few years ago, we invited him back to occupy the McEver Visiting Chair. During those intervening years, he established himself as one of the prominent slam-spoken word artists in the country and has since earned an MFA degree in poetry at New England College, in Henniker, New Hampshire. Also reading was A. E. Stallings, a brilliant young formalist poet originally from Athens, Georgia, but then (and still, I believe) living in Athens, Greece. On the bill too was R. J. McCaffery, a young poet who has since published a few books and is now a lawyer as well as a poet, a public defender, I believe, in Miami. Al Letson, a performance poet, spoke a brilliant monologue of a homeless man, which was part of his one-man show touring nationwide at the time. The reading was at a place called the Actor's Express. About three hundred people showed up.

The next readers, at the 14th Street Playhouse, were Coleman Barks, poet and translator of the great Persian poet, Rumi; Kathleen Stripling Byer, from North Carolina but recently teaching in Georgia; Turner Cassity, whose early book, *Watchboy, What of the Night?*, I remembered reading with joy as an undergraduate; and John Stone, a cardiologist at Emory's School of Medicine and well known not only as a poet but also as one of the first MDs (in a position to do so) to introduce literature, particularly poetry, into medical school curricula. (Note: wouldn't you rather have a doc who knew a little about poetry, maybe even read and wrote it, than a doc who didn't? I would. Except I'd want my doc to be familiar with other people's work rather than *my* poetry: what if he or she didn't like it?) Sadly, for their loved ones and for the Atlanta poetry community, both Turner and John died in the past few years. Rest well, comrades, your books are still here, under lamps and by daylight, being read.

As I've said, all the poets that semester were Georgia poets. (Note: Since 2002, about a third of all the poets who have read for Poetry@Tech and about a third of the McEver Visiting Chair holders live in Georgia.) At this point, "we" is Ginger and I, and we figure we can have four readings with two, three, even four poets at each reading. And pay decent honoraria. Honestly, no way was I going to invite poets from here and there. I felt anything other than honoring Georgia poets would contradict the spirit of McEver's great gift, and no way was I gonna come off to the poets in Atlanta and Georgia as a gottdamn Yankee carpetbagger! I'm not sure what the Yankee word-equivalent to a carpetbagger is. Maybe hustler, operator, one unencumbered by a conscience? So we had the readings at different venues around Atlanta: the 14th Street Playhouse, I've mentioned. It was rare to see poet's names on a marquee. Also the aforementioned Actor's Express, the Margaret Mitchell House (where I also taught my community class), and the Academy of Medicine, a historic Atlanta building. People came: 300, 400, 350, 300.

At one reading, Georgia Tech's president at the time, Dr. Wayne Clough, and his wife, Anne, attended. It was at the Margaret Mitchell house. Nearly 350 people attended, and it was quite a bill: Leon Stokesbury, a nationally known poet in the Southern narrative tradition; Judson Mitchell, a widely known poet and novelist from the Macon area; Kevin Young, then an emerging young poet, now a powerhouse of his generation; and a duo that made the bill particularly unusual, Steve and Ronnog Seaberg (unfortunately, and a great loss to the Atlanta arts community, Ronnog passed in 2007). To describe what they did is difficult, but I shall try. First, picture a couple in their mid-seventies wearing multicolored acrobatic tights. Steve makes his way onstage, very laboriously, using a walker. He gets it, finally, to center stage and proceeds to use it to do a full handstand! This is when you first notice he is ripped, his upper body about as close to a young gymnast's body as a seventy-four-year-old man's can be. He lowers himself, slowly, in a movement that looks as though it takes the strength and control of an iron cross. The crowd is going nuts. Then Ronnog, similarly attired, walks onstage, climbs onto Steve's shoulders, and begins to recite her poems. They're both acrobats; she's the poet. She climbs all over him and recites different poems in different positions, some of which make advanced yoga look simple. It's hard to tell whether the poems have anything to do with the sculptures they make of their bodies, but nobody cares.

I and a few other members of the audience who knew Steve and Ronnog—longtime performers, internationally, on the alternative art scene—were concerned they might take their costumes off and perform in the nude, which they often did. We conferred with them beforehand and assured them we wouldn't censor them in any way but that it might be a good idea if they left their clothes on this time. They did.

I believe it was Dr. Clough himself who sometime later told me he had enjoyed the reading and had been particularly pleased and surprised that so many people had come to a poetry event sponsored by Georgia Tech.

Our final reading that spring, held at the Academy of Medicine, was by David Bottoms, then, still, and should be forever, as far as I'm concerned, the poet laureate of Georgia; Pearl Cleage, a poet and best-selling novelist; and Bette Sellers, a former poet laureate of Georgia. It was a terrific reading at a beautiful venue. (Note: Georgia Tech recently bought this property—it's right on the eastern edge of the Tech campus, on West Peachtree, and we're going to have all our readings there from now on, after some restoration work this spring.)

I won't describe every reading we've done (though I'll list, at the end of this, whoever has read for Poetry@Tech, as well all the previous McEver Visiting Chair holders to date). The point of describing the first several is this: let's try different things, places, see if we can get our own students *and* people from the city to come. To let people know how many first-rate poets live and work in the Atlanta area, in Georgia in general. To makes readings accessible—hell, even fun!

Later that spring, our dean at the time, Sue Rosser, asked me if I'd accept the permanent position of the Bourne Chair. (The McEver Visiting Chair was designated a one semester a year rotating position.) They were ready to get that going too. It had never occurred to me to leave Sarah Lawrence, which I love and from which my daughter recently graduated. Eventually, we worked out a way I could still teach, in a minor way, in the Sarah Lawrence MFA program and also accept the position at Georgia Tech. I went back to Sarah Lawrence (while I was gone, Stephanie Strickland held the McEver Chair) for a year to fulfill a contractual and ethical obligation. For the entire 2001 to 2002 academic year, Ginger Murchison (still not making a dime and without an office or access to a phone, computer, etc. at Tech) worked to prepare things for the new beginning of Poetry@Tech in the fall of 2002.

We decided to start with a bang. Endowment funds had been gathering interest in the bank for a few years, and frankly, then, we were pretty flush. Our first reading would be Lucille Clifton, Billy Collins, Stephen Dobyns, and Rita Dove. Andrew Young, a former mayor of Atlanta and former U.S. ambassador to the United Nations, agreed to do the introductions. On October 28, 2002, twelve hundred people filled the Ferst Center for the

Arts, the largest amphitheater on the Tech campus. A few hundred more people, we learned later, had been turned around by fierce thunderstorms in the area. We've never had a reading with that many people since—though Billy Collins alone drew nearly one thousand in April 2004.

Wayne and Ann Clough became important supporters of Poetry@ Tech when we started up again in 2002. In 2003, after a reading by Mary Karr and Gerald Stern, I heard two people behind me singing the Georgia Tech fight song: "I'm a rambling wreck from Georgia Tech...." I turned around to see Gerry Stern and Wayne Clough, arms around each other's shoulders, singing "and a hell of an engineer...." The Cloughs came to readings whenever they could. They, and I, are baseball nuts, and we sometimes ran into each other at Tech baseball games. One time in particular was just after the terrible tragedy at Virginia Tech (where Dr. Clough had been a professor and a dean; he was also a friend of Virginia's Tech's president). Among other things, one of us said, there but for fortune. Every college and university administrator, I bet, was saying or thinking the same thing—or should have been. Another time at a Georgia Tech function, Mrs. Clough was following a Tech baseball game on a BlackBerry or something (it was a big game!) and signaling the score to me across a few tables while someone, quite possibly her husband, was speaking at the podium. Once, Dr. Clough hosted a gathering of Georgia college and university presidents, provosts, etc. For a speaker, he didn't want an educator or a scientist or an engineer. He wanted a poet: Billy Collins. Billy gave a brilliant reading. On another night, Dr. and Mrs. Clough and Billy and I went out to dinner. Dr. Clough grabbed the check. I referred to him as the "President Who Loved Poetry."

Why did he love poetry? Maybe because of the way it can transform lives. It did transform lives at Georgia Tech—the lives of our audience members and of our students. I worked with one, an undergraduate aeronautical engineering student, officially in class and when he was no longer in class. Most Tech people (with the exception of the physics people) will say that aeronautical engineering is the hardest major. When he was taking final exams his senior year, he wore an old-fashioned alarm clock around his neck and set it to go off every fifteen minutes so he wouldn't fall asleep. This particular kid had a 3.99 GPA and several job offers right out of Tech, including one from NASA. He could have walked into a job making about a hundred grand a year. What did he want to do? Write poetry. He spoke to his father. His father said something like "You know what, son? I've been doing something for the past twenty-five years that I don't really like that much, so go for the poetry thing!" The kid finished his MFA at UNC Greensboro. Broke, as a young poet should be, he's still in Greensboro, writing poems and working for his landlord to cover his rent.

Another undergraduate student, a young Indian woman, a biology major and brilliant, with another great GPA, decided to give up her parents' dream, and her own, that she become a doctor. You guessed it; she had decided to be a poet. I don't think her parents were ecstatic about this decision. I am not even certain it's what Georgia Tech has in mind for its students. But she got an MFA in poetry at Sarah Lawrence College and is now back in Georgia, writing and teaching writing and literature in the university system. She is happy, doing what she wants to do.

If the poetry project one is trying to do is at a university and the president of that university—by his or her occasional presence alone—is a supporter of that program, well, that's very lucky. No way to plan that. Lucky.

One of the last times I saw Dr. Clough was after a reading a few years ago. He came up to me and said, "You guys got me my new job." He had recently been appointed secretary of the Smithsonian Institution. By "you guys," he meant Poetry@Tech. He said, "They asked me what I knew about the humanities, and I said, 'Well, I started this poetry program at Georgia Tech,' and they hired me!" He was being kind, of course. They hired him because they knew he could get the Smithsonian, the most important repository of American culture and history, back on track. People at Tech knew he was leaving. He'd been a great president at Tech for thirteen years. He was ready for another challenge. I get to say it right here, in print, whether you ever read it or not: Wayne and Anne Clough, we miss you both. And we're grateful to you both. (Note: the point of these anecdotes regarding Dr. and Mrs. Clough, I assume, is obvious: if the poetry project one is trying to do is at a university and the president of that university— by his or her occasional presence alone—is a supporter of that program, well, that's very lucky. It was, for Poetry@Tech, very lucky. No way to plan that. Lucky.)

As you probably have gathered from the above, Poetry@Tech evolved through trial and error, hard work, luck, and the simple reality that here was a place where a university-based poetry program, with an outreach element, didn't exist. It felt like a hole to fill. We didn't know how many other people even knew or cared there was a hole to be filled, but we were going to try to fill it anyway, one shovelful at a time.

In addition to traditional poetry readings, we've tried many other things. We had a poetry festival, geared for kids as well as adults, with stilt-walkers, fire-eaters, clowns. We've had two major spoken word performances. Some of our McEver Visiting Chair holders are spoken-word artists. We had a program of readings by physicians who are poets. We had a program of three young poets from the UK. We had Patricia Smith perform with her band Bop Thunderous. We combined poetry and music in other ways, most memorably, for me, Kurtis Lamkin (who was on the same program as Gerald Stern and Mary Karr) playing a handmade (by Kurtis) *kora,* a West African stringed instrument, and reciting his poems.

In the past year, through a student's suggestion and help, we put most of our readings on YouTube (or Tube Face or something like that). Some readings are on university radio and TV stations. I think, generally, it's a good idea to try to figure out how young people, college students, communicate via the Internet, texting, and so on and ask them for help, ideas, on how to get the news out: poetry exists and is thriving at Georgia Tech! I'm shameless: sometimes, after thanking people after a reading, I'll say to the young men in the audience (after admitting it's a bit sexist), "Dudes, chicks dig poetry, it's a cheap date, she might end up thinking you're sensitive."

Our theory is this: if you can bring them to water, some will drink; some will even want to taste more of this particular water! From the beginning, however, we operated on the basic principle of inclusion, which, of course, started with the great generosity of the Bournes and Bruce McEver. We were determined to honor their generosity by sharing it with Tech students and any members of the larger Atlanta community who wanted to take part. All kinds of poets and poetry, room for all kinds of poets and poetry.

By now "we" includes, crucially, Ken Knoespel, a senior member of our department, who later became department chair and is now interim dean. Poetry@Tech is under the auspices of Ivan Allen College (named for the great mayor of Atlanta during the turbulent '60s), Georgia Tech's liberal arts college. The specific department is called LCC: literature, communication, and culture. About a decade ago, a new major was created at Tech called

STAC: science, technology, and culture. It is our equivalent to a humanities degree, and it is the fasted growing major at Tech.

Slightly paraphrasing Theodore Roethke and, as I implied earlier, "We learned by going where to go." The McEver Visiting Chair was held for the first three years by one poet each spring term: 2001, me; 2002, Stephanie Strickland; 2003, Stephen Dobyns. Since then, we have broken the job into three or four smaller jobs: a poet comes for a month and teaches four classes at Tech, gives a reading, teaches a community class, goes to a middle school or high school to visit classes and read.

It creates a course like no other in any other university I know of: a course taught by three or four poets—working, widely published, younger, older, the whole range of inclusion. We take a visiting professor to the classroom and introduce him or her. The poet does as she or he will with the class for the allotted residency. It's one of the hottest courses on campus. I teach two courses a term at Tech: a larger poetry reading class and a small poetry writing class. I also teach a community class and visit schools, Rotary clubs, poetry societies, etc. around Atlanta. If a group gives me supper, I sing about Poetry@Tech.

Our crisis? About three and a half years ago, Ginger Murchison stepped down as associate director of Poetry@Tech and since has gotten her MFA degree in poetry from the Warren Wilson College MFA Program for Writers. She's been publishing in magazines, giving readings, teaching classes (including, this term, an eight-week community class for Poetry@Tech), and still helping out at the office. She published her first chapbook. She continues to edit *The Cortland Review*, a highly respected online literary magazine. (Note: We also have an ongoing class this year being taught at an Atlanta retirement home by a recent Tech graduate and gifted young poet, Shawn Delgado.)

Remember: it wouldn't have happened, hardly any of it, without Ginger's work, her intelligence, and her good, good heart. Note: Every program like ours, any literary magazine, small press, reading series, needs at least one person smart enough and dedicated enough who loves poetry so much that he or she will do whatever is possible to serve the art form. Ginger Murchison was that person for Poetry@Tech. (It's a character flaw of mine: I believe credit should go where credit is due.) I don't think you can *hire* people like Ginger. Again, lucky.

My job is easy. I teach classes. I love to teach classes. I get to talk about this thing I love—poetry—and I even get paid for it!

Sometimes I feel like Mickey Rooney or those kids in a '30s movie saying, "Let's put on a show!" *Poof,* a whole stage, set, costumes, props are there! It doesn't happen that way. There's a huge amount to do: book venues and flights for poets, advertise—regular flyers, thousands of e-mails, etc., etc. and always, *always,* the Kafkaesque university bureaucracy and red tape, cruelly redundant. To help me sign forms I have to sign, kind people attach little "sign here" stickers in consideration of my...attention span, or lack thereof, for certain things. (I can think real hard about things I want to think hard about.) I thought that without Ginger Murchison, Poetry@ Tech would be screwed.

I believe the need for poetry is not much different from the need for bread or air. If one has a chance to deliver a little bread or air or poetry somewhere, one should do so as best one can.

No way could Ginger be replaced. But Poetry@Tech got lucky again. We hired Travis Denton, whom I'd gotten to know in Atlanta. He's a talented young poet who just published his first book, loves poetry deeply, and is super competent. He's now the associate director of Poetry@Tech and for the past few years has served a stint as one of the McEver Chair holders. Ginger will hold the Chair in 2011. They've both done a splendid job.

As I've said, it's a lot of work, and it also takes people skills. You have to be kind to the people you work with at a university, such as the people who take care of cutting the checks for the poets! It takes bargaining skills—both Ginger and Travis are brilliant at making deals on things such as catering, printing, photos, videos, hotels, travel, etc. In these times of tight budgets, saving a hundred there, fifty here means a little more wiggle room on how many poets we can bring to read and/or teach and how much we can pay them. With the current recession, our endowment monies, like everyone's, took a serious kick in the ass. Like most who survived, we are going forward. Since 2002, the associate director has been paid. I should say *underpaid*. Only my summer salary comes out of endowment money—the rest of the Bourne and McEver proceeds go toward bringing poets to read and teach, to continue our outreach to community classes and school visits.

I just reread the "Description of Duties" regarding the writing of this document, and I think I have covered the "values" (a good and honest word, by the way) that drove the project and why the project was needed in the specific place and time that gave rise to it. I hope I have essentially answered that in this bumpy narrative, but I'll put it in a nutshell again: Georgia Tech received those two gifts. When one receives great gifts, one should share them with one's neighbors. It would be churlish to do otherwise. It would be against the nature of what I believe poetry is. Don't ask me to explain that, because I can't, but maybe I will be able to in a few poems before I'm done.

The "Description" has another point I'll reiterate, this time in a thimble. It was needed at the specific time it began because it didn't exist at Georgia Tech at the specific time, and it began because of the gifts. I believe the need for poetry is not much different from the need for bread or air. If one has a chance to deliver a little bread or air or poetry somewhere, one should do so as best one can.

In seven full years, as of December 2009, we have brought approximately ninety poets to read at Georgia Tech:

Kim Addonizio, Coleman Barks, Robert Bly, Roger Bonair-Agard, David Bottoms, Kurt Brown, Kathryn Stripling Byer, Elena Karina Byrne, Turner Cassity, Pearl Cleage, Lucille Clifton, Judith Ortiz Cofer, Billy Collins, Mike Dockins, Rita Dove, Ross Gay, Regie Gibson, Doreen Gildroy, Albert Goldbarth, Jon Goode, Beth Gylys, Karen Head, Edward Hirsch, Tony Hoagland, Bob Holman, Andrew Hudgins, T. R. Hummer, Chezon Jackson, Naomi Jaffa, Mark Jarman, Van Jordan, Ilya Kaminsky, Mary Karr, Collin Kelley, David Kirby, Steve Kowit, Kurtis Lamkin, Blake Leland, Martin Lammon, Dorianne Laux, Al Letson, M. L. Liebler, Alessandra Lynch, Taylor Mali, R. J. McCaffery, Marty McConnell, Jeffrey McDaniel, Bruce McEver, Heather McHugh, Joseph Millar, Cherryl Floyd-Miller, Judson Mitchell, Opal Moore, Eric Nelson, Marilyn Nelson, Dean Parkin, Ed Pavlic, Patrick Phillips, Christopher Reid, Tania Rochelle, Neil Rollinson, Patrick Rosal, Lawrence Rubin, Michael Ryan, Steve and Ronnog Seaberg, Bette Sellers, Megan Sexton, Alan Shapiro, A. E. Stallings, David St. John, Leon Stokesbury, John Stone, Sharan Strange, George Szirtes, Quincy Troupe, Memye Curtis Tucker, Charles Harper Webb, C. K. Williams, Ralph Tejada Wilson, Karen Wurl, Ellen Bryant Voigt, Gypsee Yo, Dean Young, Kevin Young, and Adam Zagajewski.

Eighteen different poets have held the McEver Visiting Chair in Writing: me, Stephanie Strickland, Stephen Dobyns, Brooks Haxton, Vijay Seshadri, Patricia Smith, Kurt Brown, Stuart Dischell, Natasha Trethewey, Kurtis Lamkin, Chard deNiord, M. Ayodele Heath, Anthony Kellman, Sharan Strange, Laure-Anne Bosselaar, Travis Denton, Opal Moore, and Katie Chaple.

We've sponsored about thirty-five community classes and approximately the same number of school visits. All of our events and classes are free and open to anyone.

section•three

DRAWING BREATH

Programs at Large and at Home

THE THREE GOAT STORY

Notes on Poetry and Diplomacy—University of Iowa
International Writing Program

Christopher Merrill

First, a disclaimer: I am not a diplomat, just a poet who happens to work in the field of cultural diplomacy, which is defined as "the exchange of ideas, information, art, and other aspects of culture among nations and their people in order to foster mutual understanding." Cultural diplomacy falls under the rubric of public diplomacy, which is sometimes described as the art of winning hearts and minds. Since 9/11, these forms of what the political theorist Joseph Nye calls "soft power" (in contrast to the exercise of hard—military and economic—power) have generated considerable debate in foreign policy circles. The University of Iowa's International Writing Program (IWP) has played a role in these debates, developing models of soft power rooted in the practice and pedagogy of creative writing, in artistic exploration, which may offer an alternative to the dictates of extremist ideologies. In these reflections, I wish to share stories from the front lines of what has been called a war of ideas, a clash of civilizations. This is in my view not a war, at least not yet (though war is one way that nations resolve competing claims and ideas), but a dialogue, with far-reaching cultural, political, and spiritual implications.

Dialogue depends upon listening, and listening is essential not only to cultural exchange, which ideally courses in both directions, but also to any literary enterprise, especially poetry, which may begin with a poet hearing something—a word, a phrase, a rhythm—that holds the promise of exploration and the prospect of linking one thing to another in a system of correspondences that may resonate not only for the poet but for the reader as well. Hence E. M. Forster's advice to novelists—"Only connect"—is an organizing principle of the IWP, where we connect writers to other writers, students and scholars, translators, and editors. During the Cold War, the IWP was a meeting place for writers from the Soviet Bloc. Chinese writers started coming soon after the Cultural Revolution ended, and after 9/11 we began to invite more writers from Islamic countries. So many books have been written in the IWP that one writer called the University of Iowa a narrative nursery.

The World Comes to Iowa—this was the title given to a pair of anthologies of writings selected from the first three decades of the IWP, and in recent years the State Department, which provides a significant portion of our funds, has encouraged us to bring American writers to the world. Thus we have hosted symposia in Greece and Morocco, on topics such as what we hold in common, justice, home, and the city, and organized tours of American writers to Syria, Jordan, Israel and the West Bank, Turkey, Cyprus, Oman, Saudi Arabia, Tunisia, and Kenya. In the last, we visited a Somali refugee camp, where the importance of connecting, of cultivating better relations between one people and another, cannot be underestimated.

No one ever dies in Dadaab, humanitarians say, at least not in the Somali refugee camp, which is the largest in the world. Here a food ration card is a precious item, the final and perhaps most valuable legacy inherited by the family of the dead, representing for some the difference between life and death. The refugees subsist on aid provided by the international community, which translates into 2,100 calories a day, plus cooking oil and soap.

Here is another truth: almost no one ever leaves Dadaab.

The camp, which is actually three camps (Dagahaley, Hagadera, and Ifo) constructed in northern Kenya near the border with Somalia, was designed to temporarily house ninety thousand men, women, and children fleeing the conflict touched off by the collapse of Somalia's central government in 1991. A succession of failed governments, fourteen in all, turned the camp into a more or less permanent home to 275,000 refugees, most of whom traveled for weeks by bus and car, on foot and camelback, in searing heat and the red dust that covers everything in the badlands north of Dadaab. The border has been closed since early 2007, but in the first half of 2009, more than five thousand new refugees arrived every month to live in tents and endure chronic shortages of running water, electricity, and toilets. Each month, seven hundred babies are born in the camp, and thousands of teenagers have spent their lives in what one aid worker called a fenceless prison. The Kenyan government does not allow refugees to move about the country. Thus there is nowhere to go and nothing to do; with unemployment running at 80 percent, parents fear their children will return to a homeland they have never seen to fight a war that goes on and on.

It is the forgotten war. No doubt the lasting image of Somalia for many Americans comes from the 1993 Battle of Mogadishu, a failed operation to root out a powerful warlord that cost the lives of hundreds of Somali militiamen and civilians and eighteen American soldiers. It was a military and political fiasco for the Clinton administration, recounted in Mark Bowden's best-selling *Black Hawk Down* and later brought to the screen by Ridley Scott. The conflict prompted the White House to withdraw troops from Somalia and made it reluctant to employ force to stave off humanitarian catastrophes in Bosnia and Rwanda. A disaster-relief specialist involved in the planning for military action in Bosnia and Somalia told me that it was possible to make a difference in Bosnia, not Somalia; after the Battle of Mogadishu Americans largely forgot about Somalia.

However, another image of the war-torn country had formed by the time we arrived in June 2009; Somali pirates were seizing ships in the Gulf of Aden, prominently the *Maersk Alabama*, an American container ship carrying five thousand metric tons of supplies for refugee camps in Kenya, Uganda, and the Democratic Republic of the Congo. The pirates held the captain hostage in a covered lifeboat, setting the stage for a drama on the high seas. Days passed as an American warship sailed into the Gulf and television crews camped outside the captain's house in Vermont. When Navy SEALs shot three of the pirates and freed the captain, there was the sort of jubilation in America that in earlier ages might have attended the death of Blackbeard or Captain Kidd. In Dadaab, where rations had to be reduced by five hundred calories a day, a relief worker pulled aside a local leader. "You know your brothers are doing this to you, don't you?" he said. The refugee smiled, shrugged his shoulders, filled his canvas sack with grain.

What happens when ad hoc arrangements take on the patina of permanence? This is a question that my colleagues and I confronted in Dadaab. The essayist and translator Eliot Weinberger, the poet and novelist Terese Svoboda, and the poet Tom Sleigh joined me for what a State Department official had described as a slightly fantastic (and perhaps dangerous) cultural diplomacy mission: to conduct creative writing workshops for secondary school students in the refugee camp. So one summer morning, we met an American diplomat at a small domestic airport in Nairobi to board a turboprop leased to the United Nations for the hour-long flight north. The plane landed on an airstrip, where a press officer from the U.N. High Commissioner for Refugees (UNHCR) greeted us, and we climbed into white SUVs for the drive through the dingy town of Dadaab, up and down deep dips in the sandy road. Men sat on truck tires half-buried in the dirt outside each shop—crescents demarcating businesses that had sprung up to serve the Non-Governmental Organization (NGO) community. Nailed to a tin shack was a sign: *Baghdad Enterprises*. There were hand-lettered signs for hotels, which offered food, not housing. And we learned that the UNHCR was negotiating with the local community, made up largely of goat and camel herders, to lease land for a fourth camp. The discussions were not going well, though; years of drought, which had hastened the Somali exodus, had bred resentment among Kenyans, who envied the international largesse bestowed upon the refugees. They wanted ration cards, too.

The sun was blazing when we filed into the mess hall at the UNHCR compound for our security briefing. An Irishwoman newly arrived from a stint with the relief agency in Afghanistan spelled out some of the hazards her staff and visitors faced—an aid worker had been shot not long before, and there were always red spitting cobras and scorpions to worry about. She then explained that tensions were running high in anticipation of the impending verification process, a UNHCR census in which 10 to 15 percent of the refugees would likely lose their identity cards, costing many families their extra ration cards. For recreation, we could use the gymnasium or the tennis court or run on the path circling the perimeter of the compound. The press officer advised us to take flashlights to the bar unless we wanted to step on a snake.

I wondered how in the world we were going to share our experiences of writing and the creative process—the life of discovery, as the poet Brewster Ghiselin called it in his symposium *The Creative Process*, which has sold more than half a million copies since its publication in 1952. "Simply, the self-interest of mankind calls for a more general effort to foster the invention of life," Ghiselin argues in an introduction synthesizing ideas from a range of thinkers. "And that effort can be guided intelligently only by insight into the nature of the creative process."

Thus he gathered together writings from poets and writers, mathematicians and scientists, composers and artists, which in their totality suggest that a common set of principles applies to every discipline: the importance of preparation—that is, mastering skills and techniques, acquiring a body of knowledge, learning how to translate experience into wisdom—and the necessity of remaining open to different approaches and ways of understanding. How to glimpse what may lie on the periphery of vision, where heretofore unimagined connections may be made? That is the task of artist and scientist alike. "There is a right physical size for every idea," the sculptor Henry Moore reported, and this holds, figuratively speaking, for every discipline. If there is any truth to the idea that the cultivation of creativity, "the invention of life," is crucial to our collective future, there was no better place to explore this than in our meetings with students trapped in a place lacking just about everything that might make life bearable. We ate lunch, returned to our rooms to set up mosquito tents, and then drove off to our first workshop.

The issue, said the diplomat on the way to Hagadera, was that al-Shabaab, an extremist Islamist group believed to be affiliated with al-Qaeda, was offering young men in the camp five dollars a day and a Kalashnikov to join their countrymen and a small band of foreign terrorists (some of whom had honed their fighting skills on the battlefields of Iraq and Afghanistan) in an attempt to overthrow the government in Mogadishu, which the international community had gone to great pains to establish the previous autumn. Some Somali Americans had heeded the call to take up arms, and one had just been killed near the capital. The diplomat had seen a group of Somali Americans breeze through immigration at the airport in Nairobi. He feared that they were heading north.

We arrived at the community library, an octagonal building with a tin roof, and took our places at old wooden tables; taped to one wall was a UNHCR poster that read TOGETHER, and next to it was a Macmillan map of the world, the top half of which was missing. There was a scattering of books on the shelves; what light there was filtered through the open windows. The young men in blue shirts and black or white trousers sat on one side, the young women in blue or red *hijabs* on the other, and Ali, a

Kenyan Somali, translated for us, our English accents being mutually incomprehensible. The 1993 riots in Nairobi had curtailed Ali's studies, dashing his dream of becoming a journalist, and as the students introduced themselves I wondered what he made of their grand ambitions. "I want to be prime minister," said one girl. "I want to be a pilot," said another. "I want to be a heart surgeon," said a third.

To be a writer," said Tom, "all you need is a pencil
and a piece of paper."

"To be a writer," said Tom, "all you need is a pencil and a piece of paper."

Then we handed out pencils, notebooks, and lollipops—Tom said that he liked to suck on something sweet when he was working—and the students began to write.

It turned out that the exercise we had assigned them was too complicated, and in our eagerness to make it work, we threw out one idea after another, which added to the confusion. It was a wonder that the students came up with anything at all. But as they read their stories aloud, we were struck by the sophistication of their writing, all subordinate clauses and compound structures, and then by the revelation from one student that each camp had its own writing club, the entrance requirements for which were quite stringent: applicants had to turn in stories on a variety of subjects—local and international news, sports, culture—which were judged by what sounded like high standards. After the workshop, on our drive back to the UNHCR compound, there was some tension in the SUV—we wanted to succeed, we knew we had not—which did not begin to dissipate until we tried to devise a new exercise for the next workshop.

"Let's have them write a three-goat story," said Terese.

"What's that?" said Tom.

"We'll find out when we get to Dagahaley," she replied.

And so we did. Her instructions to the students who passed through the barbed wire gate to meet us in a bare cinder block building were wonderfully simple: put three goats into a page of prose or verse. The results were often moving. Here is what Abdi Kadar wrote:

The Three Goats

Once upon a time there were three goats. The three goats were called Blacky, Horny and Shouty. They lived in the forest where many predators like the hyena, the lion, and the leopard existed in a larger population.

The three slept together, grazed together, and helped each other in terms of hardships.

It was not long when one of their enemies, Hyena, decided to eat the three goats. In fact it was difficult for the hyena to eat the three goats because they were always together. Hyena thought for day and night but he could not get a way of eating the goats.

One day Hyena went to his friend Hare to discuss the issue of eating the goats. Hare who had a character trait of trickery and wisdom suggested to his friend that he would bring tonight Shouty alone so that Hyena can eat her alone and the next night Blacky so that the brave Horny will remain alone.

Hare went to the three goats and made good friends with them. He told Horny that Hyena was going to eat him tonight and you can't hide away from him unless you chase Shouty away because she will shout and help Hyena to easily discover your hiding place.

Horny without thinking started chasing Shouty. Since she was afraid of Horny she went away. By nightfall Hyena came and ate Shouty. The next day Hare went to Blacky and told her that last night Hyena ate their friend Shouty and tonight he is going to eat Horny and if he finds you with him he will also eat you. Blacky thought for a while and decided to leave Horny alone.

Again Hyena came and ate Blacky after finding her alone in the forest followed by Horny the next night.

My story ends there.

"No party is complete without a goat," is what the UNHCR T-shirt says, so one night at an Ethiopian restaurant run by a refugee we ate goat. The conversation turned to piracy—a student had sent Terese a poem praising the pirates—and it occurred to me that I knew next to nothing about the students, except that for all intents and purposes they had no prospects. The chances of resettling abroad were slim—only fifteen hundred refugees are issued permanent resident visas each year to the United States and a handful of other countries; it is equally difficult to secure one of the few university slots available. But perhaps it was better to jaw-jaw than to war-war, as Winston Churchill famously said. I hoped that in the scheme of things some good might come of our attempts to describe what it feels like to engage in the creative process.

Thus in each workshop Eliot cited the example of Chinese poets' taping their writings to communal walls during the Cultural Revolution; Terese read her translations of Sudanese poems; and Tom praised the heroism on display in Nadezhda Mandelstam's memoir, *Hope Against Hope*, recounting how she and Anna Akhmatova kept alive the poems of Osip Mandelstam, a victim of Stalin's gulags. I told a story about the Greek poet Yannis Ritsos: how he had prepared for his looming imprisonment during the military dictatorship by removing the stuffing from a winter coat and then writing poems on cigarette papers, which he hid inside the hollowed-out coat. When he was released after a year, he gave the coat to his editor, instructing him to publish all the poems because he needed the money to pay for his daughter's wedding. In short, each of us felt called to invoke the witness of writers who had testified to some of the darkest chapters of human history, for this was what our students faced in Dadaab.

What could we offer besides anecdotes about writers bearing witness to oppression, imaginative exercises, and encouragement to read and write?

There came a moment in each workshop when a student would ask what we would do for him or her. The students were accustomed to well-meaning foreigners promising them this or that. But what could we offer besides anecdotes about writers bearing witness to oppression, imaginative exercises, and encouragement to read and write? Eliot said that as writers we could barely tie our shoes—a line that always elicited stunned silence and then general laughter, which changed the dynamics of our encounter. The atmosphere lightened as we found ourselves to be on more equal footing. We suggested that they translate literary works from English into Somali and vice versa. (All the students were bilingual, and some were fluent in three or four languages.) We smiled, we told jokes (which lost something in translation), we listened: hope against hope. We were exploring together the contours of the life of discovery.

★ ★ ★

The line outside the camps' registration tent stretched as far as the eye could see—individuals and families arriving from their war-torn country, hungry, thirsty, exhausted, sometimes sick, often scared. Children sat on their mother's laps, waiting to be vaccinated, to have their eyes swabbed with medicine. And then another line into a building, where there was paperwork to be filled out and questions to answer. Religion. Nationality. Languages. What are your main needs? What did you encounter along the way? What made you flee your country? Please tick as appropriate:

- ❑ Lack of Food
- ❑ General Insecurity
- ❑ Family Members Killed
- ❑ Financial Difficulties
- ❑ Lack of Education
- ❑ Loss of Employment

Other (specify)_____

Other reasons included membership in a militia. These men were interviewed separately from the rest of the population. Some have a lot of blood on their hands, said a relief worker—which put into perspective the logistical difficulties that we faced in conducting writing workshops.

First we needed permission from the UNHCR to work in the camps, fly on its planes, stay in its compound, and use its security detail. Then we had to gauge the risk of working in a volatile environment, with inadequate communications and a lack of supplies—books, paper, pencils—that belonged to an overall picture of dearth: the camps were short forty thousand latrines, and there were not enough doctors, medical facilities, medicine, schools, or teachers, to say nothing of clean water. No wonder the humanitarians looked harried at the end of the day.

That night in the bar at the compound, I fell into conversation with the press officer, who told me stories about snakes: how a refugee working in the kitchen had killed a red spitting cobra and hung it outside the mess hall to deter other snakes, how an aid worker had nevertheless been sprayed in the face by another spitting cobra, how they had saved her life by lighting the airstrip with headlights from their vehicles so that a plane could fly her to Nairobi. I realized that I had forgotten my flashlight, and when I left the bar I wandered down one path and then another in search of my room, praying that there were no snakes out.

The diplomat and I went for a run one afternoon on the dirt path surrounding the perimeter of the UNHCR compound. A herd of black-faced goats—with *hijabs*, went the local joke—rooted in the scrub under a silver water tower, and thirty or more marabou storks perched in an acacia tree, a congregation of huge carrion-eating birds that thrive on human activity. There is a story that when a butcher in Kenya laid aside his bloody knife for a moment, a marabou swallowed it whole. We could see the birds circling above the camps or walking near the heaps of garbage. An aid worker blamed the garbage on a kind of camp-induced lethargy, the chief beneficiaries of which seemed to be the marabous. I asked the diplomat if he thought that what we were doing had any merit, and he replied that giving 250 students the opportunity to listen to American writers speak from the heart about their work was nothing to sneer at. He picked up the pace. "Can you run another lap?" he asked. "Yes," I said, panting. And so we did.

Morning and afternoon, we would drive from the UNHCR compound to the police station in Dadaab and wait for the Kenyan police officers to escort us to the camps. "They're probably drinking tea," the press officer would say, shaking his head. "They'll come when they feel like it."

The police officers accompanied us after the last workshop in Ifo to N-0, the newest camp, where the latrines placed between two rows of tents were used by forty people. Thorn branches served as gates to each tent, some of which housed as many as twenty people. Three students joined us, one of whom had opened the question-and-answer session earlier in the morning at the community center by saying that because he was giving up his time to study for exams, he wanted to know what was in it for him. We had praised the pleasures of aesthetic exploration, but I had the feeling that we had not convinced him or his friends that this would be time well spent. But here they were, now translating for a wizened man who recited a poem about businessmen in Somalia sending their families out of the country and doing nothing for refugees, now helping us wade through the crowd that swarmed around us. An old man harassed me for failing to visit sooner, and after he said his piece he shook my hand in the traditional way and led me on a tour of the camp. A woman surrounded by children took up the theme of his tirade, saying that at the hospital she could not get any medicine. "What are you going to do for us?" she demanded to know. I said that I could write about what I had seen—and then one of the students said that he and his friends could write about this, too.

"That's right," I said, brightening. "I've been here three days; you've been here years. You know this story better than I will ever know it."

I said that I could write about what I had seen—and then one of the students said that he and his friends could write about this, too. "That's right," I said, brightening. "I've been here three days; you've been here years. You know this story better than I will ever know it."

On our last day in Dadaab, fighting in Mogadishu left at least forty dead, including the police chief, and more than 130 wounded. The next day, the internal security minister, the former ambassador to Ethiopia, and many others were killed or wounded in a massive suicide car bombing in the city of Beledweyne, where they had gone to meet with tribal and religious leaders, hoping to stem the violence. The Somali president blamed foreign terrorists for the attack, and indeed there were news reports that some members of al-Qaeda had moved to Somalia and Yemen to escape the military offensives in Afghanistan and Pakistan.

The U.N. plane lifted off from the airstrip outside Dadaab and flew over the parched land. Peter Matthiessen titled an account of his travels in East Africa *The Tree Where Man Was Born,* and I had just opened his book when one of the pilots turned to me and said, "Are you OK?" I caught the eye of the diplomat seated across the aisle. "I can't say I've ever heard a pilot ask that before," I said—and then began to read about the land below, which contained the origins of our species: its vast natural resources, its terrible history of bloodshed. The plane rose through clouds—the first sign of rain in months—and by the time we landed in Nairobi the sky had darkened. Near the terminal, ambulances were lined up beside a military cargo plane from which soldiers were unloading the victims of a gruesome accident.

For the third time in two months, a fuel truck had crashed, and as people siphoned up the fuel, something—a cigarette, a spark—touched off an explosion, killing and maiming dozens of men, women, and children.

A van was waiting to take us to our hotel, and on the drive through town the diplomat called his office to pick up his messages. He asked his secretary if she had heard anything about the explosion. She had not. The road wound up a hill lined with nurseries, and at the top, not far from the American embassy built after the 1998 al-Qaeda bombing that had killed hundreds of Kenyans, there was the smell of burning charcoal. Men walked on the side of the road, past jeeps in which sat Kenyan police officers. A Somali had lately been arrested here on suspicion that he was doing recon-naissance for another attack. On we drove.

ONE HEART AT A TIME

The Creation of Poetry Out Loud

Dana Gioia

I.

Poetry Out Loud is now probably the largest poetry program in the United States. Last year, approximately 325,000 high school students participated by memorizing and reciting poems in organized competitions held in all fifty states as well as the District of Columbia, Puerto Rico, and the U.S. Virgin Islands. Not only is the program supported by every state arts agency; in most states Poetry Out Loud has become the signature public arts education program. Similarly for the competition's two founding sponsors, the National Endowment for the Arts and the Poetry Foundation, Poetry Out Loud now represents their most visible arts education program. The program's high public profile is hardly surprising given the huge media coverage it now receives at every stage, from local school competitions to the national finals in Washington, DC. By almost any standard, Poetry Out Loud constitutes a huge success in a period when cultural success stories seem rare.

In retrospect, successful ventures often seem inevitable. Our society particularly prides itself on innovation and entrepreneurial energy, and it loves stories about great ideas that triumph over every obstacle. Such successes do happen—look at Microsoft, Pixar, or iTunes—but it has been my experience that excellent notions often fail to take hold and prosper, especially in the arts. For every Poetry Out Loud, there are hundreds of worthy endeavors that never survive or achieve only a local presence. For that reason, it may be helpful to provide a short history of the program, explore its rationale, and discuss some of the key decisions that led to its ongoing success.

For clarity's sake, however, let's begin by describing the program itself. Originally called the National Poetry Recitation Contest, the now more evocatively named Poetry Out Loud is a partnership between three very different sets of organizations—the National Endowment for the Arts (a federal agency), the Poetry Foundation (a private nonprofit), and state arts agencies (state government bureaus). The NEA created the program's curriculum and materials in collaboration with the Poetry Foundation, and it distributes them free to all participating schools. Students choose the poems they wish to memorize either from the free classroom anthology or the Poetry Foundation's special website, which now offers seven hundred diverse selections. Beginning with classroom competitions, winners advance to individual school contests and then to city, regional, and eventually state finals. The state winners then go to Washington, DC, for the national finals. There are prizes and certificates awarded to winners at each level, with the largest prizes distributed at the final competition. The national champion receives a $20,000 scholarship, second place earns $10,000, and third place, $5,000. The semifinalists (places four through twelve) each receive $1,000 with an additional $500 for their schools. The national champion and several finalists usually return to Washington the next fall to perform in the NEA's literature pavilion at the National Book Festival.

II.

Poetry Out Loud began at the National Endowment for the Arts as a personal project. As the first poet ever to chair the agency, I was concerned about the declining audience for serious literature, especially poetry. Having grown up in a working-class home in which poetry was enjoyed and recited, I had never accepted the notion that poetry was an elitist art whose pleasures were available only to intellectuals and academics. I had long felt that poetry's diminished popularity was at least partially due to the analytical ways in which it was generally taught. One can learn many important things about a poem through critical analysis and term papers, but simple enjoyment is usually not one of them.

When I look back on what created my own appetite for poetry, two early experiences stand out. The first was my mother's habit of reciting or reading poems. She was a Mexican American raised in brutal poverty who had never gone beyond high school—exactly the sort of person the literary establishment usually assumes has no interest in the art. She knew dozens of poems by heart—Poe, Byron, Whittier, Tennyson, Kipling, and Shakespeare, as well as now mostly forgotten popular writers such as James Whitcomb Riley, Ella Wheeler Wilcox, Robert Service, and Eugene Field. She would recite poems with great relish and genuine emotion. It took me years to understand how deeply her favorite works connected to the private joys and sorrows of her life. My mother not only instilled in me a love of poetry, she also taught me how mysteriously poetry communicates things about the reciter as well as the author.

My mother not only instilled in me a love of poetry, she also taught me how mysteriously poetry communicates things about the reciter as well as the author.

The second experience occurred a few years later in eighth grade under the tutelage of Sister Mary Damien, a small but formidable nun of inexhaustible energy. One day early in the school year, she complained that she could hardly understand a word I said and told me to stay after school. There I discovered that I was not the only notorious mutterer. I found myself with three other boys—all of us Mexican Americans raised mostly among nonnative speakers. We expected to be yelled at. Instead, the assiduous sister announced that we needed basic elocution lessons. Three days a week after school, she worked with us to improve our speech. The lessons soon took the form of listening to recordings of actors reciting poems and then memorizing and performing the poems ourselves. She pushed us to achieve the same clarity of speech and emotional expressivity as the actors. In that pursuit we failed notably, but we did improve greatly from our mumbly beginning. More important, we loved hamming it up and belting out Tennyson and Shakespeare. Within a few months she even had us compete in a local speech contest. It would be hard to exaggerate how much those late afternoon lessons transformed my life. Using the words of dead poets, Sister Mary Damien gave me the gift of self-expression. Without knowing it, she also nudged me toward a life of poetry.

Using the words of dead poets, Sister Mary Damien gave me the gift of self-expression. Without knowing it, she also nudged me toward a life of poetry.

What strikes me about both these life-changing encounters with poetry is that neither came from a book. They were primarily oral, auditory, and performative. My love affair with poetry began not on the page but in the ear and on the tongue. I experienced it physically before I comprehended it intellectually. Poetry was also a social rather than a solitary activity—something to be shared with family and friends. And what we shared was primarily pleasure—a deep-rooted joy at hearing magnificent language spoken expertly, perhaps even thrillingly, in our presence. (It was the same sort of joy we experienced watching great athletes or fine dancers.) There was nothing unique in my case, I now realize. This was the way most people came to love poetry in the past, but in my childhood, such an initiation was already becoming relatively rare.

III.

The guiding vision of Poetry Out Loud was to create an arts education program that introduced students to poetry experientially—rather than analytically—using memorization, recitation, and performance. Poems speak to us in many ways, including intellectually, but much of poetry's power is physical, emotional, sensual, and intuitive. Those dimensions are communicated more directly through performance than analysis. Poetry now often seems to appeal mostly to intellectual readers. I suspect that situation has less to do with the nature of poetry than with the highly intellectual way in which it is taught. It is not coincidental, in my opinion, that the decline of poetry's popularity paralleled the dismissal of memorization as a pedagogic technique and the rise of close reading and critical analysis as the primary techniques for studying poetry. I believe in close reading and critical analysis—and even in term papers—but if those methods constitute a young person's primary encounters with poetry, it is no wonder so few people develop a lifelong love of the art. Those educational methods originally rested on an assumption that students brought earlier experience and familiarity with poetry to the classroom—from family reading, elementary school recitation, and general cultural currency. (Fifty years ago famous poems were still quoted and parodied in cartoons, television, and in popular magazines.) Those conditions no longer apply for today's teenagers. Most young people now first encounter poetry, at least in any serious sense, in a classroom.

IV.

For most students, the impact of participating in Poetry Out Loud is not solely, or even primarily, literary. In terms of the human energies it summons and develops, the program resembles music or sports more than English class. Poetry Out Loud revives the ancient art of memorization, which until recently was always a central element of education. By studying and reciting poetry, students learn to master language as well as develop skills in public speaking. This practice also helps students build self-confidence and expand their knowledge of literature. Social and intellectual growth occurs simultaneously. By internalizing great models of language and imagination, students increase their appreciation of the power of language, both intellectually and emotionally, to communicate complex truths. This insight has practical advantages for young people, whether they continue in the humanities or in other fields, such as law, business, government, ministry, or even sales. There is nothing especially rarified about an education through poetry. It develops the whole human being, not just the analytical mind.

Learning to recite poetry also invites personal growth. The very process of reading through many poems to find the right one to memorize can prove a catalytic experience for most students. Choosing the right poem may even help some students address inner needs of which they are not yet entirely conscious. Although some students are initially nervous about reciting in front of their peers, the experience can prove valuable—for both school and life. Much of their future success may depend on how well they present themselves in public. Whether talking to one person or many, public speaking is a skill people use every day in both the workplace and the community.

Poetry as a competitive event surprises some people nowadays. The notion of competition certainly shocked and dismayed many educational specialists when they first encountered the program, but poetic competition is as old as the Olympic Games, probably older. Along with wrestling, long-distance running, javelin tossing, and other athletic events, the ancient Olympics included contests in music and poetry. Rhapsodes, the ancient performers of poetry, trained for years and traveled great distances to attend the games. The winners were honored like sports champions, and they, in turn, composed poems in honor of the athletic winners. Poetry competitions were not limited to the Olympics but figured in most religious festivals with young men or women often performing choral odes in competition. Poetry Out Loud was consciously designed to recapture the special excitement—for both performers and audiences—that occurs when poetry is recited competitively.

V.

Poetry Out Loud began as an idea for a national recitation contest, but ideas are fragile things. To grow into something large and effective, they must be developed carefully and subjected to ongoing critical evaluation. Any national program needs to be tested locally before it is expanded. No matter how well an organization plans a new project, there will be things it misses or misjudges. The National Poetry Recitation Contest, as the program was initially called, first reached the public in early 2004 as two pilot programs in Washington, DC, and Chicago. Only one of the tests succeeded.

The Poetry Foundation tested the idea in Chicago by using a consultant who did not work the competition into classrooms but established it in an after-school program. Without the regular structure of an English class and the oversight of teachers trained in literature, the program lost focus. Contest rules were difficult to establish in the loosely structured environment. (This problem provided important learning for creating a successful national program.) Rather than focusing on competitive memorization and recitation, the program allowed almost any sort of poetry-based activity. Different students were allowed to do various things, often with little preparation. This approach resulted in a generic after-school program that lacked both individuality and competitive energy. Participation and public response were so poor that the Poetry Foundation felt that the program probably did not merit further investment.

Ideas are fragile things. To grow into something large and effective, they must be developed and subjected to ongoing critical evaluation.

Meanwhile in Washington the NEA conducted a pilot program in ten local high schools. Dan Stone, the program coordinator, and Cliff Becker, the literature director, elicited the support of teachers and administrators to make sure the competition began at a classroom level. Teachers took ownership of the program, and it proved an immediate hit with students. Participation exceeded our highest expectations, with over four thousand students entering the competition and teachers enthusiastically embracing the idea. As the Washington finals approached, we learned of the poor results of the Chicago test. I phoned John Barr, the president of the Poetry Foundation, and asked him to fly out and see the Washington finals, which were to be held in the Folger Library's elegant Elizabethan Theatre. We wanted him to see another city before making his final decision. Barr graciously agreed to come.

That evening in the Folger, everyone involved in the project witnessed for the first time the power of what we were creating. As the ten finalists took their turns on stage, reciting Yeats, Donne, Dickinson, Pound, and Brooks, we were reminded of the primal magic of poetry. There was nothing dutiful in the recitations. Some students performed better than others, but they all displayed a significant quality in common. The students quite literally embodied the poems, and the authenticity of their connection to the words was often startling.

What also surprised me during the first final was the intense attention of the audience. Having attended countless poetry readings over the years, I was accustomed to the polite but hardly rapt attention one generally finds at such events. The Folger audience was visibly engaged from start to finish, something I have noticed consistently at all Poetry Out Loud competitions. There is a special attention people—both competitors and spectators—bring to competitive activities. The audience not only experiences the recitation, but it pays special attention to the various qualities that guide the best performances as it observes and compares the contestants. The citizens of ancient Greece believed that competition encouraged excellence—not only in sports but also in the arts. Poetry Out Loud demonstrates the soundness of that idea.

That evening I noticed something else that has struck me at every subsequent competition I have attended—namely how diverse the finalists were. They came from every cultural and ethnic background with a disproportionate number of first-generation Americans. They also comprised every type of high school kid—jocks, scholars, actors, debaters, slackers, class clowns, hipsters, gangbangers, and loners. Their passion and excellence were simultaneously inspiring and chastening. I realized how much we underestimate the potential of our teenagers, how little we often expect from them, how, given the choice, they can astonish us. There was a reason that poetry, especially memorization and recitation, had played such a large part in education across the ages. Poetry awakens and develops the potential of young hearts and minds.

VI.

Having escaped one cancellation notice, the program soon faced another. The Arts Endowment felt that the best partners for the competition would be state arts agencies, the official state institutions dedicated to arts and arts education. The state agency executive directors listened to the idea positively—not with great enthusiasm but with interest. If the NEA and Poetry Foundation were going to invest additional money in state arts budgets, the state agencies would consider giving the National Poetry Recitation Contest a try. State arts education specialists, however, generally disliked the program. They insisted that students would not willingly memorize poems, that teachers would reject memorization as an antiquated, even repressive technique, and that competition was anathema to arts education. They suggested that the NEA should create a program in which students would gather to read their own original poems without judgment—"no winners or losers," one specialist said, "just sharing." By then the program had been renamed Poetry Out Loud, but one state arts official down south referred to it only as "Cryin' Out Loud."

A large program not only requires many partners, it also requires a consensus—a shared notion that everyone has something to gain by its success. Our task now was to overcome widespread skepticism about this new program and create a mutual decision to try it. Dan Stone conducted a series of conference calls with every state, using his considerable charm and intelligence to explain why students might enjoy memorization, performance, and competition—the triple taboo of arts education. He not only cited the excellent participation in the DC schools pilot program, but also pointed out the popularity of hip-hop and poetry slams among teenagers. Stone also flew to Boise to address a gathering of all the state agencies to plead our case. He faced some hostility, but he gradually made converts. Slowly, our diplomacy and advocacy worked. The state arts agencies agreed to try Poetry Out Loud—with only a few arts education specialists still prophesying doom and disaster.

Having now built a national institutional partnership with the Arts Endowment, the Poetry Foundation, and the state arts agencies (which would soon be joined by the Mid Atlantic Arts Foundation as program coordinator), we now approached some invaluable individual partners—the state poets laureate. In April 2003 I had addressed the first national gathering of state poets laureate. Talking with them about their activities, I learned that most states had created the laureate position but provided no funding for meaningful public programs. There was, therefore, a nationwide network of prominent poets in public office who needed a visible and effective program. I wrote all the laureates, asking them to lead Poetry Out Loud competitions in their states. The NEA and the Poetry Foundation then set up a national conference call to solicit their comments and support. The laureates quickly and unanimously joined the program. It is hard to overestimate the importance of their enthusiasm and advocacy. Their involvement at the state level not only provided the program with expertise and commitment but also helped give Poetry Out Loud local character and leadership.

Once the national program got underway, the negativity almost immediately vanished. State arts personnel soon observed that both students and teachers liked the program. Initial participation was excellent with 100,000 students competing in the first year. Teachers and students loved and used the free classroom materials. Press coverage was surprisingly strong, especially at the local and state levels. Reacting to the competitive nature of the program, the media gave Poetry Out Loud the level of attention it usually bestows on school sports. Local winners found themselves featured in the press like varsity athletes—a benefit not lost on school or state officials. Many state arts officials, whose good works had mostly gone little noticed for years, excitedly reported that mayors, state representatives, and even governors had become enthusiastically involved in the competition.

VII.

One key to the program's success was the strong publicity. From the beginning we took public relations seriously as a necessary means of building awareness and appreciation of the program. Cultural organizations are often ambivalent, even squeamish, about courting the media. Although they crave publicity, they worry there is something undignified, even unsavory, about seeking it. Sometimes there is even a sense of irritation with the press and the public—the organization is doing such valuable work that the public should already know about it! The problem is that in a society supersaturated by information and entertainment, both the media and the public need to be specially engaged and educated. Few nonprofit literary organizations have money for advertising, so any broad effort to inform the public can only occur through media coverage. The bad news is that successful publicity requires discipline and hard work. The good news is that press coverage is free.

> The bad news is that successful publicity
> requires discipline and hard work. The good news
> is that press coverage is free.

Poetry Out Loud was an entirely new program. If the public, especially teachers and students, were to learn about it, they needed not only to be informed but made interested. The state arts agencies sent out e-mails, but low-impact communication is insufficient to launch and sustain a broad national program. We needed to solve a problem that all poetry organizations face—how could we engage the interest of the general media, local and national, which almost universally believed that poetry no longer merited their attention?

Our first challenge was how to position Poetry Out Loud clearly and concisely to a general audience. The best way to explain something new often is to strike a chord of familiarity with something already established and then explain the differences. We initially positioned Poetry Out Loud as a literary equivalent of the National Spelling Bee—a multitiered, competitive program that developed individual intellectual excellence in an arresting way. The media immediately understood our concept and knew how to cover it. (Many journalists have a great fondness for poetry that they have little opportunity to exhibit.) The extensive coverage not only increased participation, it also recognized and rewarded participants—to the special delight of their parents and teachers. It also strengthened the support of school administrators, state arts personnel, and politicians. (The extent of the local and national coverage became more evident when *Poetry Daily* joined the program in 2008 by posting the best articles on their popular website.) Finally many newspapers quoted from or reprinted winning recitation pieces, thereby creating a new and unexpected place for poetry in publications that rarely or never otherwise presented the art.

Media attention is a powerful way of motivating and rewarding students who participate in the program. There are few ways that artistic excellence is recognized and celebrated in high school. State officials almost immediately understood the inspirational quality of the program—not just for students but also for teachers, parents, administrators, and politicians. State winners frequently recited the winning poems at large public functions—traveling around like the literary equivalents of state beauty queens. Suddenly poetry recitations became a part of public functions, a revival of an American tradition Whitman, Emerson, and Longfellow would have understood. The public, which is so often characterized as disliking poetry, turned out to enjoy the recitations. At the National Book Festival, for instance, the Poetry Out Loud winners proved second in popularity only to the Poet Laureate's reading. Likewise when the state finalists come to Washington and visit their representatives in the Senate and House, they are often asked by members of Congress to recite their poems.

Program materials were also important. Much educational material is lackluster and perfunctory. We wanted ours to be both artistically substantial and engaging. A conspicuous advantage of a national program is that it can cost-effectively develop materials that no local program can afford. For Poetry Out Loud, the Arts Endowment and the Poetry Foundation created beautifully designed and produced posters, teacher's guides, audio CDs, and eventually DVDs. American culture is celebrity driven. Celebrities give programs or products visibility and credibility, especially among teenagers who have grown up in a media-saturated society. To demonstrate the broad appeal of poetry, the NEA approached well-known actors with a passion for the art—Anthony Hopkins, James Earl Jones, Alyssa Milano, Alfred Molina. We matched them with well-known writers, including Richard Rodriguez, N. Scott Momaday, Rita Dove, Kay Ryan, David Mason, and David Henry Hwang. We then recorded both groups reciting favorite poems. The purpose of the "audio guide" was both to communicate the pleasures of the art and to provide diverse models for effective performance. As the program developed, we also filmed some of the national finalists to illustrate the wide variety of successful approaches to poetic recitation.

Meanwhile, at the Poetry Foundation, Stephen Young led the development of a classroom anthology for the competition. The book, which he and Dan Stone edited, included 114 poems, carefully selected to present a diverse range of themes, styles, historical periods, and cultural traditions. The Poetry Foundation supplemented the printed anthology with a website containing approximately four hundred selections. Gradually this online anthology has grown to seven hundred poems, providing contestants and instructors with an enticing range of possibilities for every level of the competition.

In creating an enduring public enterprise, validation fosters validation. Any new venture must successfully display the standards by which it wants to be judged. In developing the national finals, we carefully crafted a series of public events that would support the program's visibility and importance. They had to hold their own in Washington, a city crowded with exceedingly well-executed public programs. The final events also needed to appeal to multiple constituencies—students, poets, teachers, politicians, and the press. Poetry has become such a specialized activity in our society that some literati might doubt that an inclusive and exciting public event can be created without dumbing everything down. The Poetry Out Loud finals have demonstrated that a compelling and artistically rich event can be created for a general audience. Special care each year has gone into selecting a diverse, distinguished panel of judges, which has included Garrison Keillor, Azar Nafisi, Tyne Daly, Caroline Kennedy Schlossberg, and Natasha Trethewey.

Author and National Public Radio host Scott Simon has served as master of ceremonies. A live jazz trio has provided musical breaks and accompaniments. The U.S. Senate has hosted a lunch for state winners. Each year, the NEA program manager, Leslie Liberato; the Mid Atlantic Arts Foundation's director of external affairs, Karen Newell; and Poetry Foundation's program director, Stephen Young, have found new ways of adding excitement and glamour to the national finals. Each year, all fifty-three finalists have distinguished themselves by sheer excellence from hundreds of thousands of competitors. They deserve an unforgettable finale. So do their parents and teachers. And so, too, does the underappreciated art of poetry.

VIII.

The future of Poetry Out Loud looks reasonably secure. It has become a signature program for all its major partners. Now in its sixth year of national competition, it has become a familiar part of high school culture. Teachers across the country have made it part of the curriculum, and some have even declared it their favorite classroom activity. Although today no arts education program is entirely safe from elimination, the immediate future for Poetry Out Loud seems auspicious. With the program now successfully established, it may be useful to ask what it has achieved for literary culture.

The first important thing that Poetry Out Loud has accomplished is to demonstrate that large and ambitious literary programs of the highest quality are still possible. Properly planned and executed, they can succeed with both artistic integrity and broad democratic reach. There is now so much fatalism among American intellectuals and academics about the decline of serious literary culture. It's one thing to note the negative trends in literacy and reading—an informed perspective is invaluable—but it is quite another to assume that the cultural problem is irreversible. Poetry Out Loud demonstrates that a hugely popular program can be launched and sustained nationally—even on a relatively small budget. Such enterprises require long-term partnerships, careful planning, and creative promotion, but Poetry Out Loud suggests that the public will respond to serious literary ideas when they are well presented.

The second significant impact of Poetry Out Loud has been to expand the conventional strategies of literary funding. In the case of the NEA, for instance, the program took the agency into new territory. Before Poetry

Out Loud, virtually all of the Art Endowment's support for poetry focused on assisting its creation—individual fellowships for poets and translators, subsidies for presses and magazines, subventions for artists' colonies, poetry organizations, and writers' centers. While the NEA helped support poetic creativity, the audience for poetry declined substantially. Between 1995 and 2002, for example, the percentage of U.S. adults who read any poetry fell by an alarming 30 percent, from 20.5 to 14.3—almost one-third of the audience vanished in less than a decade! It was time to try a new strategy. Perhaps one way of helping poets and poetry was to rebuild their audience. Art does not easily thrive in isolation. As Walt Whitman observed, "To have great poets, there must be great audiences, too." Poetry Out Loud focused on developing a large, new audience among American teenagers—and through them among parents, teachers, and the general public.

Third, Poetry Out Loud has expanded the audience for poetry. The program has inspired hundreds of thousands of American teenagers to memorize poems. Bringing these students into a deep and personal relationship with poetry at a point in their lives when they are exploring their adult identities will surely create many new lifelong readers. The 2010 student participation of 325,000 probably constitutes a cohort almost as large as the core adult readership of American poetry. As the program continues across the next decade, its alumni will number in the millions.

Fourth, the program's popularity has helped refresh and expand the way poetry is taught in high school. Memorization and performance are rightly regaining their place beside critical analysis—making the art more accessible to many students who might otherwise find it overly cerebral and intimidating. Poetry Out Loud also includes an element few people mention—listening. Students not only memorize poems but also hear them recited by classmates and competitors. During the weeks of the competition, they are immersed in a culture of poetry as intense as any college course. This experience broadens their familiarity with and deepens their connections to the art.

Finally, the activities fostered by Poetry Out Loud have helped bring poetry back into public culture—in newspapers, on radio and television, at civic events and school assemblies. The media coverage is not only enormous and growing; it is also surprisingly smart. The media love annual events and they tend to improve such coverage each year. Poetry Out Loud has also given thousands of journalists, commentators, programmers, and editors a chance to air their love for poetry. Because of its size, excellence, and popularity, the program has provided the general media a chance to improve arts coverage. All these activities create a meaningful place for poetry outside the classroom and bring millions of Americans into contact with excellent poetry.

This is how poetry grows its audience—on heart at a time.

All of these larger trends are important, but their greatest value rests on something very small and true that goes to the core of why poetry matters. Culture is not a marble museum; it is human energy. The true value of Poetry Out Loud is the sound of a young man or woman speaking the words of a poem he or she chose to learn *by heart*. Standing in a classroom or auditorium, among friends and family or strangers and competitors, the student momentarily becomes the embodiment of culture. Poetry has no better bridge between past and present, poet and audience. As this small affirmation repeats itself hundreds of thousands of times across the republic, the mysterious power of the art radiates "like shining from shook foil," and "gathers to a greatness." This is how poetry grows its audience—one heart at a time.

PEOPLE, HABITAT, POETRY

The University of Arizona Poetry Center

Alison Hawthorne Deming

We owe what we are to the communities that have formed us.
—Habits of the Heart

Thirty years ago, I made a cross-country road trip from northern Vermont, where I had lived for a decade of self-exile in the clarifying North, drove to New York City to pick up my then-lover who was studying art at the Cooper Union, and rolled out into the American West. This was my first trip west of the Mississippi. My daughter was in boarding school, a scholarship-induced reprieve for me from the burdens of single parenting. My companion and I were broke, in love, and happy for the road. We pitched our tent in a cow pasture in Pennsylvania, waking to a circle of curious Holsteins watching our sleep. We kept rolling on out into the open possibility of the Great Plains. I'd been writing poems for years and reading hungrily to try to figure what this art was that drew me, first serving as a modernist acolyte in love with Eliot and Yeats; then falling for the emotional extremism of Lowell, Plath, and Sexton; then landing in the backyard of poets associated with the San Francisco Renaissance and Black Mountain College. I had become snobbish about my poetic affections, which strikes me now as an offensive narrowness, an aesthetic parochialism that made me identify myself with one group by opposing others. I was looking for something larger in myself, some vista more expansive than the worn-out New England hills and a poetics true to my own character and experience. I did not want to be a caricature of poets who had come before me.

We camped on a dirt road in Texas after a freak ice storm, pitching the tent in sleet that coated the ground, weeds, fence wires, tent struts, and nylon with sheening ice. We were exhausted to the bone from the ice-road terror. In the gray morning, we woke to a melting world and found that we'd pitched our tent beside the corpse of a dog, a traveler less fortunate on that perilous road. By the time we got to Tucson, we were ready to be housed once again and took up the invitation to stay with my lover's brother, a graduate student in arid lands. When he heard I was a poet, he told me that the University of Arizona had a Poetry Center. He had that look on his face that said he knew I'd be surprised to find such a thing out in the desert. He boasted that the Center had an archive of poetry recordings. I was snobbishly skeptical, certain the place would have none of the poets who mattered to me.

I was at the time excited by Kathleen Fraser, whose book *New Shoes* had just come out. I loved the Magritte poems and the way others ranged across the page, allowing air and uncertainty into the poems. She wrote of "feeling pulled along by forces not quite even in one's control," and I understood myself to be an apprentice to that feeling, the desire to be self-possessed and recklessly open all at once. I made my way to the weedy bungalow on the edge of campus, browsed the rickety shelves lined with poetry books, and found the small plastic file box holding twenty years' worth of cassette tapes, including a recording of Kathleen Fraser reading here on September 29, 1977. As I write this, I pull the book off my personal library shelves and find that *New Shoes* sports Jon Anderson's endorsement—"These are stunning poems…[which] form a kind of latticework or exterior nervous system…a great gulp of pure oxygen"—and cover art by Tucson's Gail Marcus Orlen. The Poetry Center, from my very first visit, changed my sense of the national literary map and made me realize that what I was seeking was not just a self-actualizing voice but literary community.

If a place isn't careful, it can become a caricature of itself, falling for a canned version of its history that leaves it bereft of whole categories of collective experience. Tucson as "Cow Town" and Santa Fe as "Pink Coyote Land." A place can lose track of its story and so its future. This can happen to literary organizations, which can sprout up like field mushrooms in the rain and shrivel as quickly. In the twenty years I've lived in Tucson, I've seen dozens of journals, reading series, community workshops, and writers' groups form and dissolve. A few have sustained. This is not a surprise: artistic affiliation follows the patterns of growth, connection, and decay that cycle through nature and culture. Life spans vary; dynamism is all. Looking over the past fifty years of the Poetry Center's history, I can't help but marvel at its constancy through periods of institutional distraction, fiscal insecurity, aesthetic contentiousness, the tired jabs at "academic poets" (as if such a category could be defined and remain so from 1960 to 2010), the privatization of public education, and the call for arts audience development in the age of entertainment.

What has carried us through all this weather, so that we begin our second fifty years standing in the breezeway of an artful new building that is the fulfillment of a long collective dream in this community, spawning a wealth of programs serving diverse audiences and building a living archive of poetry, photographs, and recordings of more than one thousand readings hosted by the Center since 1961? "Why here?" we ask, even those of us closest to the life of the Poetry Center, why here in the arid and malled landscape of desert and Sunbelt sprawl? What key values shaped the Center and might serve others who wish to create something in their own communities that says poetry matters?

The Poetry Center was established on an aesthetic idea passionately held by founder, poet, novelist, and editor Ruth Walgreen Stephan—"to maintain and cherish the spirit of poetry." When she spoke of the spirit of poetry, she meant not the art's ethereal aspect that "makes nothing happen" but rather the animating force that lends strength and purpose to individuals and movements. "Poetry," she wrote, "is the food of the spirit, and spirit is the instigator and flow of all revolutions, whether political or personal, whether national, worldwide, or within the life of a single quiet human being." She spent winters in the 1950s writing in a rented cottage near the university campus. In 1960, she bought this cottage and an adjoining lot, donating them on the same day to the university to launch the Poetry Center. In her Connecticut home, she had a small poetry room, and she noticed how it encouraged her young son to read poetry "without intermediaries." She also saw that the university was devoting more and more of its resources to science and technology, and she wanted to protect a cultural space for poetry.

"Poetry," she wrote, "is the food of the spirit, and spirit is the instigator and flow of all revolutions, whether political or personal, whether national, worldwide, or within the life of a single quiet human being."

Stephan was not the kind of donor who writes a check and disappears. In addition to her original donation of property, between 1960 and 1972 she made gifts of poetry books, lists of books to purchase, a secretary, a housekeeper, curtains, furniture, Southwestern art and artifacts, money, and Walgreen stocks (she was the daughter of Charles Walgreen, Chicago drug store executive), and she secured a bequest of Walgreen stocks from her mother. She purchased five additional lots and donated them to the Center, envisioning construction of its permanent home. She wrote an illuminating essay on collection development in which she emphasized the beauty and physicality of the book and the importance of poetry's roots in indigenous song and its flowering in world literatures. "The nucleus of the collection," she wrote, "should be the acknowledged great poets of all countries in the world together with the foremost living poets in our country. This is essential in America whose population is multi-ancestral."

Stephan lived by the tenets of her vision and remained a fierce steward of its values. From 1947 to 1949, she and her husband, painter John Stephan, coedited the avant-garde journal of art and writing *The Tiger's Eye*, which was celebrated in a 2002 exhibit at the Yale University Gallery and which David Anfam called "a seismograph to the complex cultural moment of the late 1940s in America." Stephan traveled to Peru to collect Quechua songs and tales, published as *The Singing Mountaineers* in 1957 by the University of Texas Press. She published two historical novels. She traveled to Japan in search of a quiet place to write and found herself a student of Zen Buddhism, publishing the essay "The Zen Priests and Their Six Persimmons" in *Harper's* in 1962 and making the documentary film *Zen in Ryōkō-in*. Decades before the buzzwords of multiculturalism and diversity became ubiquitous, Stephan articulated a vision and practice that embodied them.

The process of building community opened up and changed over time, as it will do. Stephan was not in favor of hosting readings, fearing that they'd turn into faddish celebrations of favoritism. But it was the reading series, launched in 1961 with visits by Stanley Kunitz and Kenneth Rexroth, that brought the community together—following the auspicious dedication ceremony at which Robert Frost and then-U.S. Representative Stewart Udall presided. John Kennedy had just been elected president, and, at the Tucson gathering, Frost and Udall cooked up the idea of having a poet read at the upcoming presidential inauguration. From its first public ceremony, then, the Poetry Center was linked to the national theater of politics. It did not hurt the broader cause that the first director of the Center sent a letter to more than one hundred poets worldwide inviting them to spend time in the Center's guest cottage. On the local scene, audience development through the 1960s and 1970s was a homemade affair of making phone calls to professors and writers, running posters around town, and hanging them in commercial venues, including, with Ruth Stephan's help, Walgreen's drug stores. Audiences for literature were strong from the start: a couple hundred for Kunitz and Rexroth, four hundred for Robert Duncan in 1963, a stunning twenty-six hundred for Archibald McLeish in 1965. Tucsonans like to joke that there was nothing else to do in town in those days. But that's not the whole story.

The dominant story of the American West carries the flag of Manifest Destiny—that sense of "divine" purpose that led the eastern Anglo culture to expand its political and economic influence "from sea to shining sea." It was an ethos bearing blades and bullets, iron rails and steel wills. It usurped land inhabited by Mexicans and American Indians, taking and using whatever it wanted, mining and grazing to the nub, then moving on. A familiar story by now, this ethos has long been demoted by the anguish and diminishment that came with its sense of progress. But this was never the only story of the West. Small stories have emerged within this large one, stories in which distinctive cultures and landscapes drew artists, writers, anthropologists, and scientists—the Taos of Mabel Dodge, D. H. Lawrence, Marsden Hartley, Georgia O'Keefe—people who brought learning and culture from their home places but were also hungry to learn from the land and the people who knew the place intimately through generations of living by its terms.

In Tucson, one such influence, as ethnobotanist Gary Paul Nabhan reminds me, was the Carnegie Foundation's launch of the Desert Laboratory on Tumamoc Hill in 1903, the first research site devoted to the study of arid lands. At the time, Tucson's population was seventy-five hundred, and the influx of scientists focusing on this place helped enrich the town as it began to grow. I think it is fair to say that Ruth Stephan's contributions to Tucson are part of this cultural flow, newcomers expecting a level of culture they had known in larger cities such as New York and Chicago but who also made an effort to celebrate the older cultures that were in place. She valued the communal identity experienced in art that crosses generations and continents. She did not foresee how significant the community's role would be in the life of the Poetry Center.

> She valued the communal identity experienced in art that crosses generations and continents.

I've emphasized Stephan's role because I believe her passion has been translated and carried on by many people who shared in the Center's stewardship over the past fifty years. Lois Shelton merits special mention, as she served as the Poetry Center's director from 1970 until 1990. While being a vigilant overseer of the Center's endowment, she offered warm hospitality to writers; she and her husband, poet Richard Shelton, took poets on outings into the desert, to the Arizona-Sonora Desert Museum, or to the San Xavier Mission. They never lost sight of how remarkable the desert is to newcomers. The collection of poems written by visiting writers (May Swenson, Lucille Clifton, Carolyn Kizer, Al Young, etc.) in the Sheltons' honor—and in that of the Sonoran Desert—testifies to the quality of experience their hospitality offered. In 2002, Gail Browne became director, offering precisely the set of leadership skills in organization and development, and the brilliantly steady temperament that made the elegant and inviting new facility a reality.

When I moved to Tucson in 1990 to become director of the Center, a tenth-generation New Englander who had lived for forty-four of her forty-five years in New England, I knew I had a lot to learn. I had been working as coordinator of the writing fellowship program at the Fine Arts Work Center in Provincetown, where I had been a poetry fellow, the last stint of a decade-long transition from a hard chapter of life that began when I was a pregnant college dropout and ended after two decades of work in family planning and public health programs in northern New England. I fell into this work during Lyndon Johnson's War on Poverty, first as a paraprofessional outreach worker for Planned Parenthood of Vermont and last as a researcher and writer for the Governor's Task Force on Teen Pregnancy in Maine. What I had experienced as a teen mother—poverty, struggle, judgment, and deep personal reward—was not represented in the professional face I wore in those positions, which were all about helping others, all about being of service to those who lacked health care information and services. I had struggled through a doomed teen marriage, raising my daughter mostly on my own in a life that now seems to have been bewilderingly difficult. At the time, it seemed right to make physical challenge the starting point of self-invention.

Get up before dawn, build wood fires to heat the permeable old farmhouse, wake daughter in cold, hike to barn to milk goat, gather eggs, water and grain the horse, scare away the fox scouting the henhouse, breakfast the daughter, pack up her lunch, take her to school, drive an hour in the snow to get to work. Repeat chores in the evening. Read stories and more stories to daughter who hated bedtime. Find still and quiet hours in the night to write. Bank the fire. Stack wood for morning. Sleep in the cold. For a dozen years, I understood the desire to be a writer as the hunger for what Virginia Woolf taught a woman she needed: a room of her own.

Through these years, I wrote and read poetry: Wendell Berry's "Mad Farmer" poems, Jerome Rothenberg's *Technicians of the Sacred,* Plath and Sexton and Lowell, Kinnell and Merwin and Levertov, Duncan and Creeley and Dorn, Stein and Apollinaire and Neruda. I understood that language was the tether that held poets to life and to the human family in all its anguish and contradiction. I read anything my friends—fellow urban refugees—handed me, and I wrote by hand on a desk made of old, weathered barn boards, woodstove bracing me against the night. I wrote list poems about the junk I had cleaned out of my woodshed in that ramshackle home—horse harnesses and canning jars, the front page of a newspaper from the day the *Hindenburg* crashed in flames, and jars full of square-cut homemade nails. I wrote poems about the cold, farming, stars, muskrats, and loneliness. I imitated everything I read. I fell in love with the silence at the end of my pen, the sense that could spill from that silence, and the music that could drive language out of its dark habitat in the neural forest of my mind and onto the open field of the page.

I understood that language was the tether
that held poets to life and to the human family
in all its anguish and contradiction.

I wrote that way for years, showing work to no one but a few other closeted poets who shared my enthusiasms for the beauty of words and their tendency to fall into form. I did not understand that language was a communal possession, that to write was to join in a collective enterprise that reached all the way back to clay tablets and papyrus, to the deeply old human desire for sharing story and song.

I know this is a long digression into terrain apparently alien to the matter at hand, which is to explore the values that shaped the life of the University of Arizona Poetry Center. But it is a necessary digression because though the details vary, stories of artistic apprenticeship often leave out the importance of finding community. One can sit in a room of one's own until the wallpaper peels from the walls, never knowing if one's words have the capacity to bridge the distance between oneself and others. Without the communal sense of art's force, one can weaken into faithlessness when facing the blank page. It took me a long time to realize that nearly every advance I made as a writer came in concert with someone's passing along the work of a beloved author, of my attending a poetry reading or lucking into a writing community—first and foremost the wonderful vortex of anarchistic energy that was Poet's Mimeo Cooperative in Burlington, Vermont, during the 1970s and later on other groups (Vermont College MFA, the Fine Arts Work Center in Provincetown, and Stanford's Stegner Fellowship programs)—that led me to feel the power of a collective experience of art.

Poet's Mimeo was founded by poets Tinker Greene and Bud Lawrence. They didn't really have an aesthetic ax to grind, except to bring spirit and play into the life of art. Publications (run off on the drum of an old mimeograph machine in editions of less than a hundred) were an afterthought to sharing a certain energy about the art. The poets hosted readings at galleries, coffeehouses, and a firehouse that had become a community center. Tinker led classes, which often as not met in someone's living room, focusing on Gertrude Stein, Ed Dorn, Guillaume Apollinaire, Robert Duncan, Frank O'Hara, Andre Breton, cut-up and concrete poems. For a 2001 article on this micro movement (http://www.7dvt.com/2001/time-passages), Bud Lawrence said, "It was a very yeasty time, a sort of settling down out of the wildness of the '60s without getting rid of too much of the wildness in terms of art and literature." Coming out of a period of self-exile, I became committed to the social function and pleasure of art.

I gained from that experience a greater conviction that artists, in a manner that might well be impossible to quantify, can help shape what a community means to itself and to others.

I took these values—experiences that had begun to solidify into values—with me to Tucson. I had come from the Fine Arts Work Center (FAWC) in Provincetown, where I been a poetry fellow and then writing program coordinator in the 1980s. FAWC is a notable arts institution founded by writers and artists, among them Stanley Kunitz, whose spirit hovers over several of the projects described in this collection. The idea to offer long-term (seven-month) residencies to twenty writers and artists early in their careers was spurred by the founders' belief that what artistic vocation required most of all was the freedom to work among like-minded others. But the FAWC founders were also committed to investing in Provincetown as the nation's most enduring arts colony. As commercialism was diluting that legacy, they felt that the influx of the fellows and visiting artists would help seed a future in which that legacy would not be lost to shops and condos. I gained from that experience a greater conviction that artists, in a manner that might well be impossible to quantify, can help shape what a community means to itself and to others.

The University of Arizona Poetry Center had a distinguished thirty-year history by the time I arrived in Tucson. Its collection had continued to grow thanks to the Stephan endowment, the reading series had flourished, funding had been diversified among public and private supporters, the guesthouse walls bore the beloved graffiti of visiting writers who had slept there.

> *Yevgeny Yevtushenko in 1979 wrote*
> *"I bless everybody unblessed by God*
> *Those in shoes and those unshod."*

> *Edward Albee in 1980 wrote*
> *"The least dishonorable defeat*
> *is the only honorable goal."*

> *William Matthews in 1981 wrote*
> *"Isn't it great,*
> *Not being dead yet!"*

> *And Denise Levertov in 1984 wrote*
> *"The poet-ponies sniff the breeze;*
> *They scent a friendly stable . . .*
> *No bit or bridle there to tease*
> *And oats upon the table."*

Richard Shelton was running his prison writing workshops, the MFA program was established in 1974, writers in the reading series routinely made visits to local high schools to read and give workshops, the Walgreen endowment grew to more than one million dollars dedicated to library acquisitions, student awards and readings helped build audience for new writers, community and student writers hung out and loafed at their ease on the Center's couches, and visiting writers quite literally left marks of gratitude on the guesthouse walls. The constellation of programs and resources the Center offered was unlike any other poetry facility in the country. I felt immediately both the dignity of its history and the potential for its future.

However, the fates of urban development and university expansion set up a few detours. This led to one of the Center's most challenging decades. In 1989, the Poetry Center's original two buildings were demolished for a city project to widen Speedway Boulevard, long infamous for its 1970s *Life* magazine designation as "the ugliest road in America." *Sic transit gloria mundi.* The collection and guesthouse were moved to temporary quarters—then moved again when those temporary quarters were demolished to build a parking lot for the university's medical center expansion. It is easy to claim that the needs of a small and quiet center can be glossed over and forgotten in the growth spurts of a large and rapidly expanding institution.

The Center's plans to build a permanent home were at this time linked with other campus projects slated for construction with state money. Our project met delay after delay, as state resources became more pinched. For the purposes of this essay, I won't give even the barest outline of the arcane, tiered procedures involved in getting a building project approved, funded, and built with the support of state government in a state boasting a legislature that places little value on higher education. A few informal proposals were floated our way suggesting models in which the Poetry Center would be subsumed into other university identities—the library or college—proposals that did not offer much promise that the unique characteristics and values and history of the Center would be given a priority.

The Arizona Board of Regents gave conceptual approval to the construction of a new Poetry Center in 1990. By 1996, with one-third of the collection in storage because of space constraints, we still had no new building and faced the prospect of being folded into a state-funded humanities office building at an unknown future date. That year, with the support of our community-based development board, I made the recommendation that the Poetry Center separate from this larger project, which meant we would also separate ourselves from the prospect of having a state-funded building and so would need to commit ourselves to raising four or five million dollars. This was truly a test of our capacity to reach the community and of the community to respond to our need.

The dual challenge—to hold on to aesthetic integrity while drawing major donors to the cause—can be a perilous passage for an arts organization. Will the organization's core values be compromised? If we changed from a being a "poetry" center to being a "literary" center, would we attract more money? Would that dilute the strength of what we'd accomplished over the years, making us less distinctive and worthy of support? The prospect of raising several million dollars for poetry was chilling—and the estimated cost kept climbing the more years our project was delayed. Though the Center had a firm financial footing in its library endowment, its programs had been supported over the years by a mix of public and private funding—small grants and contributions from Friends of the Poetry Center. By the time construction commenced in 2006, we were looking at a

$6.8 million dollar building, with university support covering only $1.9 million. The success of the campaign, which stretched over a decade, had everything to do with community board members who contributed time, money, and influence, as needed. In addition, the Center partnered with the Humanities Seminars Program, which offered noncredit courses "for community members in serious pursuit of intellectual stimulation and enrichment" and lacked a permanent home on campus. Its constituency joined ours in common purpose and raised funds for an elegant presentation space at the new Center.

The dual challenge—to hold on to aesthetic integrity while drawing major donors to the cause—can be a perilous passage for an arts organization.

My confidence in community support grew over the years I served as director (1990–2002). It seems worth backtracking now to consider a moment in the Poetry Center's history when I began to appreciate the robust interest in poetry and the unique strengths of our community. In 1992, Larry Evers and Ofelia Zepeda launched a semester-long course and reading series out of the American Indian Studies Program, cosponsored by the Poetry Center and the Department of English. "Poetics and Politics" brought thirteen of the most accomplished American Indian writers (including Simon Ortiz, Joy Harjo, N. Scott Momaday, Leslie Marmon Silko) to campus for readings. The series began with standing room only in the customary lecture hall, which seated a few hundred people. Each week, the reading was moved to a larger hall as audiences swelled. We wondered if we'd end up in the basketball stadium. It did not quite come to that, but the point was made out loud that there was a much more committed audience for poetry in Tucson than even we partisans had suspected. Beyond that, I became more convinced that special interests in the audience for poetry are a good thing and need not be a source for contention. There are indeed multiple audiences for poetry.

A reading by an avant-garde poet drew a different audience than did a populist poet or a Latino poet or a new formalist poet or a bioacoustical composer or a celebration by high school students of the traditional *corrido*, a border ballad form. Some audiences were large and some small, some constituencies overlapped and intersected with one another, but our audiences were always varied and in love with the art of the poetry. One tends to celebrate only the big numbers, but in the life of poetry, it is essential to also celebrate the many small traditions that exist within this large and encompassing and unfolding form of expression. This ethos reminds us to continue asking, "Who's included? Who needs to be included?" Perhaps our longest-standing program addresses some of the most neglected citizens, participants in the prison writers' workshop. All these experiences with the poetry audience in Tucson spoke, as we considered our expansion, about a community—both the city and the university—that wants to be a great place for the arts and understands how deep and broad its legacy in the arts goes. Though state support for both education and the arts in Arizona is dismal and diminishing, we continue to have enough citizens who care about these values for us to know that their support will be there.

The design challenges for the new building were great: how to make a space large enough to house the collection and its anticipated growth while retaining a feeling of intimacy; how to provide access to an irreplaceable collection of books, recordings, and photographs while protecting and preserving these resources for the future; how to provide a welcoming space for public events hosting several hundred people while offering silence and refuge; how to foster interaction between community and university members while leaving space for solitary reading and reflection. It will come as no surprise then that the overarching theme of the building's design, as conceived by our gifted architect Les Wallach and his firm, Line and Space, was "contradiction = inspiration."

The building has become a landmark, its opening celebrated by more than two thousand people who attended the day of festivities and performances in fall 2007. Landmarks serve as navigational guides, and the new Poetry Center serves that function well, drawing in a growing range of audiences. New stories of artistic apprenticeship are finding a habitat in which to grow. Local writers offer classes and workshops that support the work of other local writers. In addition to library patrons and reading series audiences, new constituencies that frequent the Center include young children and their families who come for Saturday programs called Poetry Joeys, K to 12 students visiting on library field trips, high school poets on a Corridor Field Day or in a Poetry Out Loud competition, and retirees attending the burgeoning Humanities Seminars Program who join in Shop Talks on poetry and prose.

Early in the design process, the Poetry Center held a salon with staff, community volunteers, and architects to brainstorm about the relationship between poetry and architecture. Gaston Bachelard's *Poetics of Space* came into the conversation. Poetry is a form of "protected intimacy," he wrote. "The house allows one to dream in peace." The private life of the mind is the province of the poet, and the core principle governing this province is the faith that by attending to inner imperatives, framing them within the constraints of artistic/linguistic form, the poet reaches out to reveal our shared humanity out of which the spirit of community rises.

The private life of the mind is the province of the poet.

Bachelard tells the story of the French poet Saint-Pol-Roux, who bought a fishing cottage perched on a dune of the Breton coast. The poet designed and built around this humble hut a many-towered manor where he and his family lived. "And soon, bound up in my egotism," Saint-Pol-Roux wrote, "I forget, upstart peasant that I am, that the original reason for the manor house was, through antithesis, to enable me to really see the cottage." I think often of that relationship between hut and manor when marveling at our spectacular new building and all the responsibilities it places on us who are, for the moment, custodians of its future. Our origin as an institution rose quite literally out of a couple of rundown cottages. And poetry is a humble citizen of the art world, not given to commodification or stardom. How the small art/language/culture is to survive with integrity within the large is a question for our time that has many resonances. I take the metaphor to heart and celebrate one particular resonance: poetry is the hut; community is the manor.

A PLACE FOR POETRY

Building Models for Poetry Programming in Communities—
Poets House

Lee Briccetti

When schoolchildren visit the Poets House library, I sometimes feel I am present at the birth of poetry. A palpable energy manifests itself during a class trip as the students understand that poetry is alive and belongs to them! Or when a program audience listens to something surprising in language and the gathered attention creates an invitation to listen more deeply. Not to say that place is necessary to this kind of discovery, but it certainly can—and does—facilitate a means of entry and sense of community.

When Poets House opened its new home, my colleagues and I were surprised as the crowds of people touring the space started reading in excited quiet almost immediately—even during the grand opening celebrations—as if they had been hungry for a long time. The complications of our capital project had made it necessary for our collection to go into storage for two full years during construction. So it was joyous to see the books "in conversation" with readers again. The teenager with a nose ring reading Giacomo Leopardi. Families with young children enjoying the tactile pleasure of sitting close together and reading out loud. Reading is relationship.

And you never know where the connections will be made. This is an essential plea-sure of arts administrators, educators, and librarians—to create entrée and witness the growing engagement that follows.

For me, this work has many antecedents. In my twenties, I had a job at a "resi-dential facility" for troubled children. I will never forget a group of girls who could barely keep their heads off the classroom desks—from boredom and an expectation of boredom. When we read Lucille Clifton together, they discovered what reading was about for the first time. The line "these hips are big hips," from "homage to my hips," made them quake with laughter. They repeated the line all summer long and carried the poem with them. Suddenly someone was speaking directly to them. The way I look at it, once Clifton reached them, they wanted to be more reachable. And I was hooked too. This is the joy that is repeated daily in my work at Poets House.

INTRODUCTION

How poetry matters is a question worth asking, not just for practitioners and nonprofit service workers who seek to invite wider audiences into its pleasures but also for child psychologists, linguists, and anthropologists. This may already sound like a statement bordering on faith. I hope so because it's a useful introduction to the spirit of the programs I will talk about and to Poets House, which has just settled into its new "green" home on the bank of the Hudson River, housing one of the country's great poetry collections—50,000 volumes—and welcoming a constant flow of visitors of all ages, conversations and programs.

I have been the longtime executive director of Poets House. Though the organization has benefited from the combined energies of many, its original inventors always conceived of it as a physical *place for poetry* from which programs would radiate. In 1986, when Poets House first opened its doors—before the full impacts of the Internet and computer technologies were felt—its founders, former U.S. poet laureate Stanley Kunitz (1905–2006) and visionary arts administrator Elizabeth Kray (1916–1987), sought to make a physical space that would nurture poets and enlarge the role of poetry in the culture.

Like other nonprofits represented in *Blueprints*, Poets House provides something that would not otherwise exist in the marketplace. Stanley, Betty, and a host of poets who met during the early 1980s felt that poets were lonely in our culture and needed a spiritual home that would embrace a wide range of practice. Their blueprint balanced democracy and openness, tradition and contemporary practice. The organization first provided services in its own local context. Then, later, we communicated what we had learned by developing models for the creation of places for poetry within other institutions: libraries, community centers, and wildlife conservation organizations.

Poets were lonely in our culture and needed
a spiritual home that would embrace a wide range
of practice. Their blueprint balanced democracy
and openness, tradition and contemporary practice.

In this essay, I share observations from a signature Poets House initiative: Poetry in The Branches, our model for poetry services in public library systems. My hope is that teachers, poetry reading series coordinators, librarians, and community workers of all kinds will find ideas here to help them create places for poetry in their own settings or to reinforce what they are already doing. Later in this piece, there is a description of how Poetry in The Branches was born and the preconditions that made us ready to take it on, a checklist of the constituent elements of the original model, and ideas about how to extrapolate from the original recipe to create a multilayered approach to poetry in your community, wherever you are.

By way of introduction, I want to acknowledge that, obviously, making a program series or an organization is not the same as making poems or reading poems, which are the acts of imagination we serve. This essay is almost exclusively about organization making. Nonetheless, a craft is required, and I believe that craft is important, in its own way, because literary nonprofits have taken on the responsibility for creating cultural access to poetry, which was once carried out by schools.

A prized book from the Poets House archive is a 1928 primer for the second grade, *Required Poetry for New York City Public Schools,* edited by James J. Reynolds, then district superintendent of New York City schools. The short introduction, presumably written by Mr. Reynolds, clarifies the expectation: each child in the school system will pick three poems to memorize and recite and will be able to recognize and discuss other poems from the collection when they are read aloud by the teacher.

This little book charts a distance traversed. It contains about forty poems in two themed sections followed by an addendum corralling humorous offerings with a letter-by-letter meditation on the alphabet. This is not Arthur Rimbaud; throughout, there is a tendency toward the happy grasshopper and the industrious robin. All poems are rhymed. There are works by Christina Rossetti, Robert Louis Stevenson, Vachel Lindsey, and Edward Lear, and a John Keats poem with a complex rhetorical structure in which the protagonist ties a silken thread to a dove's foot. The primer is laced with such maxims as "A liar is not believed even when he speaks the truth." The impulse to moralize—or to civilize?—is on every page.

We can only conjecture how poetry may have mattered. But I think it likely that this little poetry primer, like etiquette handbooks from the same period, offered an acceptable map to the rules of thinking and speaking that could be a means of entering more deeply into American life. Certainly, poetry mattered enough to be an assumed presence and an active requirement of mind. And certainly, the pedagogical expectation is remarkable: what school system today would insist that the formative experiences of reading be so reinforced by learning complete works by heart and then speaking them? In the second grade?

We know that there is no second grade standard equivalent to *Required Poetry* for reading and memorizing today. But how do we understand that we are also in the midst of the most active moment of poetry production in the history of the United States—with more than 2,200 books from 500 publishers represented in the annual Poets House Showcase of new poetry books last year.

> How do we understand that we are also in the midst of the most active moment of poetry production in the history of the United States?

On the one hand, we are told that the number of readers of literature is in decline. But we also hear that the state of poetry is robust, with more people having access to poems both as text and as aural acts via the web. From some corners of the literary world, we hear that there are many books of poetry produced but not enough of them are "good."

Meanwhile, Poets House audiences have exponentially increased over the last twenty years from handfuls to the millions, given our online presence and the creation of robust, reciprocal program models. I am not always sure myself how to balance seemingly opposing pieces of information about the state of contemporary poetry. But I do believe that literary nonprofit organizations are in some sense culturally remedial, aiming through their missions to do what our society and our schools do not do. As I explore the nuts and bolts of various Poets House programs in communities, the bottom line is that we nurture what we love in a particular time and place.

POETS HOUSE BASICS

> Home is the place where, when you have to go there,
> they have to take you in.
> —Robert Frost

Poets House was created to be a home in which visitors could literally step into the living art. I want to linger a moment here, in order to make the discussion more meaningful by providing some context—because, like all nonprofits, Poets House expresses both nature and nurture. That is, the genetic composition of its mission expresses itself in a particular environment. Poets House currently serves about two million people a year, online and in person and through regional and national outreach.

Poets House is at the beginning of new phase of adaptation and service. Having grown first in a spare home economics room in a high school, then in a loft in Soho, our new 11,000-square-foot facility provides more rooms for collective purpose and interior quiet. With almost twenty-five years of programming experience, the organization's permanent quarters in Battery Park City opened to the public on September 25, 2009, after many years of planning, fund-raising, and, finally, construction.

Poets House is the long-term tenant on the ground and second floors of Riverhouse, a LEED Gold-certified building surrounded by beautiful parkland. In a city where real estate dealings are aggressive and expensive, this move creates a level of security that is necessary for a space-based organization. And with a sixty-year rent-free lease, we have an extraordinary opportunity to shift resources from rent to programming, to invite more people in, and to secure the collections for future generations.

The new space features almost a full city block of windows facing the Hudson River and the Statue of Liberty, attracting more people than ever to the library and programs. Well-known poets work on their laptops side-by-side with poets in the early stages of their careers, high schools students pore through piles of books, youngsters sing poems in a room built just for them, others listen to poems from our multimedia collection of two thousand distinct items. Today, the organization hosts more than two hundred programs a year—readings, forums on poetics, meetings with international poets—that create a palpable energy of exchange.

The vigor of different kinds of people participating, with distinct points of entry—children's room, program auditorium, library, multimedia area, quiet reading room—physicalizes the notion that there are many ways to apprehend this art form. This, you will see, is the approach we have modeled extensively for other kinds of communities. Our programming also presents different points of entry, from events designed for the widest possible audiences to advanced forums that are among the most challenging seminars on poetics outside the university.

Poetry in The Branches grew organically from a special library book-collecting program, which helped us to articulate a need within our field. Since 1992, Poets House has systematically gathered poetry books published in the United States through the Poets House Showcase, building one of the great libraries of contemporary American poetry. The Poets House Showcase is the only comprehensive, annual display of all books of poetry published in the country—a complete annual snapshot of the art in print—supported by a catalog of the books, presses, and poets.

During the early years of the Showcase, we realized that there was an explosion of poetry publishing activity as new technologies decentralized the means of production. We observed what has now become common knowledge throughout the field: the vertiginous increase in book production, the larger role of independent presses in creating poetic diversity, a more varied range of voices in print, and the decentralization of publishers throughout the country. We also saw the marked discrepancy between production and delivery. The books were not reviewed and had little or no shelf life at bookstores (remember bookstores?), and distribution was profoundly fragile.

Informed by intensive dialogue with colleagues in the literary, publishing, and library worlds, we began to turn to local libraries as our best natural partners to test ways of cultivating a wider audience for poetry and a better means of getting the range of poetry books being published into the hands of readers. We devised a poetry "menu" that might increase the appetite for poetry and encourage general readers in their communities to make a *place* for poetry in their lives.

Like so much of what we did at home, Poetry in The Branches was built on the premise that staged, sequential, and reinforcing program elements over the long term could create greater community engagement with the art form. On our home front, we had seen that when poetry is made more visible and people are invited to bump into it, they are able to discover it—happy to discover it. As we developed the capacity to track and then prove these assumptions, our partners' (and their audiences') engagement with the program grew.

POETRY IN THE BRANCHES

Beginning in three and then growing to nine New York City branch libraries during the early 1990s, Poetry in The Branches (PITB) is now a vigorous national movement that involves thousands of librarians. After eight years in the field as a full-service "poetry laboratory," when the tides of arts funding and public library budgets ebbed, we began new ways of delivering the program. It is alive and well as a vigorous training model for librarians from all over the country, in both urban and rural settings. The PITB concept creates a synergy among books, events, writing workshops, and professional training. All of these elements, reinforcing one another, create multiple audiences over time.

Preconditions for Program Development

Poetry in The Branches has now been reconfigured and regenerated many times, but at each new beginning, we found that there were some necessary preconditions for doing good work:

- articulation of a need or service potential
- identification of partners and the strengths they bring to the program
- planning process
- program plan
- timeline development

- identification of internal leaders, management structure, and/or governance
- networking and socializing
- pilot programs
- evaluation procedures
- documentation and distribution.

What follows is a mini case history, loosely charting the way the program was born and began to have a life of its own.

ASSESSING NEED AND IDENTIFYING PARTNERS

The Poets House Showcase manifested the abundance of book production and the limitations of distribution and readership. However, based on what we had seen at our own site, we believed more general readers could be interested in poetry if they were "invited in." Just as we were articulating this field-wide imbalance to ourselves, we met Kay Cassell, who was then a highly placed administrator in the Branch Libraries of the New York Public Library (NYPL). Kay had a background in literature and was willing to think creatively with us and to open her institution.

From the very start of our conversations, there were multiple attractions in working with the Branch Libraries. First, branches are perceived as community centers attached to books. Second, the installation of a new circulation-tracking system at NYPL branches made it possible to develop evaluation tools to study our initiative's impact on poetry *readership*. And, oh yes, we were eager to repackage what had worked so well at home to learn if it could work beyond our walls.

Poets House developed the model and phased program plan. Kay and her leadership team weighed in to provide insight into the structures and institutional culture of the branches and found satellite branches with the staff capacity to take on a new assignment. There was a full year of planning as we developed early networks of relationships between leadership teams. A pilot program at one of the selected branches featured Philip Levine reading from his own work along with that of poets he admired (such as Edward Thomas and John Clare). This closely followed the model of our home-grown Passwords—a template we have used over and over again—which features poets reading and discussing work they love from the living tradition of poetries. The goal was to help audiences experience poetry through the enthusiasm of poets and to make a bridge back to their own collections of books, as we had been doing successfully at Poets House for years.

Poets House applied for and received funding from the Lila Wallace–Reader's Digest Fund and acted as the organizer for the project. In the vernacular, we became the "poetry mommy."

THE PLAN

As I have written in other places, our early mantra was "You can't create love. But you can create the conditions for love." So too for poetry. And the first condition is always exposure. This is what the PITB program provided to each participating branch each year for three years:

- at least three public programs for adult patrons
- two after-school poetry writing workshops for young adults (multiple sessions)
- support for marketing services and publicity
- a "special needs" budget for each site
- assistance in collection development and display
- professional development opportunities for staff
- system-wide training
- assiduous evaluation.

Each site was required to purchase at least $1,000 worth of poetry titles during the course of a project year. Each branch was also required to aggressively *display* poetry books from the collection throughout the year and to integrate at least one book of poetry into every display presented in the library. Poets House gathered a one-time "seed collection" of forty selected titles at the beginning of the program so each branch could create an immediate poetry presence on shelves and in displays.

In addition, Poets House did the following:

- created a name-capture mechanism, building a poetry mailing list for each site that grew with each program
- developed support resource materials, tip sheets, project reports, and evaluation materials
- provided extensive planning assistance to branch sites

- hosted team meetings
- facilitated system-wide training for librarians, at which participating librarians reported on their work to their community of peers
- mapped out an annual timeline so that everyone had a clear sense of the pacing and expectations.

Two notes about the individual elements of the program. First, "special needs" grants. These were mini discretionary grants giving librarians the authority to go beyond the model and add elements specific to their sites. Some sites bought electronic message boards to "publish" poetry written by teens in workshops, others bought display hardware or created poetry corners, and still others created poetry bookmarks that were slipped into each patron's books at checkout. Whatever the librarians came up with was discussed at team meetings in the spirit of an exchangeable "idea bank." The emphasis was always on an integrated, reinforcing, and visible presence for the art form—and the creation of a group culture of experiment and exchange.

Second, system-wide training. These programs provided individuals participating in the project with an opportunity for recognition in their own branch systems through presentations to all their local colleagues. Those who excelled were given an opportunity to participate in presentations at national conferences. This element of the program encouraged participants to engage in a level of analysis and articulation and encouraged them to share what they found meaningful. The seeds of the future life of the program were planted at the very beginning.

PROGRAMS

Obviously, we treasure the book. But one of the ironies of our era is that new technologies have revolutionized access to poetry as an aural art form. Penn Sound, the Academy of American Poets, and the Poetry Foundation are used by millions to find poems as text and as spoken acts. At the same time, poetry slams, rap, and spoken word are manifestations of a deep tradition because the orality of language is permanent,[1] and sound is one of the essential elements of our craft. Multiple modes of entry to and dissemination of poetry are the rule—if there is a rule. In later iterations of the program, librarians were urged to create a presence for web-based resources, just as they were creating a presence for new books and journals and live events. The emphasis, always, was on creating a synergy among people, programs, and the various modes in which poetry is now disseminated.

In the early years of on-site work, we facilitated poetry readings based on the Passwords model, but as we went forward librarians tried many different formats—"memory circles" for recitation, open mics, poetry discussion groups, and events that combined poetry and music. Whenever librarians presented readings, they encouraged poets to include poems of other poets they loved and wanted to share.

We asked librarians to think carefully about the demographics of their neighborhoods and to find ways of including voices that reflected the experience of the residents. This is also a way of bringing in an audience that might not think of itself as poetry loving, giving it an opportunity to have a new experience. Not that bringing Dominican poets to a Dominican neighborhood should supplant William Carlos Williams. The idea, always, is to enlarge the conversation.

Poetry is a bridge builder. Because it speaks from and to our inner lives, it has a remarkable ability to create empathic connection between perceived differences.

In one of our original sites in the Bronx, there had never been a poetry program before, and the poetry book collection amounted to a few books by Walt Whitman, Emily Dickinson, and Edna St. Vincent Millay. Because the neighborhood had a population of elderly Jewish people mixed with Caribbean families, we diversified the collection to reflect some of the identity communities in the neighborhood. I will never forget the fourteen-year-old Caribbean girl who stumbled into a Yiddish poetry event and said she was going to begin reading poetry even though she didn't know Yiddish *yet*.

Poetry is a bridge builder. Because it speaks from and to our inner lives, it has a remarkable ability to create empathic connection between perceived differences. One library in New York City found that the only program that mended many years of mistrust between its two main user groups,

senior citizens and inner-city, at-risk teenagers, was an ongoing poetry pro-
gram.[2] We often suggested pairing a reading with a feature that would bring
two different groups together—reinforcing community connectivity, which
joyously, oddly, interactively created a remarkable aesthetic range. In a
diverse community setting, it is imperative to engage with the notion that
standards are plural.

NETWORKING

First there was the Listserv, then the project wiki. Newer iterations of our
project models rely on technology more, especially when working long-
distance with disparate cities. But regardless of the power of technology,
in-person meetings create an opportunity to deepen team building and
have an important place in creating shared goals.

Again, in our original PITB program, the lead staff at each branch—an
adult programs specialist and a young adult specialist—became trainers for
colleagues at their branches and throughout the system. This made it possi-
ble for the individuals who were willing to do the extra work to get profes-
sional recognition and lateralize learning throughout the network of eighty-
two branch libraries.

Participating PITB librarians become expert mentors for their extended
communities, and the poetic wealth and learning spreads throughout each
participating library system. Hundreds of librarians benefit from this train-
ing annually and, over many years, the system as a whole has become more
confident about poetry's place.

EVALUATION

Through disciplined, regular evaluation, the librarians became their own
best teachers and learned to tailor program elements to the specific needs
of their sites. Partners from early branch sites submitted progress reports,
compiled quarterly circulation statistics, and evaluated each poetry event
presented at their branches.

Poetry book circulation tripled at each branch during the first year. We
particularly noticed that circulation spiked after programs were presented
or when new books were added to the collection and displayed. Because
strong evaluation tools were in place, Poetry in The Branches was able to

document a dramatic relationship between poetry program delivery and *readership*—and we were better able to tell the story. As a result, buy-in throughout the system grew.

DOCUMENTATION AND DISTRIBUTION

Throughout the life of a project, online and in-print documentation helps to share the story and create community engagement. But summative documentation of a project cycle helps to capture and share the learning.

As we gained more experience, Poets House's *Poetry in The Branches Source Book* became an important way of documenting best practices. Revised every year, it serves as the curriculum for our Poetry in The Branches (PITB) National Institute, a full weekend seminar for librarians from all over the country to learn how to bring the complete model to their home sites.

The *Source Book* contains twenty-five nuts-and-bolts tip sheets.[3] It addresses some of the basics of program planning and program production from setting up an open mic or a "memory circle" to creating an introduction for a live event. Though evaluation leads to reassessment of the performance of the model, summative documentation can lead to new program cycles.

As I have said before, a significant building block of the PITB model was a level of funding that allowed us to work closely with our partners and spend adequate time in creating a robust plan. The original funding lasted for six years. At that time, the program was flourishing throughout New York City, and we were able to expand services by engaging our partners in active financial support of the project for another two years. That put us on a path toward marketing the model as a fee-for-service program so that as libraries throughout the tri-state area became interested, they could bring it to their communities.

At the same time, we began developing system-wide trainings and pre-conference presentations at the American Library Association's national conventions. In fact, one strand of the ongoing life of the PITB model is our Poetry in The Branches National Institute for librarians from all over the United States, which continues to this day at our own site. Graduates of the Institute are now doing important work all over the country—leading poetry festivals and reading series, expanding collections, and changing lives in communities.

> For me, one of the beauties of nonprofit community building is going back to articulated purpose and creating new relevancies as the world changes.

Another strand in the development of the PITB model is its continued reinvention to meet new funding opportunities and new opportunities for service. For me, one of the beauties of nonprofit community building is going back to articulated purpose and creating new relevancies as the world changes. The simultaneous trick almost always requires building engagement and the financial participation of many individuals to support the work. The goal is to have a mission, services, and the ability to support them all aligned.

EXTRAPOLATING FROM THE PITB MODEL

If you want to pilot writing workshops for seniors or if you are an administrator at a natural history museum—and if you are reading this—you already have an intuition that poetry can help your constituency enter into a different kind of conversation. Poets House has enacted this kind of connectivity in many ways. Baseball poetry contests and readings at minor-league stadiums. Special children's programs on ecopoetics in park settings. Poetry in zoos. The list could go on and on. It is yours to add to and activate.

Happily, sharing great poems does not have the attendant expense of mounting a production of *Madame Butterfly*. But it is also true that whatever we cook up will have some cost. Honesty about the costs will help everyone have a better experience. Volunteering to create a poetry corner at your company would not be expensive. But supporting it by developing an annual in-service for poets to work with the entire staff would probably require discretionary funding. (Poets should be paid for their work!)

At the heart of the PITB concept is willingness to experiment with interlocking program elements to create a more nuanced exposure to poetry. If you are just getting started, outline your overall program goals. Who are the partners? What kinds of programs would you like to see and in what sequence? How can you reinforce them with a more visible daily presence for the art? How will you get the word out? Essentially, it comes down to this: What is the work? Who will do it? What will it cost? For each constituent piece of the plan, ask yourself what your first three actions need to be. Plot these on a timeline, and you will have the beginning of a plan.

By making a place for poetry to be shared in community, people make a home together in language, and they find new sources of affiliation, creativity, and knowledge. The following checklist can provide a jumping-off point for coming up with your own poetry recipe for your community.

★   ★   ★

Excerpted from *The Poetry in The Branches Source Book.*

CHECKLIST

Poetry in The Branches: The Original Model

This is an outline of the model that Poets House brought to New York City's public libraries beginning in 1995. The basic formula of poetry programming for teens and adults, acquisitions and display, and ongoing staff training is still going strong in many of the original locations. As you consider how to duplicate or adapt the model to your own circumstances, remember to adjust the acquisitions and special-needs budgets to reflect today's costs.

Programs

In working with libraries, Poets House has used programming as an audience development tool, providing at least *three* programs for an adult audience at each site annually. If you are borrowing from the model to create your own initiative, you will need to decide how many programs you can sustain. (We have found three to be the bare minimum in creating visibility for the art.) Then, for each program—reading, open mic, or special book discussion, poetry "memory circle"—you will need to engage in the following behind-the-scenes activities:

- identify poets
- coordinate invitations, travel, lodging, and fees
- confirm your arrangements in writing
- coordinate publicity and flyers; list each event on the system-wide season calendar

- coordinate advertising (if applicable); provide printed programs (if applicable)
- develop name-capture techniques
- send e-mails or direct mail pieces to your site-specific mailing lists
- provide coverage and setup
- create a presence for the event at your site through both flyers and book displays
- evaluate the program, and set goals for the next.

Young Adult Poetry Workshop/Discussion Groups

Poets House provides *two* workshops/discussions for young adults (of at least three sessions, though five is much better) at each PITB site annually. You will need to engage in the following behind-the-scenes activities:

- identify workshop leaders
- coordinate invitations and fees; schedule the dates
- publicize through a centralized press list, if applicable
- contact local schools directly to publicize and network
- coordinate a sign-up sheet or reservations list
- publish (photocopy) a small booklet of poems written during the workshop
- display the publication in your branch, letting copies circulate
- host a publication party and reading at which the students read their work
- evaluate the workshop experience, not the students' work.

Acquisitions and Display

Poetry in The Branches increases a *presence* for poetry at each participating site. Poetry book acquisitions are at the heart of the program. Poetry displays help to create a synergistic relationship between on-site programming and the collection. You will need to do the following:

- evaluate your collection; assess your needs
- identify an acquisition budget that can be dedicated to poetry; PITB sites spend a minimum of $1,000 per year on poetry acquisitions
- articulate a goal regarding the number of poetry books you will buy each year
- acquire basic reference materials for the collection

- familiarize yourself with annotated bibliographies, such as Poets House's Directory of American Poetry Books (www.poetshouse.org) or Small Press Distribution (www.spdbooks.org) catalogs
- procure additional signage
- display at least one poetry book in every topical display.

Requests for Special Resource Allowance

In the original Poets House program, each participating branch had access to an annual allowance from Poets House of up to $1,500 for special needs during the first two years. This stipend was used to support the Poetry in The Branches project in creative ways tailored to the specific community. Each site had to write a brief plan detailing how it would use the funds. Even if funding is not immediately available in your community, dream about what you might need and articulate it. You may find a contributor or a local vendor willing to help later on. Here are some possibilities:

- signage, posters, banners
- poetry reference materials
- book-display hardware
- receptions in support of programs
- staff support, i.e., travel to meetings or model poetry programs
- site-specific poetry brochures
- additional press mailings
- mailing list purchase
- electronic message boards.

Evaluation

Evaluation is a critical component of developing any new program. But in the case of Poetry in The Branches, the information gathered was useful to other librarians in creating a national dialogue about poetry in diverse settings. Even if you are working on your own, written evaluation is part of giving yourself credit and learning how to improve your work. Here are the basic mechanisms for evaluation that we used in the original program:

- regular progress reports, including audience numbers
- program-specific evaluations from audience members
- poetry workshop and discussion group evaluations
- circulation statistics.

★   ★   ★

BUILDING FROM A MODEL

Various program models will be worth readjusting so they can be tested in new formats or on new ground. PITB proved to us that when poetry is made visible, people are more likely to make a home for it in their own lives. Since 2001, it has been hybridized many times: as a weekend-long training institute, as a traveling in-service for state library conferences, and as various national initiatives that matched programs to a *poetry presence* in partner library systems across the country.[4]

In this era of stretched resources and economic downturn, it is assumed that cosponsorships of all kinds will create opportunities to explore new content areas and cross-fertilize audiences. Cosponsorship creates associate thinking and affiliation and is good business practice. But we also know that cosponsorships can range from intense comarketing to slapping a logo on a piece of paper. Poetry in The Branches required cooperation of a different order, and the participating organizations and leaders needed to be ready for it. Institutional partnership demands joint planning and good communication over years—*it brings the whole institution to the project*. It is impossible to make a multiyear commitment for partnership without being open to change.

Though many of the elements in the PITB model may be used in an à la carte fashion, the totality of the original model required constant interorganizational decision making. For example, in our initial partnerships with the New York Public Library and other large library systems, we had to adjust to more complicated decision trails and bureaucracies. Consequently, we revised our timelines to accommodate their more layered protocols. *It is easy to underestimate the true costs and variables of partnership during the start-up phase.*

But I don't want to under-articulate the potential results either. Long-term partnerships are generative, building an infrastructure for poetry that enables larger audiences to continue to access poetry even after there are changes in staffing or in funding. In our early PITB work, a legacy of books was left at the branches and the integration of poetry into system-wide acquisition priorities was much improved. *Partnership creates a deeper infrastructure for poetry and changes the participating partners' ways of doing business.*

Because so many of the librarians had inspirational professional experiences with PITB, they carried new tools with them throughout their subsequent careers, leading to an emphasis on poetry (reading series, poetry clubs, acquisitions) at diverse institutions far beyond New York City. One librarian, taking to heart our message that poetry could be integrated into everything, routinely read poetry to her knitting club. Another started poetry-reading groups at American schools all over Europe. Another brought her expertise to a library in the Southwest where she started programs for teens. Another started a prestigious reading series in a high school. Another was on the Poets House staff for six years, after her retirement from the NYPL.[5] The true impacts are exponentially magnified over years.

With a teacher's happiness, I recall the young man who
heard Emily Dickinson recited and said fervently,
"People need to know about her!"

How poetry mattered to the thousands in PITB audiences is an open question. The evaluations from those audiences say that enjoyment would lead them to read more poetry, and the circulation statistics proved it. Let's get the cognitive psychologists, childhood development specialists, and social scientists to study the case. But with a teacher's happiness, I recall the young man who heard Emily Dickinson recited and said fervently "People need to know about her!"

NEW MODELS

The secret.
and the secret deep in that.
—Gary Snyder

The versatility of a new project will help me make some final points. The Language of Conservation features the installation in five zoos of inventive poetry signage matched with nature and conservation resources and related poetry events at libraries, and a poet in residence at each site.[6] The installations were inaugurated in 2010, and we anticipate that millions of people will experience poetry in the zoos of New Orleans, Milwaukee, Little Rock, Jacksonville, and Brookfield, Illinois, just outside of Chicago. This themed urban synergy among institutions uses poetry as the catalyst—and the language of poets to articulate the most essential message of wildlife biologists to the public.

Art can create new kinds of affiliation and understanding in our communities. The Language of Conservation installations will function as flexible anthologies throughout the zoos and reinforce a basic assumption that poetry can help people apprehend any subject with greater pleasure and understanding. The arts, whatever else they may be, are about how we live in the world. In my view, this kind of generative, associative work will become more necessary as we seek to create new modes of engagement, understanding, and value in our cities and in our towns.[7]

This new model comes out of a successful project at the Central Park Zoo in the late 1990s, when poems were placed throughout the zoo on benches, rafters, and stairs,[8] creating another set of connections through which visitors could enter into relationship with the living creatures they were apprehending. Finally, it is because poetry *is* an intellectual and emotional complex in an instant of time that the art form has been so associatively rich.

At the Central Park Zoo, professional evaluators did interviews with zoo visitors before and after the poetry signage was installed. When visitors were asked what they took away about conservation after the poetry installation, most frequently they would recite a few lines from a poem or approximate a poem fragment. When asked directly if they liked the poetry, some of those same people did not know that what they were saying *was* poetry. Nonetheless, researchers found that after the poetry was installed, visitors had a significantly increased awareness of human impacts on ecosystems and, more important, a deepened sense of themselves as participants in a larger world.

Scientists and zoo workers who had been suspicious of poetry at the beginning of the project began to think of it as a "conservation tool." Because it *works*. (Personally, I don't care if scientists call a Gary Snyder poem a tool—if they love it and go back to it and make it their own.) By the way, this does not signal an end to scientific signage about polar bear gestation at zoos. But it does indicate that science and poetry can be two strands in a conversation and that by engaging with both, the conversation is deepened.

CODA

Because anthologies like *Required Poetry for New York City Public Schools* are no longer articulating an educational expectation, entrée to poetry is encouraged by passionate librarians, teachers, community workers, presses, nonprofit literary organizations—and directors of zoos and botanical gardens, and others—that create a visible presence for the art. We nurture what we love in a certain time and place.

Writing immeasurably expanded the potential of language and, therefore, thought. The printing press immeasurably expanded the reach of writing. We are in a moment like that now, as new technologies change human interactions and institutions globally. What will this mean for poetry?

How can we know? From the times when our ancestors made imprints of their hands on the walls of caves, they probably chanted words. Was it poetry? Did they call it poetry? I cannot help but think that poetry, like human dance and song, has so many variations that it may be expressed and apprehended in many ways. The modes of poetic production may change, but the roots are deep in human identity, and the audience continues to be potentially unlimited.

NOTES

1.   Walter Ong, *Orality and Literacy: The Technologizing of the Word* (London: Routledge, 1982), 7.
2.   *The Poetry in The Branches Source Book: A Guide to Creating a Complete Poetry Environment in Diverse Library Settings*, rev. ed. (New York: Poets House, 2009), 18.
3.   *The Poetry in The Branches Source Book* is available through Poets House, www.poetshouse.org, or by calling 212-431-7920.
4.   A partnership with the Poetry Society of America reinforced humanities programs in libraries with Poetry in Motion placards of subject poems throughout the city's transit system. A speaker's bureau of contemporary poets delivered talks (Kay Ryan on Emily Dickinson, Robert Pinsky on Robert Frost

and William Carlos Williams, Martín Espada on Pablo Neruda, to name a few) with reader's guides available through the web. Two distinct cycles were funded for two years each by the National Endowment for the Humanities.

5. Marsha Howard was the Poets House Poetry in The Branches coordinator from 2004 until her recent retirement. She was the librarian at whose site we did the original PITB pilot event in 1995, when she was working for the New York Public Library, and has been a "saint" of the program.

6. The poets in residence are Mark Doty in New Orleans, Joseph Bruchac in Little Rock, Alison Hawthorne Deming in Jacksonville, Pattiann Rogers in Milwaukee, and project leader Sandra Alcosser in Brookfield, Illinois. The Chicago-based American Library Association is collaborating with Poets House to share the outcome of the project—which was designed to be replicated—with libraries throughout the United States and beyond.

7. I began my career in town and urban planning and believe that some of the most fascinating reading about arts and community building is coming out of an integrated, city planning approach from Charles Landry. I have found his recent book, *The Creative City*, to be particularly inspiring.

8. Special thanks to poet Sandra Alcosser, the poet in residence at the Central Park Zoo in 2002, and to the visionary Dan Wharton, who was then director of the zoo. They are now team leaders for zoos and poets in the national Language of Conservation program.

section·four

APPRENTICE YOURSELF

A Toolkit for Poetry Programmers

Katharine Coles, Susan Boskoff, Tree Swenson,
Orlando White, and Elizabeth Allen

PART I

AN IDEA, A PENCIL, AND PAPER

Tools for Practical Dreaming

When you want to build a house, or even remodel a bathroom, you begin with an intuition that, however much you like your life now, a new kind of space could make it even better. You spend a lot of time thinking about how you want to live and what kind of space will make this possible. When the ideas begin to come together into something like a palpable image, chances are you will sit down and begin to make lists and drawings to capture and refine their shape. The first part of this Toolkit offers you some tools for doing a similar thing with your ideas for bringing poetry into your community, whether you are a poet yourself, a community activist, an arts administrator, or simply someone who has a hunger for more poetry in your life.

IDENTIFY PASSIONS, DEFINE VALUES, CREATE GOALS

You may be tempted to skip this stage. Chances are, you are looking to start a poetry program because you are passionate about the art or because you have become convinced it will help you bring your community together in important ways. This is obvious to you. You've already decided you want to do the work, and you're ready to dash ahead.

All the essays in this book make clear that passion and values are the fuel for the engine of any poetry program. They keep you connected with why you want to do the work in the first place, and they help you do it well. You can help yourself now as you're getting started and also down the line if you take a little time to articulate why this work matters to you, why you value it, and, from there, why it might matter to others. Having done so will also help you when the time comes to persuade others to come on board or give you money. Finally, it will give you a touchstone to return to in moments of growth or crisis, which will inevitably arise.

Even more than this, examining your own motivations—the *why* of what you are doing—can help you begin to define the *what* and the *how* in a way that increases your chances of success.

Begin by asking yourself some basic questions—preferably in the company of other, like-minded people who might be interested in working with you or at least in sharing their ideas with you.

Does a passion for poetry itself make you want to do this work?

If so, ask yourself what first got you engaged with poetry in a passionate way and what that early experience was like. What makes poetry feel essential and important to you? How can you best communicate and share that essence and importance with others?

At the beginning of "The Flywheel," Bas Kwakman says, "It was the sound of a poem that made me fall in love with poetry once and for all"—"the sound of a poem," he says, even though it wasn't even the poet's own voice and language he was hearing but rather a translation read by a translator. Still, it's no accident that Kwakman's essay begins there; as a musician, he is deeply sensitive to sound, and in the rest of his essay he writes eloquently about how, since that moment, he has tried to bring people into poetry through "the sound of [poems]." Because this value is so important to Kwakman, he works especially hard to find new ways to let audiences experience poems in translation while hearing them in their original voices.

Alison Hawthorne Deming, on the other hand, tells us that she was originally drawn to administrative work through her own powerful sense of how community had been integral to every important moment of her growth as a poet. A desire to bring that sense of community to others led her to work first at the Fine Arts Work Center in Provincetown and second at the Poetry Center at the University of Arizona.

Dana Gioia came to Poetry Out Loud through the memory of early experiences with poetry, both at home and in school, that were natural and embodied, not intellectualized, and a desire to re-create that experience for young people.

Orlando White, a member of the Toolkit group, remembers how powerfully the experience of working intensively with poets who visited Santa Fe's Institute of American Indian Arts for weeklong residencies influenced him as a young poet. At Diné College, he now works to create the same kind of experience for his students.

"Values," according to Thomas Lux, is "a good and honest word." Notice that, in each of these cases, a sense of values, of the importance of a certain kind of experience, led people to a programming commitment and vision. So, again, what experience brought you into a passionate relationship with poetry? Can you imagine replicating that experience where you are?

On the other hand, a passion for your community and a desire to strengthen that community may make you want to create poetry programming.

Of course, this desire isn't necessarily separate from a passion for poetry—in fact, it implies a belief that poetry offers something special to those who encounter it. Susan Boskoff, a member of the Toolkit group, directs the Nevada Arts Council and helps rural communities within Nevada build arts programming. She feels strongly about the power of poetry "to animate democracy, create dialogue and discourse, and bring people together through falling in love with the sound of poems." She remembers her experience of "falling in love" when she lived in Utah and was first regularly exposed to poetry readings and the way of speaking that is unique to poetry, at once public and also personal and intimate. Mark Strand expressed the same idea in his 1991 introduction to *Best American Poetry*[1] when he said about poetry that "[W]e still depend on it in moments of crisis and during those times when it is important that we know, in so many words, what we are going through."

In his essay, Luis Rodriguez writes powerfully about how he came to poetry after leaving prison and how this experience led to his making a connection between poetry and freedom. "The first move from chaos isn't order," he writes, "—it's creativity." Through his work with Tia Chucha's Centro Cultural & Bookstore, he comes to understand the transformative power of poetry in drawing together the members of an underserved community and in connecting that community with the values of freedom and civic discourse. He tells of one young woman in his neighborhood who was literally saved from taking her own life and so restored to herself and her community through an accidental introduction to the Centro.

Patricia Smith talks about how the Chicago slam provided her with a passionate experience with poetry and connected her with a larger community. In particular, she recalls how Gwendolyn Brooks, who served as a sort of presiding spirit for a memorable Chicago event, helped her understand how she could express her experience as a young, African American woman from Chicago's West Side—and how she could do so as a member of a larger poetry community.

And Sherwin Bitsui writes about poetry as the vehicle uniquely able to help young Navajo students connect with school by encouraging them to bring the rich language and stories of their own culture into the classroom.

Rodriguez, Smith, Bitsui, and Boskoff have the experience of working with and in communities in which people may feel isolated and alienated, socially or geographically, by poverty or segregation or other factors. In these cases, poetry itself isn't the point so much, at least at the beginning; it's more a means to an end. In a way, isn't it always? Even those of us who are animated by a passion for poetry are so animated because we've had the experience of poetry's power to change our lives and our relationships with our world and ourselves. But to achieve any of these ends, we still have to create the conditions for the intimate experience that is poetry. We still must come to the question: How does one create the conditions for the "falling in love," for the restoration to self and thus, perhaps, to community, to occur?

Recognize that your passions and your values are intimately connected

Articulating what you are passionate about and why can help you identify and articulate your values and perhaps answer the next question: Why me? Do you value and want to create the conditions for individual, transformative experiences with poetry? Do you value and want to create a community gathering place around poetry? These are anything but mutually exclusive—there's a good chance that if you do the one you might also accomplish the other. Knowing what aroused your passions will help you understand what you value, and understanding what you value will help you decide what kind of program to create, how to go about it, and perhaps whether and why you are the right person to do this work.

Toolkit group member Tree Swenson recalls her experience at Copper Canyon Press and the many times she decided to persist in her work in spite of seemingly insurmountable obstacles. She kept going because of her passion for poetry, a passion she had discovered as an isolated teenager in Montana, and her sense that if she didn't do this work, nobody would, and that if nobody did the work, something important might be lost to the world. Hers was values-driven work.

Tom Lux began his work for Poetry@Tech with this value: if someone gives you a gift, you shouldn't waste it—in fact, you should share it as widely as you can. From this, he came to his goal of bringing as much poetry of different kinds to as large and various an audience as possible. Another value of Tom's is that programs should be made with the same care and attention to detail that poems are. We'll say more about this later, but for now, it's useful to point out that this is a good value to adhere to in the early stages of any program. As for why he should do the work himself—in his case, the answer is simply because he was asked, and the invitation looked to him like an opportunity to build something real.

Robert Hass began the River of Words project with a value and a conviction: we should do all we can to connect with our local natural environments, in this case specifically with watersheds, and poetry has the power to help us do this by linking what we observe and know with what we feel through language. From this, he arrived at the goal of bringing kids together with naturalists and other experts who could help them explore and understand their watersheds both through fact-based investigation and through writing poetry. Why him? In this case, in a way, because he could. He had a passion for the work, and as U.S. poet laureate, he was in a position to make something large and enduring.

Out of personal experience, Alison Hawthorne Deming developed the value that community is important, and through both the Fine Arts Work Center and the Poetry Center at the University of Arizona, she developed the conviction that community is tied to place. When it became clear that the Poetry Center's physical home would be lost, the Center faced a decision: would it allow itself to be subsumed into a larger campus entity? This would have been the easiest, least expensive course and the one most certain to preserve the Center in some form. But if it lost its independence, would it lose touch with its values and mission? In the end, the Center raised millions of dollars so it could remain a home devoted specifically to poetry.

Luis Rodriguez's beginning was different. Instead of rising to an opportunity, he created one out of his own desire and need. Everything began with a press he started in order to publish his own work. Soon he realized that if he needed a publisher, so did other poets who, like him, belonged to communities and groups often overlooked by mainstream publishers. He began publishing them too. To do so expressed the value that their words were worth hearing, even if—maybe especially if—they came from the margins. From that value, everything else came. Moment by moment, like Tom, Robert, and Alison, he was there: present, passionate, and willing.

Perhaps that sentence describes you: you too are passionate and willing, whether you are stepping into an opportunity that presents itself or creating your own opportunity. If so, this is a good time to begin to keep a written record. If you're working alone, identify and write down your passions, motives, and values. What effect are you looking to create? Why? If you haven't already done so, begin to look around for others who share some of your passions and values and who might be able to help you think about them. During your discussions, make sure to take notes.

Make your passions and values concrete

This is not just an abstract exercise. These conversations are interesting to have over coffee or a glass of wine, but your ultimate purpose is to make something happen. To do this, you need to identify possible avenues for expressing your passions and values. Once you identify those that are most important to you, discuss how best to re-create those passions and enact those values in a concrete setting.

Perhaps you want to try to duplicate your own original experience or to import a program from elsewhere into your community. This approach has advantages. For one thing, you can ask those who have already done what you want to do for advice and ideas; you can also find out what mistakes you should try to avoid.

There are potential pitfalls in this approach. Different communities have different makeups and needs, and you will want to make sure you're able to adapt any program to the resources and needs of *your* community. A program that brings visiting writers to a venue in Brooklyn or even in Santa Fe will probably have to be tweaked to work on the Navajo reservation, if only because the closest airport may be an eight-hour drive from the program venue.

In her essay, Lee Briccetti talks about Poetry in The Branches, a program Poets House created originally for libraries in New York and eventually expanded to libraries across the country. The program offers specific services to and requires specific commitments from every library. But the program also allows libraries the leeway to make adjustments based on community needs. Among the examples Lee talks about is a program that brings young and old people together and incorporates poetry in Yiddish. The first piece of this program may be appropriate for almost any community, depending on its goals; the second may not be. On the other hand, a community with many native Spanish speakers might use the second model as a template to create programming specifically for them.

If your idea is to create a program in your local library, Lee very generously gives you an outline to follow. She also makes clear that Poetry in The Branches is something Poets House already knows how to do very well and that the organization can work with you and your library to build a program that works in your location. If this is what you want to offer your community, you might save time, energy, and even money by working directly with Poets House.

You probably don't have the resources Dana Gioia had as the chairman of the National Endowment for the Arts when he created Poetry Out Loud, a nationwide program. (If you do—congratulations and good luck!) But if you want to do the program at the high school level, you can contact your state arts agency and find out how to bring it to your local schools. If you want to add something unique to your own community, you might think about how to create a way to involve others, perhaps by holding a competition on the local level for adults or younger kids that runs concurrently with the POL competition. Something like this could be done with little or no money because POL is funded by the NEA and Poetry Foundation and the states, and all the materials for POL are available for download online.

Finally, most states have arts agencies staffed with people who are experienced in bringing poetry into different kinds of communities. If you don't have a very specific vision of what you want to do, your local arts agency can probably help you develop one, especially if you have well-articulated values and goals. If you already know what you want to do, whether it's library programming, recitations, readings, residencies, workshops, after-school programs, or something else entirely, someone at your local arts agency will probably have ideas about how to get started. That person may also be able to help you with some practical issues, including providing contacts, giving you information about how to incorporate and become a nonprofit organization, and helping you think about funding. As early as possible in your planning, you should make contact with these people.

You may not be able to precisely re-create the program or idea that originally drove you—or not at least right away. It may be that your experience came out of some large, national program or the opportunity to study abroad or an encounter with a Nobel laureate. But remember, as Susan Boskoff points out, that the experience of poetry, even when it comes in company, is intimate, the experience of one person speaking to another, creating an intimate space for that other to enter.

Checklist: Identify Passions, Define Values, Create Goals
   A. With pen in hand, ask yourself these questions:
      1. What experiences led me to this juncture?
      2. If they involve my developing a passion for poetry, how did they do this?
      3. If they involve my sense of a need in the community for community building, how do I describe this need? Why and how do I think poetry might fill it?
      4. What do my passions tell me about my values?
      5. Why am I doing this—why me?
      6. What do I hope to achieve?
   B. If you began by asking these questions alone, continue by asking them in company, again taking notes.
   C. Together, you and your group members should compare experiences, passions, values, and goals. Find where they overlap, and decide which are most important.
   D. Relying on your previous experiences to guide you, imagine what kinds of programs might achieve your goals. Remember that a given program might fulfill more than one goal. For example, an afternoon reading series might give young people a place to go after school and also engage them in civic discourse or bring them together with

elderly members of the community. Whether you re-create the same kind of program that originally connected you with poetry or decide to do something new, the most important thing is that you work out of a sense of what matters most to you.

E.   Ask: can we begin any of these programs under current conditions, with available or easily obtained resources? If not, how can we break them down into smaller parts that can be tackled one at a time?

ASSESS NEEDS

You've begun the work of assessing needs. You may not have performed a formal needs assessment, but in the section above, you and your group members responded to your needs, your sense that something is lacking in your lives or in the life of your community, and you would like to address this lack.

It's a good idea to get as precise a sense as possible of what the need actually *is*. If several readings a week are held in your town, yet you still feel the need for another, identify for yourself and your group just what is missing. Readings by local poets? Emerging poets? Poets writing in Spanish, Yiddish, or some other language? A kind of event that is either more or less structured than what you have? You need to know. Thus, it's a good idea to do a needs assessment that is as thorough as you can manage.

Consider Your Community

If you live in (or want to create a program for) a very small community—a small town, a single school, a neighborhood, a school, even a geographically spread out but otherwise well-defined ethnic group—this may appear to be a fairly simple matter. Assessing your community includes looking at demographics, habits, and activities. But even in the case of a small community, it doesn't hurt to look around, maybe even to make a few calls, to both prevent duplication and avoid unnecessary competition among different programs. Even if your high school program focuses on literary poets, there's no point in discovering too late that you've scheduled an event on the same night as the weekly high school slam.

In a very small community, you probably don't want to schedule your events against any other community event or gathering. In this case, your assessment will survey not only literary events but also all events taking place within a given period and geographical area. Even if the events are not all literary, you might ask yourself if they are nonetheless fulfilling needs you have identified, especially if these needs have to do less with poetry itself than with the development of community and civic discourse.

If you live in a large community, sometimes you may not be able to avoid competing with other literary events. Many large communities can support multiple events in a given week or even on a given night. A city the size of Tucson might need only one big poetry center, at least for now, but it can, both in spite of and because of having such a center, sustain several coffeehouse reading series grounded in different neighborhoods and directed at different audiences. Even in smaller communities, events of a certain kind aimed at seniors might not compete with similar events needed for kids.

Regardless, it's a good idea to figure out how what you want to offer is different in kind from what is already out there—or how it might replicate other programs. To know this, you have to do a thorough survey of the terrain.

Use the Resources Around You

No matter the size or demographics of your community, it's a good idea to get in touch with your local and statewide arts agencies. Their programmers should know much of what is going on in poetry and the other arts in your area. If you live in an area where cultural programming happens through local or county governments or through existing private groups, get in touch with them too. Don't leave out libraries and schools.

You should also pay attention to the community calendars in your local and neighborhood newspapers and to announcements on radio and television (especially local and locally run public stations). There may also be an arts-oriented website in your community. Check all of these regularly.

Be Proactive—Learn from What You See

Then—this is important!—go to events. If you are looking for a greater connection to community, you can begin to satisfy this need by participating more fully in what is already offered and by thinking about your own work as belonging in this larger context. At the same time, you will be able to analyze the difference between an event that is run well and one that isn't, an organization that is working out of passion and commitment and one that is only going through the motions. Beyond this, you may discover groups doing pieces of what you've considered doing yourself and doing them well. You can use these events to meet people who are experienced in making programs. They may become important advisors or partners.

Use Assessment to Identify Potential Partners

As you have already gathered, whether your community is small or large, your survey will not only let you know what needs are being fulfilled and what might draw audiences away from your events but also might give you ideas for partnerships, both those that are obvious and those that aren't. No matter what size your community is, it probably doesn't make sense to schedule a reading at the same time as a large, multiday arts festival if your goals are artistic or against a voter registration evening and political debate if your goals involve community building and civic discourse. But it might make sense to coordinate with the festival or the community and civic organizers to create a jointly sponsored reading or event.

Checklist: Assess Needs

A. Look at the community you mean to serve. Be as specific as you can at this point; for example, don't begin with "my state" but with "teens in my city" or even "teens in my neighborhood high school."

B. Develop a plan for finding out what kinds of programs are available to this community. Notice how much easier this is once you've identified your community precisely. Then assign group members to follow through on specific action items, which could include the following:

1. Conduct Google searches using keywords that will bring up relevant programs in your area.
2. Phone your local arts and cultural agencies, and ask programmers about what is happening and what nonprofits they're aware of in your area.
3. Contact nonprofit agencies, possibly including not only those specifically devoted to literary programming but also those providing, say, arts experiences for kids or seniors, after-school programs, etc.
4. Phone other related organizations (in the above case, libraries) to find out what they are doing.
5. Check with other local government and community agencies.
6. Call businesses, such as bookstores and coffeehouses, that might be involved in literary programming.

7. Check community bulletin boards and calendars, both physical and virtual.

8. Check local newspapers, both dailies and weeklies.

9. Ask other people—teachers, friends, local business owners, civic boosters, etc.—you think might be aware of programs that haven't caught your attention.

10. Attend events, with an eye to learning both what is being done and how.

C. Then, if possible with a group, sit down with paper or computer and do an honest evaluation of what your community already has to offer.

1. List the programs you found.

2. Identify what they offer and to whom.

3. Identify areas where what is being offered overlaps with what you have in mind, with an eye both toward refining your goals and toward developing potential partnerships.

4. Identify what still remains to be done.

5. If your list includes more than one item, prioritize.

ASSESS RESOURCES

Building a poetry program is anything but an orderly, linear process. You've already begun resource assessment if you followed the steps in the previous section.

To begin with, you need to know what you have. At the moment, it may be only your own willingness and your own ideas. This is a good place to start, but it's not enough to get something off the ground. You need to develop access to concrete resources as well.

Find Space

No matter what your program is, you need a place to do it. This is especially true if you are planning to host readings, workshops, conferences, or other events. Even if you plan to launch a website, you need a place to sit and a place to set up your computer.

At the beginning, your space needs may be less elaborate than you think. City Art in Salt Lake City hosts both readings and workshops. Though it now partners with the gorgeous new downtown library, the first reading space was a basement room donated by a local Lutheran church. It was

Spartan but fully adequate. And, in those early days, City Art often held workshops in the homes of board members. Literary magazines and presses have been started in spare bedrooms or even in spare corners of bedrooms in use. We imagine you could run a website from wherever your laptop is, whether it's on your kitchen table or a table at the local independent coffeehouse, but we don't necessarily recommend that you do this forever. You can think of space needs in two ways: what is essential now and what your goals are as you move forward.

A partner has always provided space for City Art. Unless and until your organization has its own space—which may not be necessary or even desirable—partnership is an excellent way to leverage what your community already has to offer.

Find Partners

Because you have already engaged in identifying your resource needs, you began making partnerships almost immediately in the process, connecting and talking with people whose values and goals align with yours and then using your needs assessment activities to scope out potential partner programs. Never underestimate the value of good partnerships; they are essential. You will need to develop several kinds of partnerships.

Build Partnerships With Individuals

It's never too soon to reach out to individuals who have priorities and passions similar to yours and who might be willing to help you. This becomes very important when there is actual work to be done, but it is also important at the idea stage of any project. Like-minded people can help you both articulate a vision and priorities and identify resources. They can help relieve the burden of the substantial labor involved in getting a program up and running. In addition, they may bring needed expertise to the project. In writing this Toolkit, Katharine Coles brought on partners Susan Boskoff, Tree Swenson, Orlando White, and Elizabeth Allen, all of whom offered skills and knowledge she didn't have. In such a case, you can think of your time with partners as a kind of mini apprenticeship. With this in mind, you may want to seek out individuals in your community whose work you admire, who have specific skills or connections you can use, and whose values mirror or complement your own. Remember, if you are approaching people you don't know well to ask them to collaborate with or advise you, it's a good idea to have a well-developed and articulated plan before you ask them to spend valuable time with you. They will want the answers to all the questions we have posed: Why this? Why here? Why now? Why, for heaven's sake, me? What resources do I have?

Build Partnerships With Organizations

Organizations often have resources individuals don't, and if they share your goals and values, they may be willing to share resources. If you want to start a reading series but have no space, you will want to look for an organizational partner that does have an appropriate space and is open to, even enthusiastic about, your idea. This may be a business, such as a coffeehouse or bookstore. It may be an organization, such as a library, a theater, or an art center already invested in promoting culture generally or literature in particular. But you don't have to stop with the most obvious partners. Susan Boskoff tells a story about how the Nevada Arts Council found a space partner for its Poetry Out Loud competition. The NAC had succeeded well in aligning its Poetry Out Loud competition with the national finals in Washington, DC, but less well at making it attractive to Nevada high school students. Then NAC arranged to hold the finals at the Reno Knitting Factory, a franchise of the New York City–based concert venue. Suddenly, Nevada teens had the chance to compete on the same stage where their favorite bands performed.

Senior centers, high schools, hospitals, even prisons—all may be open to the right kinds of partnership programs, especially if you can offer them good programming that will help them further their missions at little cost to them. Some may even be able to provide a portion of a poet's honorarium or travel costs. If your partner is a nonprofit organization, there might be an opportunity to establish your program under the organization's umbrella and apply for grants even if you haven't yet established your own status as a nonprofit. If you do this, be careful not to compete with your partner for grants—make sure you target different organizations and programs for your funding.

The key to making these partnerships is to ask yourself what's in it for the potential partners and be able to articulate these benefits persuasively. Make sure, before you approach, that you've considered things from their point of view, that you've thought about how your program fits into their missions and needs.

Build Partnerships With Local and State Agencies

You got in touch with your local and state arts agencies during your needs assessment. The good news about arts councils is that their job is to bring the arts to communities. If you've done a thorough assessment and assembled a convincing case that there is a need for your program, chances are your local arts council will be willing at least to advise you on technical matters (such as how to obtain nonprofit status, for example) and possibly to lend material support. They might do the latter through planning assistance, through connecting you with other potential partners, or even through funding.

Arts agencies may have various ways of providing financial help, depending both on agency rules and on the structure of your program. Though most arts agencies require formal grant proposals and nonprofit status from programs they fund, some may be able to help less formally, perhaps by helping arrange and pay for travel or providing honoraria directly to the poets involved in your program. Make an appointment with the literature programmer at the agency to talk over various possibilities. Be prepared to articulate the needs your program will address, how you plan to fulfill those needs, what resources you have, and what you need. Be ready to discuss how your program will fit into and help further the overall mission of the agency.

The issue of staffing—who does the work—may be to some degree addressed by your partnerships, especially when you are just getting started. But you can't count on your partners to do everything for you. Many, if not most, arts organizations and programs run on shoestring budgets, so they begin with all-volunteer staffs. Thus, the trick at first is finding a way to make sure that your all-volunteer staff isn't all you all the time. You don't want to burn out before you even start.

In the beginning, your staff might comprise only you and one or two friends. A small program with occasional events can run under such circumstances for a long time—as long as the people involved remain interested and available and as long as the program doesn't grow significantly.

Moving from a volunteer staff to a paid staff is another matter; this requires significant and stable funding. Nuts, Bolts, and Widgets: Tools for Tinkering, at the back of this book, provides an extensive list of resources that can help guide you through this and other transitions.

Find In-Kind Resources

If someone offers you a venue and a sound system for no fee, that is considered a resource provided in kind. Your partners may have other skills and resources to bring to the table as well. For example, partners whose operations already include advertising and public relations may be willing to provide those services for you. The same may be true of recording, photography, and any number of other services that might enhance your program. A local hotel or motel might provide free rooms; a restaurant might donate meals for visitors. As you consider what you need to make your program happen, remember that asking for in-kind donations can be an excellent way to let people help you without writing you a check. In-kind donations can be as valuable as any others, if not more, because they save money and both create and demonstrate community involvement. Make sure to get documentation from the in-kind donor that describes the donation and verifies its value.

Find Money

You will probably need to ask for money. Notice, though, that we put money last. This is because it's hard to determine just how much you will need before you know what partnerships, volunteer staffing, and in-kind resources you already have in place. However, even if you have free space, free advertising and other services, and a volunteer staff, you will need money. Artists make a living from their work and both need and deserve to be paid for it. (This is one value driving the work of everyone involved in this book.) You may not be able to pay market rates at the beginning, and some writers, if they believe in your project or believe they have something beyond money to gain by participating, may accept reduced fees. But your goal should be to pay all artists something and to pay them as near to market rates as you can, with a very few exceptions we'll go over later.

Fortunately, funding sources are out there. As we said earlier, local arts councils and other organizations might be able to chip in for honoraria on an ad-hoc basis. Most arts councils and humanities councils also give formal grants to nonprofit organizations involved in literary programming. (Note that there is a process involved in becoming a nonprofit organization for tax and grant purposes, which we address in part 2 of this Toolkit. You can also find useful websites about how to undertake this in Nuts, Bolts, and Widgets.) In addition, most states and many communities are homes to private nonprofit foundations that fund the arts. Your arts council will probably have information about which ones might be appropriate for you. Non-profit listings are also available at your local library and online.

If you know people who are especially interested in the kind of work you are undertaking, you might approach some of them for private dona-tions, whether large or small. In the old days, City Art passed a literal hat at readings; it still keeps a donation box on the refreshment table. You could hold fund-raisers, perhaps particular readings for which you charge admis-sion; you could also charge a very small admission fee for every reading, a practice that is rare but becoming more common in the new economy.

Checklist: Assess Resources

A. Space: ask yourself what kind of space you need right now, just to get going. This could be a reading space, a workshop space, a space to house a computer, or a space to house a collection. Then ask the following:

   1. Do I already have access to a space that would work for what I need to do right now? Be flexible—not all readings need to take place in auditoria, and a computer and a phone take up only the corner of a desk.

   2. If you don't have access to an appropriate space, do you know about any existing spaces owned or managed by potential partners?

   3. If so, are these spaces out of use and available during times you could hold your programs?

   4. If you locate a space that might work for you, make an appointment to talk to the person responsible for managing it.

   5. In preparation for your meeting, develop a pitch:

      a. What do you want to use the space for?

      b. Why is this space especially appropriate (close to your community, located in a building already used by your target audience, particularly well suited to your purpose because of size, shape, flexibility, or other characteristics)?

      c. What plans do you have to make sure the space is used respectfully and left clean and undamaged?

      d. How does your program fit into the space holder's mis-sion; how will the space holder benefit from hosting your program?

6. Be prepared to hear "no" from one or more places, and have backup plans.

7. Be prepared to be flexible or to negotiate (for example, offer to changes dates or times or to pay a damage deposit) to get the space you want.

B. Partners

1. Build partnerships with individuals.

    a. If you haven't already, identify people among your friends who share your values, have good ideas, and are reliable, and invite them to join you.

    b. Working with them, identify others in the community, perhaps people you know less well or mostly by reputation, who have specific skills or resources to offer. Don't cultivate relationships based only on money—even if you bring people and organizations on board that may eventually give you money, right now you're looking for shared values and passion combined with something only specific people can bring to your project.

    c. Arrange formal meetings with these people.

    d. Prepare your pitch:

        i. Describe your program.

        ii. Tell people why you are approaching them in particular—their expertise, skills, connections, ideas.

        iii. Be specific about what you want from them and the roles they might play.

        iv. Tell them what they have to gain from their involvement.

        v. Ask them what they think they might have to offer that you haven't thought of.

        vi. Let your passion engage theirs.

        vii. Ask them to recommend other people you should talk to.

    e. Make sure to follow up right away with a note and a phone call.

2. Build partnerships with nongovernment and government organizations.

a. Begin by identifying organizations that do good work, share your values, and have resources they might bring to bear.

b. Arrange formal meetings with the appropriate people.

c. Prepare your pitch.

   i.   Describe your program.

   ii. Tell people why you are approaching their organizations in particular—their places in the community, their missions, their expertise, skills, connections, ideas.

   iii. Be specific about what you want from them and what you imagine their roles might be, whether you want them to help with funding, with the actual work, or with in-kind donations.

   iv. Tell them how what you're doing fits into their mission and what you think they have to gain from their involvement.

   v.   Ask them what they think they might have to offer that you haven't thought of.

   vi. Ask if they know others you should speak with, either in their organizations or elsewhere.

   vii. Let your passion engage theirs.

d. With government organizations, remember that one organization may have a literature coordinator involved specifically with literary programming, an arts in education programmer working with schools, and a community development person with expertise in building organizations, gaining nonprofit status, etc.—or one person may wear many hats. Don't forget that the director of any organization is the person in charge and the person who can make decisions. What's more, directors of government agencies work for you, the taxpayer. Call the directors! They will send you to the right people.

   i.   Keep asking if there's anyone else you need to talk to.

   ii. Keep asking whether you need to know anything else about an organization and its services.

      3. Remember that your partners won't do all the work.
         a. Assess the contributions of your partners.
         b. Decide what else has to be done.
         c. Consider how to distribute the remaining work among the staff (including volunteer staff) you have available.

C. In-kind resources
    1. Assess the ready resources of willing partners, including both physical resources, such as space and sound equipment, and less tangible resources, such as expertise.
    2. Approach your partners to ask whether they might make these resources available. Understand that they may be either unable or unwilling to do so.
    3. Look beyond your partners to local businesses for resources such as hotel rooms, food, etc.

D. Money
    1. Think about money after you know what other resources you have.
    2. Carefully consider what expenses you will have for goods and services beyond what is already covered.
    3. Make a plan to raise money to cover these (see Part 2: Hammer, Saw, Nails: Tools for Framing).

NOTE

1. Mark Strand and David Lehman, eds., *Best American Poetry 1991* (New York: Scribner, 1991).

HAMMER, SAW, AND NAILS

Tools for Framing

You have gathered materials to begin framing your organization. If you've ever done home repair or building projects yourself, you know that you will need to make uncountable trips back to the hardware store when you find that a given part just isn't what you need. This is simply the bootstrap nature of the work. Don't worry if everything doesn't happen in perfect order—if, say, you've already mounted an event and haven't even thought about incorporation or mission statements. Regardless, it helps to keep the issues addressed here in mind from an early stage so you don't miss opportunities down the line. As Susan Boskoff points out below, there are many good reasons to undertake these tasks earlier rather than later, not the least of which is that becoming a 501(c)(3) nonprofit will help you get grants and raise money. For this reason, we put organizational development and fund-raising together here, before events. If you are not yet ready to tackle these activities, go straight to the next section.

BUILDING AN ORGANIZATION 101

You already have a vision, which is one thing all successful organizations and businesses have in common. You've animated that vision and developed projects or programs that have been inspiring, motivating, and successful in their own right. At some point, you will need to engage in systematic planning to nurture the health and growth of your organization.

If your project or program is successful, ongoing, and growing, you should probably consider becoming a 501(c)(3) nonprofit organization. If you have gross receipts of less than $5,000 per year, you do not need to apply for tax exemption. However, even if your organization still has a small budget, as a nonprofit 501(c)(3) tax-exempt organization, it will be eligible to receive private and public grants and solicit tax-deductible donations, which are critical to your fund-raising efforts. Nonprofit identity also reassures potential donors that you are a legitimate organization, and it makes you eligible for a bulk-mailing permit. In other words, there are many reasons to take this step. The reason many small organizations delay is the paperwork involved, which may seem complicated and difficult.

Don't feel overwhelmed by this stage of your organizational development. There are multitudes of wonderful resources available in print, online, or at local arts agencies, state arts councils, and nonprofit service organizations to assist you with incorporating as a nonprofit, evolving as an organization, planning, developing programs and partnerships, fund-raising, taking care of and feeding volunteers, accounting, and recruiting and training board members. Some organizations provide workshops, training, and even funding to assist with this type of professional development and skills training.

The following section provides an introduction to incorporation and an introduction to shaping a nonprofit organization. Remember that, as with everything else you've already done, organizational development is truly an organic process. As you undertake it, many things will happen at the same time or in a sequence that can't be dictated but arises out of, and works best for, your needs and those of your organization. This should feel very familiar to you. The things that are different here, which may feel less organic and less driven by your specific needs, are the legal requirements, the timelines, and the paperwork involved with formally changing your status.

It won't surprise you to hear that many arts people are not known for taking pleasure in filling out complicated government forms. You may be lucky enough to have a poet or poetry lover already on your board who relishes doing taxes every year and has the confidence to tackle incorporating and filing for nonprofit exemption status. Alternatively, if you know a lawyer or an accountant who is passionate about poetry, he or she may be willing to join your volunteer base or sit on your board with the primary responsibility of shepherding you through the process. If not, some lawyers will provide this service at no cost as part of their professional public service commitments. If there is a Lawyers for the Arts group in your area, it may be able to help you find one. If you can't find someone who will help you for free, you might still consider hiring a lawyer to help. If you have the money to do this, it may be more efficient and effective for your organization than doing it yourself. Almost certainly, it will save you time and aggravation.

Incorporate

To be incorporated means that your state recognizes your organization's corporate bylaws and articles of incorporation. Incorporation protects board members and other individuals in your organization from being held personally liable in case of lawsuits or other legal problems. Your organization must be incorporated before you can file for tax-exempt status with the Internal Revenue Service.

The following are the basic steps to incorporation:

- Select a name for your organization that is legally available in your state. Stay away from any name that sounds like another organization's, both to avoid confusion and because in the Internet age, you need to think about domain name considerations. Even if you don't have a website yet, you may want to reserve a domain name as soon as you name your organization. Note that your website domain name might be slightly different from your official name. AWP.org, for example, was already taken when the Associated Writing Programs (now the Association of Writers and Writing Programs) looked for a domain name. It was far too late at that point to change the organization's name. The domain name is currently AWPWriter.org, which is an imperfect solution for a group known widely as AWP. One place to search for domain names in use is networksolutions.com.
- Create your articles of incorporation (see below), file with your secretary of state's office, and pay the filing fee. At this time, you can

request a packet of nonprofit materials from that office that should include sample articles of incorporation and your state's laws on nonprofit corporations.

- Write your bylaws (see below), which will dictate the operations of your organization.
- Recruit an initial board of directors.
- Hold the first meeting of the board of directors, and officially approve your bylaws.
- Apply for any licenses or permits that your corporation will need to operate in your state and local municipality.

Develop Articles of Incorporation and Bylaws

Your bylaws and articles of incorporation are the primary official documents required for any corporation, whether it is a for-profit business or a nonprofit organization. The particular requirements for bylaws are set by the state in which the organization incorporates.

Articles of incorporation include the organization's name, the name of the authorizing official or person(s), the purpose for which the organization was formed, assurance that no assets of the nonprofit organization benefit the members (shareholders), the number and names of initial board members, and the location of the registered office where legal papers can be served to the organization, if necessary.

Typically written during the incorporation phase, bylaws are rules that govern the internal management of an organization. Bylaws are created by the organization's founders or board members and include, at minimum, how board meetings are conducted, what officers the organization will have and their duties, voting procedures, and other operational details. In the eyes of the law, your organization does not formally exist until your board of directors approves your bylaws. Therefore, at your first formal meeting of the board, your agenda should include the adoption of your bylaws and election of your officers, as well as any other business details that need to be completed to start the "formal" operations of your organization.

File With the IRS

After you have filed all the paperwork for nonprofit incorporation in your state and received a copy of your articles of incorporation, you are ready to submit an application to the IRS for your federal nonprofit status as a 501(c)(3) organization, which is the most common type of nonprofit organization.

To qualify for tax-exempt status, your organization needs to meet three basic requirements. Your organization must be organized or incorporated, must be working toward its stated goal and mission without benefiting private interests, and must have one or more exempt purposes, among which literary activities are included.

Remember that the process involves the federal bureaucracy and so can take time, even after you fill out your forms and send them off. When it receives your application, the IRS will send you a letter of acknowledgment. You may also receive one or more requests for more information before the IRS approves or denies your nonprofit status. If the latter occurs, don't give up; contact a lawyer who specializes in nonprofits and try again.

Depending on where you and your organization live, you may need to apply to your state for tax-exempt status as well. Your state may be satisfied with your federal tax-exempt status, though you may need to send a copy of your IRS determination letter to your state tax commission. However, your state may be among those that will require you to file a separate application to receive a state tax exemption.

Develop Your Organization

Create Your Mission Statement

Every organization has a mission, a purpose, a reason for being. Often, penning a mission statement is one of the most difficult tasks because it requires that you distill your vision and express it clearly and briefly. Goals and objectives are subsets of a mission. You might also hear of organizations that employ strategies and action steps. Whatever vocabulary you use to express your vision of the future of your organization, think of the resulting document simply as a road map that helps you remember and get to where you want to go.

Assess and Structure Your Organization

One size does not fit all, nor is one structure better than another. Organizations, nonprofit or for profit, come in every size, shape, and configuration; they can grow organically or by design. Organizational structure can be tight or loose, depending on the needs and culture of a given organization. Regardless, undergoing regular assessments of your organization and its programs can provide a sense of what works and what needs retooling. Assessments can be internal, engaging only board and staff, or external, involving your community as you define it. Even if you don't involve the community in every assessment, you should involve community members periodically in order to get an idea of how existing and potential audience members and donors view you. Written assessments help you review your organization's strengths and weaknesses, identify areas for improvement, and plan for the future.

Manage Operations and Finances

During the process of incorporating and filing for nonprofit status, you developed a structure and operating procedures intended to help you begin on a sound legal and financial footing in compliance with the numerous federal, state, and local requirements affecting nonprofits. Though every nonprofit needs a strong foundation for good governance, every nonprofit organization looks and feels different. One might maintain an entrepreneurial spirit; another might hew to a more rigid, establishment-type structure. Some nonprofits have small but active boards of directors and no paid staff; others are large, with professional staffs. A small organization may run extensive programming, and a large one may limit its programming and mission. A successful nonprofit may have a paid accountant or board member who provides financial services, or it may manage its budget the back-pocket checkbook way. (We don't recommend this as a strategy, but for many organizations, it is the reality.)

Plan

Most people don't jump out of bed and say, "Today I think I'll tackle my twelve-month strategic plan." Like others, arts lovers may have a notion that planning is time-consuming and boring and focuses on the budget. Not true. If you integrate planning into the work that you normally do and keep it simple, you'll be able to seize opportunities, avoid misunderstandings and burnout, and solve problems in a timely manner. By keeping you focused and on track, a plan actually provides more flexibility to do what you want to do. It can be an invaluable tool for every aspect of your programming, whether you are working with artists, audiences, venues, or, well, anything.

Plans can be simple or complex; in developing them, you can involve just the board, your full membership (if you have a membership organization), and/or the whole community. You can create a plan internally or bring in a specialist to facilitate the process. Plans can focus on budgets, programs, operations, fund-raising; they can be short-term or long-range. In Nuts, Bolts, and Widgets, you'll find many names of websites, publications, and organizations that provide information, guidance, and examples of planning processes and documents.

Recruit Board of Directors

What you need most, however, is a great board of directors. This group of people can promote your activities and programs. Your board members may often act as staff until you are able to hire staff. They come up with ideas, provide leadership, represent the interests of the community, and raise money. In addition to bringing passion to the table, board members shoulder oversight responsibilities, both financial and programmatic. Remember, their names are listed on your applications for incorporation and nonprofit status, on grant applications, and on thank-you letters to your sponsors.

Most people don't know what being a board member means. Typically, organizers ask or recruit friends and family, enticing them by promising that their involvement won't require much investment of time or money and will be great fun. The one thing you don't want to do is scare away potential board members, so it's always best to be able to back up your promise that service won't be a lot of work by providing a short job description for each position on the board (not just for the president, vice president, and secretary) and a simple board handbook. In the end, board members will feel better and work more effectively when their responsibilities are clearly agreed upon at the beginning. The job descriptions and handbook can also note that board members' roles may fluctuate throughout the year, depending on your organization's programming schedule and needs. A board member whose primary responsibility is fund-raising for an event may do much of the work well in advance; board members responsible for actually mounting an event may be busiest immediately before the event and after it is underway. No matter what a board member's specific role is, attendance at board meetings is extremely important, as board discussions and decision making require wholeness, collaboration, and participation. The success of a board is the direct result of the individual and collective participation of its members.

Asking for donations is an uncomfortable task for some people, even for causes they enthusiastically support. The reality is that all boards must raise money at one time or another, whether by writing personal checks or by opening the door to others who contribute. This is just one of many reasons board training is so important. Skills required of board members are not genetically inherited behaviors; they are learned. Numerous community and nonprofit organizations provide hands-on training for board members or specialists to work with boards. And, of course, resources abound online, in bookstores, and on library shelves. Use Nuts, Bolts, and Widgets as a resource guide.

Recruit Staff

In general, the role of the professional staff, paid or volunteer, is to develop, implement, and evaluate programs and services that achieve your organizational mission, goals, and objectives. Other tasks include supporting the work of committees, subgroups of the board, or individual board members. Staff duties, as board responsibilities are, should be clearly laid out in job descriptions and annual plans. It is important that board members understand that staff members are responsible, directly or indirectly through their supervisors, to the director, who is in turn responsible to the board. This structure may seem hierarchical and bureaucratic, but without a line of authority that allows for supervision and protection of your staff, communications and collaborations within your organization may become fraught with ambiguity and mistrust. Even with a volunteer staff, job descriptions should identify general qualifications for participation and specific qualifications for particular duties. These may include qualities such as commitment to team building and partnership activities; ability to adapt to flexible and sometimes extended working hours; ability to express oneself clearly, both orally and in writing; a talent for diplomacy, tact, and good judgment; and experience in raising money.

Be an Advocate

Taking on the direction and governance of a nonprofit organization is a way of entering the larger community by representing your values and interests in concrete ways. By undertaking this work, you become a public person whose voice matters and whose opinion may be increasingly respected. As an artist, a patron, a board member, or the voice of a nonprofit organization, you will be asked at some time to speak on behalf of your community's arts sector, public funding for the arts, and/or arts education.

Every time you speak to an individual or a group about the value of your program and of the arts or arts education in general, you engage in advocacy. We encourage you to step forward and meet the demand of this role as it comes to you. Many voices speaking on an issue of mutual concern can make a difference. People in public office value citizens who help them make informed decisions. Every time you write, call, or meet with elected officials to introduce them to your organization or programs, you provide them with information they may use in a variety of ways. Think of advocacy as educating your neighbors, your coworkers, your elected officials, or the citizenry in general about an issue—the arts—that you believe is very important. In doing this, you foster and pass on the values that led you to do this work in the first place.[1]

Checklist: Build Your Organization

A. Incorporate.
1. Select a name.
2. Create your articles of incorporation, file with your secretary of state's office, and pay the filing fee.
3. Request a packet of nonprofit materials that should include sample articles of incorporation and your state's laws on nonprofit corporations.
4. Write your bylaws.
5. Recruit an initial board of directors.
6. Hold the first meeting of the board of directors, and officially approve your bylaws.
7. Apply for any licenses or permits that your corporation will need to operate in your state and local municipality.
B. Become a nonprofit organization.
1. Check that you meet the requirements.
2. File with the IRS for 501(c)(3) status.
3. Find out if you need to fill out paperwork for your state as well.
C. Develop your organization.
1. Research mission statements, and then create your mission statement.
2. Research organizational structures, and decide on a structure that fits your organization.

3. Develop a budget and financial plan.
4. Research strategic plans and begin to develop one for your organization, keeping it as simple as possible.
5. Recruit a board of directors.
6. Recruit staff.
7. Refer to Nuts, Bolts, and Widgets for research sources.

Raise Money

Fund-raising, from grant writing to asking individuals for money, is one of the hardest parts of arts programming, perhaps especially for artists, who may be shy when it comes to talking about money. However, if you want to do anything very significant, you will eventually have to raise funds. The good news is that there are agencies, individuals, and private foundations and corporations actually looking to give money to nonprofit organizations engaged in worthy endeavors. The bad news is that even an individual or organization whose mission it is to give money to groups like yours will need to be persuaded and thus will, at the least, require some sort of request or application from you. In other words, fund-raising can be work of the kind least pleasant for artists. Potential funders that don't necessarily consider your support to be their highest calling but might be amenable to giving you something if you can give them reasons to do so will require more persuasion still.

Some rules apply to all areas of fund-raising, whether you are applying for grants from public agencies, writing application letters to corporations or private foundations, or appealing to individuals. One involves another piece of good news: as a lover of poetry, you have a secret weapon. You love words, and you probably know how to use them. When you write your proposal or request, use this gift. Your grant applications and appeal letters should be not only grammatically perfect but also thoughtful, cognizant of the values and goals of your potential donors and grantors, persuasive, lively, and all-around interesting to read. If you can make your reader misty-eyed, all the better, but remember to remain professional while you do it. Never, ever toss these things off quickly and send them out without proofing.

This same rule applies to final reports and thank-you notes. They should be interesting and well written, they should follow any guidelines to the letter, and they should clearly explain how your program successfully furthered the goals of the grantor or donor.

Access State and Local Grants

Early in your planning stages, before you were even thinking about events, you spoke with staffers at your state and local arts agencies. Such agencies often work on long schedules—for example, Utah Arts Council grant applications for programs beginning after July 1 are actually due the previous fall, so Utah organizations have to submit grants in September or October for programs that begin in September or October of the following year. Thus, if you plan to pay your poets or have any other significant expenses, such as rentals, travel, or staff salaries, you need to begin planning your grant proposals at least a year and maybe as long as fourteen months out from your first event.

Begin by noting the typical deadlines of all your granting organizations and make a calendar, including deadlines and a grant-writing schedule for each grant you plan to apply for, so deadlines don't slip by you. Note that a few agencies have two deadlines: an early one for a draft proposal and a final deadline a few weeks later. The early deadline is as serious as the later one because going through the draft process is usually a requirement for submitting the final grant. Feedback from the agency gives you an opportunity to strengthen your proposal, so use the early deadline as an opportunity.

In addition, if your program lives within an institution like a college, university, or museum, you may need to get permission and signatures from one or more internal offices, each with its own requirements. Find out which offices must sign off in what order, what additional forms they require you to fill out, and what lead time each requires to review and sign the grant proposal before it can go to the next office. When you add up all the days and count back from the official deadline, you have your own "real" deadline—the day the grant and the forms that accompany it must actually be completed. This could be a month before an agency's official deadline, so be prepared. Then turn your calendar back to at least a month before that "real" deadline and make a note to start your proposal on that day. Starting early will give you a chance to check with your partners about their participation and get feedback on your proposal, both from experienced friends and possibly from grant officers at agencies that don't build review into their processes. It will also give you time to ask questions if you're confused by the directions, which can be perplexing even to experienced grant writers.

Before starting each grant application, reread the application guidelines and the mission statement of the organization in question. In addition, check the organization's website to see what it has funded before and which programs it highlights as being particularly representative of its work and values. This will help you find the right pitch to make. For example, arts organizations generally fund poetry making and presentation directly, and humanities organizations tend to fund only discussion or discourse about and around poetry. Other organizations might be most interested in programs that are connected to education or explicitly work to strengthen their communities. **Do not** expect an organization that supports education to give you money if you haven't shown that your mission has a strong educational component. In other words, **do** tailor your application to the organization's mission. That said, **do not** misrepresent what you are planning in order to fit into an agency's agenda. Rather, think strategically about how to highlight the things you plan to do that most fit in with the agency's mission. In addition, though you never want to add a programming element just to get a grant, such research might give you ideas about programming elements that fit with your mission and values, that you want to do, and that you might be able to get funding help for either now or down the line.

Granting agencies generally require you to show on their applications how you are going to match any funds you receive with support from other sources. Especially at the entry level, agencies often allow organizations to use in-kind donations, such as donated space, staff time, etc., to match cash grants, but this isn't universally allowed or may be allowed for only a portion of the match. Often, you can use a local grant as a match for a state grant, but you probably won't be allowed to match funds from one state agency (such as the arts council) with those from another state agency (such as the legislature or governor's office) or funds from one office within the arts council with those from another. Make sure, before you begin to write your budget, that you know what the limitations and requirements of each granting agency are.

Finally, be as meticulous as you can in your budget section. If you count a space donation as in-kind funding, make sure you know what your partner actually charges when it rents the space, and get a written statement from the partner saying so. Be careful in estimating the costs of honoraria, plane tickets, and similar expenses. You can easily find the going rates for all of these things online. Most organizations know that plans change and budgets can shift for all kinds of reasons, but you want your budget to be both as accurate as possible given the information available to you and consistent with what you plan to do. Though much of this is guesswork and some of your numbers will be based on pending requests and applications, remember that the number on your income line needs to be **exactly the same as** the number on your expenditures line. In other words, in the Platonic world your proposal represents, your budget needs to balance.

Having a check in hand does not mean you're finished with a grant. Usually, agencies withhold some portion of the amount granted—often about 10 to 20 percent—until they receive your final report. The report is meant both to hold you accountable for the granted money and to help the agency hold itself accountable to its board and funders. Thus, its guidelines will ask you to show whether you did what you said you would and how successful you were in doing so. It will also ask you to show exactly how you spent the money you received and that you balanced your budget. Prepare this report as carefully as the proposal itself—and use its looming prospect to remind yourself as you are mounting your program to keep track of your spending meticulously, maintaining receipts, canceled checks, etc., and to stay within your budget. A failure to turn in good reports may result in the agency's reducing or even denying future grants.

You aren't finished with the grant process until you decide how you will publicly acknowledge your funder(s) and follow through on your acknowledgment. If a funder has specific requests, such as including its logo and/or name on public relations materials, make sure you follow through. If it has specific requirements about how it wishes to be listed (as a "sponsor" or "supporter," for example), make sure to follow them to the letter. And if it wants you to follow certain evaluation procedures, do that too. Regardless, you should always acknowledge major support both in all promotional materials and orally at your events; smaller gifts should be acknowledged in writing on your programs and website.

Develop Other Funding Sources

Given matching requirements for grants, you may need to raise money not only because you need it for expenditures but also because you need it to get other money. This is a good time to think about different ways to raise money for your organization. The methods you choose will depend both on the amount of money you need and the tone you want to set for your programs. Remember that City Art in Salt Lake City got by for years on local and state grants and a passed hat. If a hat doesn't quite fit the tone of your program, you could substitute classy little envelopes at the book table. Or you could sell T-shirts, hold benefit readings, throw benefit parties or balls with literary themes and kiss-an-ugly-poet booths, or create membership packages that offer donors privileges associated with your events.

As you think about raising money, consider the interests, values, and needs that intersect in your program, and target your efforts accordingly. For example, if you want to raise money just to keep the coffee flowing at your readings, a jar on the coffee table might do the trick. If you need money so you can move from free readings to paid readings and/or match your grants, a membership program for your existing audience might work. But for major expansions, look outside your existing circle. For example, if you want to raise money to add a program for teens, target not only people or businesses interested in poetry but also those with histories of supporting education or helping at-risk kids. For more and perhaps better ideas than these, refer to the sources in Nuts, Bolts, and Widgets.

As you consider the different options open to you, consult with your partners. One or more may be willing to help you in your efforts, whether by providing space or food, sending appeals or invitations to their regular or electronic mailing lists, writing some or all of an appeal, or actually helping underwrite your efforts with cash. Partners may have experience with different kinds of fund-raising strategies and be able to tell you what has been more and less successful in your own community—whether, for example, you're better off having a silent auction of signed books or a station where people can commission composed-in-the-moment poems on themes of their choosing for twenty-five dollars a pop.

Remember: it usually takes money to make money, and fund-raising outlays inherently involve a certain amount of risk. Expensive fund-raisers may bring in less money than they cost. Do a realistic analysis of what you will have to bring in to break even, considering expenses such as travel and honoraria if you're throwing a benefit reading, mailing expenses for direct mail, space rentals, printing costs, or maybe just the price of a really nifty hat. If your budget is in poor shape already, you probably want to minimize risk by starting with something very inexpensive to begin with.

On the other hand, remember that fund-raising is always a long-term project. It can be demoralizing to put in a lot of work for little immediate return, and you do want to identify fund-raising duds and avoid them, but early efforts that might not bring in a lot of extra money at the time can still lay the groundwork for money to come in later. Long-term success in fund-raising involves building relationships and trust with potential donors and getting them first used to the idea of and then into the habit of supporting you. Donors want to know that you will be there and doing good work they value for the long term. It can take some time, and a certain amount of buy-in, before people feel comfortable writing even the first small check, much less offering a substantial donation. If you do no more than break even your first time out, consider the effort a win, and start applying any lessons you learned from it to your next fund-raiser.

Raising money from individuals requires accountability, even if you don't have to provide them with final reports. If you're passing a hat or putting a jar out for dollar bills, make sure to thank everyone orally at the event for donating—it doesn't hurt to attach a sign saying Thanks! in as many languages as possible to the hat or jar. Beyond this, anyone who writes you a check should get a note of thanks and a brief explanation of how you will use donated money. As your organization grows, consider mounting a web page or creating an annual letter reporting on your activities and publicly naming and thanking your supporters. Saying thank you is not only good etiquette and good business but also helps you keep in touch with your donors and cultivate relationships with them.

If you have the good fortune to find an individual donor willing to make a major contribution, reach out to this person in appropriate ways. Of course, you don't want to give over your program to a donor, but if it's possible to include a donor in a reception or a dinner with a poet or to invite the donor to observe a poet's visit to a school classroom, for example, do so.

Tap Foundations and Corporations

In Nuts, Bolts, and Widgets, you will find information about how to locate private foundations and companies that give grants to arts and nonprofit organizations. There are many good resources online and probably also available at your local library.

While you are still relatively small and local, focus mostly on the foundations and businesses specifically devoted to funding programs in your area. The big national foundations and corporations tend to fund big national programs. If your program might appeal to foundations that fund programs in education or some other fields in addition to or beyond poetry, check those out as well.

As with the funding agencies discussed above, look for possible funders whose missions and values align with your own so you can emphasize the overlaps in your application. Remember, foundations and corporations look for worthy projects to underwrite, but they already know what their funding goals are. Businesses will likely also have agendas related to their corporate missions, including but not limited to raising their profiles in the community and improving problematic corporate reputations. Some people have no problem with the idea that businesses buy goodwill they may have lost through imperfect corporate citizenship. Others are not so happy about it. If you do choose to accept funding from corporations with less than stellar reputations—that will be up to you and your board—be aware of the possible downside of doing so. You may alienate your constituents by accepting money from the wrong corporate partner. For this reason, think hard about which corporations you want to associate with. Imagine the corporation's name and logo on signs and banners alongside your program's name. Are you comfortable?

Different private foundations and corporations generally have different requirements for their grant applications and reports. One might ask for a letter only. Another might want to see a bare-bones budget, and another might want extensive budget information. Some will invite you to submit letters of support from people who have benefited from your program. As with your proposals to agencies, supply all the primary information and documentation required as well as any supplemental materials you're encouraged to provide. Make sure to follow any directions explicitly.

Some foundations and corporations will require a report at the end of a program and others won't. Regardless, send out thank-you notes to all private funders as soon as you receive news of any gifts. If a final report or letter is required, follow all the directions and our previous advice on how to compose it. Even if a report isn't requested, do send a second brief letter of thanks explaining how you used the gift to further your program. As with supporting agencies, make sure to follow through on requests to include the donor's name and/or logo on your materials, and provide copies of these materials to the donor. Finally, if you have a newsletter or web page in which you thank donors publicly, make sure to include these donors there as well as on posters and other media and in introductions.

Checklist: Raise Money
A. State and local grants
1.   Very early on, get in touch with the grant officers at your state and local arts agencies and, if you host lectures and discussions about poetry, at humanities organizations as well.

2. Find out whether you are eligible for grants and under what programs (for example, some agencies have special programs to help new organizations get going, which could benefit you).

3. Find and make a note of all deadlines, including any pre-proposal deadlines.

4. If your organization lives within an institution that requires approval for grants, find out which offices must sign off and in what order and what lead time each office requires for its signature.

5. Count back to find your "real" deadline.

6. Reread the grant guidelines and the mission statement of the organization in question, and check the organization's website for information about what it has previously funded so you can tailor your narrative accordingly.

7. Make sure your budget is as accurate as you can make it and that it balances.

8. Make note of any requests for acknowledgment and follow through on them.

9. Beyond these requirements, make a plan for public acknowledgment on publicity materials and in introductions.

10. Make a plan for accounting for the money, and stick to it.

11. File all required reports accurately and on time.

B. Individuals

1. Sit down with your board and staff, and set goals for your individual fund-raising.

2. Solicit ideas for different kinds of fund-raising activities you might engage in, ranging from appeals to individuals to membership programs to benefit readings or events.

3. Check in with your partners and advisors in the community to get their ideas and find out about pitfalls.

4. Do a realistic cost analysis.

5. Identify where needs, interests, and values intersect in your program.

6. Target individuals who might be interested specifically in any or all elements of what you're doing, and make sure they receive invitations and reminders to help you.

7. Follow up with potential major donors personally.

8. If they agree to donate, invite them to be involved with your actual programs in appropriate ways and follow through if they express interest.

9. Find as many appropriate ways as possible to thank donors and to report to them on your work, and do so early and often.

10. For more specifics, check the resources in Nuts, Bolts, and Widgets.

C. Foundations and corporations

1. Use the Nuts, Bolts, and Widgets resources to identify foundations and corporations that fund arts organizations and other nonprofits in your community.

2. Look at each possible target foundation or corporation carefully for overlap between its mission and yours.

3. Examine guidelines to see which opportunities you qualify for.

4. Make note of all deadlines and of organizations that review applications throughout the year.

5. Find out whether you need letters of support, and gather them if you do; give letter writers plenty of lead time and remind them gently of deadlines as they approach.

6. Be careful in each proposal to identify and highlight those areas in which your mission and the granting organizations' missions align.

7. Follow guidelines and directions to the letter in creating proposals and accompanying budgets.

8. Follow any news of a donation with an immediate thank-you note.

9. Adhere to any requests about acknowledgement.

10. Beyond such requests, find ways to acknowledge support publicly, and follow through.

11. If possible and appropriate, invite foundation officers and representatives to receptions and other events.

12. Fulfill any requests for reports meticulously.

13. Regardless of whether a report is required, finish your program or season by sending thank-you notes that communicate what the gifts enabled you to do.

NOTE

1. Some of the information in this section is synthesized from and can be found in greater detail at several websites, which we recommend to readers: About. com; foundationcenter.org; and the Texas Commission on the Arts Tool-Kit, www.arts.state.tx.us/toolkit. Other useful sites can be found in the reference section.

PART 3

SANDPAPER, WALLPAPER, AND PAINT

Finishing Tools for the Event Itself

Much of what we have been talking about involves those things you build that are not visible to the eye. When you mount a program or an event and poets and audiences come out, you have to worry about small details that will have an impact on their impressions of your organization. This part is a commonsense guide for getting your first event(s) up and running and includes a set of reminders and checklists that may be useful even to those of you who have mounted events already. Some of what follows is extremely practical, but quite a lot of it is devoted to creating events and situations that reflect your goals and values and in which people are comfortable and happy. If some of this strikes you as pretty basic, at least once you've mounted an event or two yourself, please don't be insulted. Even the most commonsensical among us can forget to do important things, with or without lists, especially if we've been left to reinvent the wheel ourselves.

MAKE GOOD FIRST IMPRESSIONS

Your early events and the run-ups to them set the tone for your entire organization and become the foundation for your organization's reputation. The plans and management you put into these first events let both your audience and the poets you invite know that you respect them and are committed to creating good experiences for them, whether those experiences are strictly buttoned and starched or relaxed and freewheeling.

Your partners will thank you for good planning, communication, and follow-through on your commitments, whether you get out a press release on time, provide refreshments, or pick up plates and put away chairs at the end of an event. They will also be grateful if you acknowledge their contributions early and often. If you establish good habits with them from the beginning, they will trust you and be willing to build on your early partnerships.

Your audience members will thank you for accurate advance information that allows them to incorporate you into their schedules as well as for such small courtesies as good program descriptions, on-time starts and finishes, and carefully crafted introductions. If you're known for respecting them and their time, your audience members will readily forgive you on the rare occasion when something beyond your control goes wrong.

The poets you invite to participate in your events will thank you for understanding and anticipating their needs, from providing them with clear agreements and good schedules to making sure that they have plenty of food and water and that they get to the airport on time. If you treat them well and they have good experiences, they will be more likely to come again if invited and to spread the word to others.

CREATE A SCHEDULE

You've already gone a long way toward imagining the kinds of events or programs you want to create and why, as well as for whom, you want to create them. You might plan readings, poetry book groups, workshops, after-school events, slam or recitation competitions, fellowships, residencies, publications, or, eventually, more than one of the above. At this point, it's useful to remind yourself that you don't have to start with the most difficult or complicated thing you've thought of, and you don't have to launch everything you've imagined doing all at once. However, you do want to imagine what you start within the larger context of your plans for the future so you can easily build on what you create now. For more on planning, please refer to the second part of the Toolkit, Hammer, Saw, and Nails: Tools for Framing, and to the resource section, Nuts, Bolts, and Widgets.

Unless you are planning a one-time festival or symposium or publication, think of your first event as just that, the first in a series—perhaps the first in a series that will eventually be one in a suite but right now probably the first in a series that is limited and manageable. This kind of imagination will allow you to consider what kind of tone you want to set, not just for your first event but also for your organization. (Are you high literary or punk or funk or Goth or avant-garde? Casual, freewheeling, and spontaneous or formal and rigorous?) It will also help you plan in a way that will create continuity for you, the artists you work with, and your audience. This sense of continuity will make it easier for everyone to trust your organization and to build plans that include it.

Therefore, instead of deciding to schedule and announce one open-mic reading or slam or workshop or publication at a time, consider scheduling and announcing several events at once—even two can be enough, if you want to start by holding an event in the fall and one in the spring or a couple during one season. For a weekly or monthly series, it's a good idea to plan as far out as you reasonably can. If it's not practical for you to plan a whole year out, a quarterly schedule is a good way to start; some organizations that don't program in the summer work with a fall and a spring calendar, running September to December and January to May respectively.

Even if you plan one big annual event or production—a destination conference, workshop, festival, or symposium, for example, or an annual book prize—imagine and pitch it as one in a series. Begin with a "first annual," showing that you expect to repeat the following year and giving the audience confidence to invest time and emotional energy in you. Then let your audience know how you plan to keep in touch. All the above kinds of programs are large and complex enough to involve activities and announcements that can be used to engage your audience and participants throughout the year. For a conference, you will want to announce at the current year's event the date of the next and perhaps the dates when you expect to unveil your faculty, launch your fellowship competition if you have one, and open registration. For an annual book award, you will fix dates for when you will announce the judge, when the deadline will be, when you will notify and announce the winner, and when the publication itself will appear.

If your organization grows and begins to provide more than one kind of programming, perhaps aimed at different audiences, you may eventually find that you need several different but overlapping schedules—say, one for workshops, one for readings, and one for contests. This is probably a bridge you don't need to build just yet, but it's not a bad idea to keep in mind that adding a new kind or level of programming shouldn't have to mean you must completely change how you conceive of, manage, and publicize the old, at least not if you plan well now. Because making big changes in successful programs can be problematic—a major change in scheduling almost always leads to a dip in participation, at least temporarily—it can't hurt to think in advance about how new programs will build from and converse with the old. Maybe the poetry contest you're holding now will eventually become the fellowship competition for a summer poetry conference, which will eventually become the flagship event for an organization that also holds mini workshops and readings throughout the year. If you're imagining such a progression already, you may want, for example, to give your contest a midwinter deadline from the very beginning so you can fit it into the conference schedule later without confusing your regular entrants.

Establish Regularity

The more you can do to help your audiences build your events into their calendars, the more success you will have. One way you can do this is by building in regularity. For example, let's say you want to hold eight or nine events between September and May. You can build in regularity by deciding that your events will always be held on, say, Wednesday nights or Saturday mornings; you can build in even more regularity if you always hold them on the first Wednesday or the third Saturday of the month.

The downside of building in such regularity is that you lose flexibility. If you work with lots of poets who have to come in from out of town, you might discover that you can usually find a Wednesday that will work for both your organization and the poet but that limiting yourself to first Wednesdays is just too constraining. If, on the other hand, you deal mostly with local poets, chances are you'll be able to manage with more limitations because you have plenty of first Wednesdays to choose from without having to worry about travel, hotels, missed teaching, etc.

Even if you have a regular schedule, there may be times when you need to do something a little differently, perhaps because you're pairing your reading series, which usually holds events during the week, with a weekend festival, or because you want to bring in a major poet whose teaching schedule precludes a visit on your usual day. You should try to avoid such alterations, but in cases such as these, changes might be worth the inconvenience. Remember that such changes will place an additional burden on your audiences and on you. You'll need to announce the "special event" early and often.

Mind Your Manners

Your community might already have an organization mounting regular poetry programs that occur on a certain day of the week. If so, you might be tempted, because audiences are already accustomed to thinking of that day as belonging to poetry, to use the same day yourself. This is usually a bad idea, even if you are ready to promise never again to schedule directly against the other organization's programs. Such promises, however well intentioned, can be devilishly hard to keep when you're trying to juggle busy poets and busy venues. In fact, even if you choose a different day altogether, you may find yourself on a rare occasion having to schedule against the other program (or you may find the other program having to schedule against you). Good feelings are far more likely to be preserved in such cases if they are rare and the other programmers don't feel you've already poached on their scheduling turf. The truth is, if your community is large enough to support several poetry programs, it is large enough to support programs on various days of the week. Poetry lovers who have other commitments on the day in question will be very happy to have their options expanded.

Establish a Space

Just as it's a good idea to be as consistent as possible in your days and times, it's also a good idea to be as consistent as possible in your venue. On rare occasions, you may need to use a venue different from your usual one. Perhaps you are bringing in a poet who can come only on a day when your usual venue is already committed. Perhaps you expect that the poet you invited will draw a much larger audience than your usual space can accommodate. Perhaps you're doing a one-time partnership with an event held elsewhere. You've worked hard to get your audience accustomed to a particular space and time, and now you will have to do lots of extra work to get word of the change out as widely as possible.

To keep such changes rare, you want to choose a venue that is the best possible fit for the kind of programming you usually do and the audiences you usually draw. Because a huge, empty space is as uncomfortable for audiences and presenters as an overcrowded one, be as realistic as possible about the likely size of your usual audience. Attending other events will help with this, as will talking to the folks running your venue about what kinds of audiences they draw for their other programs and taking into consideration such factors as whether teachers may encourage or require students to attend your program.

Once you've selected your venue, stay in close touch with the people there as you make your plans. Early on, before you make any specific scheduling decisions, check with them to find out when the space is available and whether your ideas about scheduling mesh. If you decide you want to hold events for kids on Saturday mornings, but the venue already holds a regular children's craft class or story session on Saturdays, you will need to rethink your schedule or coordinate or collaborate with the other program. If you can't work out a good solution, think about finding an even better-fitting venue—always considering whether it's in your best interests to compete with an established program and a potential partner. After you agree on a general framework for your program, ask which specific dates within that framework are ideal, not ideal but workable, and not workable.

Before you actually contact poets, check your preferred dates for conflicts of the kind that might come back to bite you, such as Sabbaths, festivals, and holidays observed by any religious group with a large presence in your community. For example, in Katharine Coles's department at the University of Utah, a number of faculty members observe the Jewish Sabbath and holidays and an increasing number observe Buddhist festivals and holidays, so the department tries to avoid dates important to those groups as well as Sundays. This will be different in every community; any big literary, cultural, or other kind of event could present major conflicts. Understand that you will not be able to anticipate or avoid every possible conflict, but if you can at least account for what you can anticipate, your events will go more smoothly for you, and your partners and audience members will be much happier with you.

Checklist: Create a Schedule

A. Decide, based on all the work you've done so far, what your first event or series of events will be.

    1. Make sure you start with something you think you can and should do, based on your earlier assessments of need, resources, etc.

    2. Make sure it is consistent with your articulated values. Is this something you really want to do and will follow through on? Do you want the event to set the tone for your organization from the outset?

B. Arrange for a space.

    1. Given the kind of event(s) you will be mounting, carefully consider your space needs. For readings, you need only a reading space of the appropriate size; for a weekend workshop or symposium, you will need a reading space and appropriate classroom and/or gathering spaces, all in close proximity.

    2. With your board, consider spaces you know of that might be appropriate.

    3. Approach those who own or manage spaces with a plan. For more information, see the Partnerships section in part 1 of the Toolkit, An Idea, a Pencil, and a Piece of Drafting Paper: Tools for Practical Dreaming.

    4. Once you have identified a good space and partner, work closely and collegially with those who own and staff the space.

C. Decide how far ahead you want to plan, remembering that it's usually better to get a rhythm going rather than simply present one-off events.

    1. Consider how many events you can realistically mount within a given time period with the labor and budget you have.

    2. Consider the commitment and reliability of your staff, including yourself. Be realistic with yourselves and one another. If you schedule six months in advance, are you sure the staff will be there to follow through? If not, consider cutting back to three months.

    3. Consider the needs and schedules of the kinds of poets you want to invite for your events. Major poets with very busy schedules often book a year in advance or even longer; emerging poets might have more flexibility. Younger people tend to

be more mobile, though. A young local poet you approach in March to read in September may no longer be local by the time fall rolls around, so if you think relocation might be an issue, ask about plans.

4. Consider the needs of your audience members.

   a. What kind of time commitment will their participation require? The greater the commitment, the more lead time is necessary. In the case of a weeklong conference, for example, you will want to give people a year's notice; for a weekend-long event, a few months will do; for an evening event, a few weeks.

   b. How will you reach your audience members? If your target audience is made up of students at a particular school or university, you can effectively use posters, flyers, e-mail, and teacher announcements to get the word out in short order, which means you can schedule outreach closer to event dates. If your audience is spread throughout the community, you will need enough lead time to use the media effectively and pass out flyers at earlier events.

5. Consider whether staking out a particular day of the week or month is feasible.

   a. Consult the schedule of your venue, considering all its programs and the demands on its staff as well as staff preferences.

   b. Consult your board and staff—if a key person has regular commitments on a given day, select another day.

   c. Consider to the greatest extent possible the regular commitments of your target audience, including other poetry and arts events as well as holidays and days of worship.

   d. Consider the likely limitations on the schedules of poets, remembering that many are academics and have courses to teach.

6. Working with your facility, your staff, your partners, and your board, identify open dates. Double-check calendars for major competing events and holidays.

7. Working with your staff and partners, identify which poets you would like to invite to participate.

a. Prioritize this list so that your first approaches are to the poets you are most anxious to include.

b. Understand that you won't get everyone you want, and have backup names.

c. Beginning with those you have identified as most important to your project, contact your potential participants. Set dates for your key participants before moving on to the others.

d. If you can't schedule a high-priority poet in the period you're working with, ask if he or she is willing to be contacted when you are scheduling the next set of events in the series. **Make a note** so you can follow through at the proper time.

BOOK THE TALENT

Of course, the first thing you need to do is find your poets. You may already have a firm idea of the kinds of poets, or even the specific poets, you'd like to invite to participate in your events or publications. If not, or if you are looking to expand your list to create more diversity of any kind, there are plenty of people around who can help you. Most colleges and universities have poets in their English departments and creative writing programs; many of them would be happy to consult with you. You can also check with your local and state arts councils, which often have poets on their artist rosters or lists of artists in residence. Don't forget to decide with your board who will have the final word on which poets to include. Will the decision rest with one person, the board or a committee of the board, or the entire community? Be clear about the criteria you will use for selection. Are you looking only for poets with books, for young poets who are just starting out, or for some balance of the two? How will you consider racial and ethnic diversity, gender diversity, aesthetic diversity, diversity of subject matter, or any other kind of diversity you can think of? Will the process involve a competition or an application? Such decisions are generally rooted in which audiences and communities you want your program to serve. It is good to articulate a process because granting agencies will want to know all these things when they decide whether to fund you.

Never announce a poet's participation in an event or a program until you are absolutely sure the terms are clear between you and the poet. Early on in your conversations about dates, you will need to negotiate with your poet the terms of engagement. In fact, immediately after assessing a poet's initial willingness to talk with you, the first thing you should do is lay out as clearly as possible what you want (a reading, a workshop, an outreach event, a reception, a book signing, dinner with board or community members, contest judging, some combination of these) and what you will give in return.

It is best to have a signed written agreement so that you and the poet can refer to it if any questions should arise (such as the poet's waking up in the middle of the night thinking, "Oh, my goodness, I promised to go to Dubuque. Now, when was that reading?"). The agreement does not need to be elaborate, but it should recognize that among the most valuable currencies are information, time, and money. From the beginning of your contact, a poet will want clear information about what is expected and about what you, in turn, will provide and on what timeline. Clarity is never more important than when money and time are in question.

COMPENSATE THE TALENT

You already know we believe poets should be paid as much as possible, whenever possible. Some funding agencies will work only with organizations that pay artists, even those who are just starting out; fortunately, these groups are very often willing to help by providing grants or matching funds. However, unless your organization is unusually lucky, you will almost always be unable to provide honoraria that are as large as you would like; if you are very new, you may not be able to provide honoraria at all.

Regardless of whether or what you can pay your participants, be clear with them from the outset: **early in your first conversation**. Make no mistake: this is a hard conversation to have—for some people, the hardest kind and therefore more easily postponed or avoided. Those of us who are poets are used to and even proud of living in what Lewis Hyde calls a gift economy, and we often find it difficult to place a monetary value on what we do, especially aloud. Nonetheless, we all also live in a real economy, in which poets struggle to pay bills just as organizations struggle to raise money to pay poets.

The good news is that everyone is aware of this tension—poets know the groups that hire them are nonprofits in a profit-driven world, and you know that most poets want as often as possible to receive some compensation for their work. You honor that desire and recognize that if established poets, the ones you think might be able occasionally to afford to work for nothing, consistently do so, none of the up-and-comers will ever get paid for what they do—and neither will the established poets. Nobody wants this.

Remember, it is absolutely your job to raise the question of money, whether or not you have any to offer. You should not leave this to the artist, who may be as uncomfortable with the topic as you are. Our most important advice for the conversation: just get it over with. Too often, inexperienced programmers, embarrassed at how little they have to offer, leave the money conversation until later or even avoid it altogether and then mistakenly assume the poet has tacitly agreed to work for free. Avoiding the problem of money will not make it go away and will almost inevitably create misunderstandings and hard feelings down the line. Clarity has many advantages, not the least of which is that it can prevent embarrassing situations. It has no downsides at all.

The trick in negotiations, then, is to reach the sweet spot—an arrangement both you and the poet can afford. If you are not able to provide an honorarium, say so right away and express your hope that the poet will still be able to participate. Be gracious if she or he declines. If you have something other than money to offer, or if you think your event will appeal in other ways than financial, let the poet know. People often tend to feel as grubby about offering nonfinancial incentives as financial ones, especially if they don't directly involve charity, but if you're offering something the poet really wants or might even spend money on otherwise, such an incentive may actually be persuasive. Here are a few incentives that might persuade a poet to work for free, along with sentences you might open a conversation with, assuming in each case that you adapt the sentence to make it true for your situation.

- **The event is a benefit for a cause or organization the poet cares about.**

  We are planning a reading to benefit Diné College (or whatever the cause may be). We know you will be a big draw in our community and that people will pay to hear you. We also know that you're a big believer in the work the college does. We hope you might be willing and able to donate a reading to the cause. We will,

of course, acknowledge your generosity on all our materials. In addition, we prom-
ise to give you a good dinner afterward.

- **The event will help the poet reach an audience she cares about, whether because its members are underserved or because its members can help the poet in some way.**

    Unfortunately, we have a very small budget for the event and can't provide an honorarium (or are offering an honorarium we know is embarrassingly below your usual fee). However, we are aware of your previous prison work; these incar-cerated kids have responded really well to the previous poets we've brought in, and we think your work is perfectly tailored to the program.

- **The event presents an opportunity for the poet to get needed exposure (this most often figures if the poet is still essentially unknown or the event involves an unusually prestigious venue, organization, or audience) or to meet someone he might wish to meet.**

    We wish we could pay you, but we just don't have the budget right now. However, we can promise a good audience—we usually get close to a hundred people— and you'll be reading with Ms. More Famous Poet, whose new book just came out. Of course, we'll have a bookseller there, and afterward we'll give you a good din-ner—it just happens that the director of the MacArthur Foundation will be join-ing us.

- **You can provide an experience that might appeal to the poet.**

    Unfortunately, we can't yet pay honoraria, though we hope to be able to do so soon. However, we heard that you've always wanted to try parasailing, and the resort where we're holding the event offered a free lesson and equipment for the day after the event. (Don't send your poets parasailing, skydiving, skiing, or mountain climbing before events—wait until afterward.)

Even if there are no clear gains for the poet (already has access to this audience, no cause to embrace, just been named a MacArthur fellow, has no interest in bone-imperiling recreational activities, etc.), you may still ask her or him to read for nothing or for less than the usual fee. Be clear and hon-est that what you are asking for is a kind of charitable donation, even though it is unfortunately not tax-deductible, and make sure to honor the poet, both publicly and in making your request, for such generosity to your organization. And provide that dinner, a good one.

Poets can be remarkably generous with their time. When Mark Strand lived in Salt Lake City, Toolkit member (and his former student) Katharine Coles was working as an assistant in the Utah Arts Council Literature Pro-gram office. Strand had recently been named U.S. poet laureate, and he commanded in the thousands for a reading. Some students from a local community college phoned Katharine and asked if there were any chance Mr. Strand would visit their campus. At that point, the going UAC rate for an in-town reading by a local poet was one hundred dollars, the same for everyone, and others at the UAC thought the call wasn't worth making. But Katharine phoned him and laid her cards on the table: a relatively under-served local community, a request from community college students, a one hundred dollar fee (plus, of course, dinner). He immediately agreed and gave a warm, generous reading, including Q&A.

However, you shouldn't take such agreement for granted, ever. Simply give the poet the information and let him or her weigh the different costs and benefits. If the decision comes down on your side, be an excellent and grateful host, and don't forget about dinner. If not, be courteous and under-standing. After all, things might be different next time.

Set Honoraria

Different organizations handle honoraria in different ways. The Utah Arts Council simply offered set fees when Katharine Coles worked there: one for Utah poets reading in their own towns, one for Utah poets travel-ing within Utah to give readings, and one for poets coming from outside the state to read. Such a structure simplifies many things, including negoti-ations. If you can, say you pay a standard rate. Even if you have tiers for dif-ferent kinds of work or, say, numbers of books, the poet can simply do a cost-benefit analysis and decide whether to participate. Some poets are grateful when they don't have to figure out what a reasonable fee is. The downside is that there will inevitably be poets who routinely receive much higher fees that the one you offer and who will be priced out of your struc-ture. One solution for this is partnerships—you might be able to get one or more other organizations to chip in to increase the honorarium amount for a single, jointly sponsored reading. For example, your college's Middle East-ern studies unit might have funds to chip in for an Arab American poet. You might be able to add events and sweeten the pot that way (a high school might have a little money for a classroom visit or an assembly reading, or your local humanities council might send the poet to a senior center). If you pile up events, the poet will have to work a little harder, but you might be able to make a trip look worthwhile.

If you don't pay a set rate, you will need to work with the poet to come to an agreement. It helps if you know whether a poet has a standard fee and what it is. This is usually negotiable (you should ask before beginning to barter), but at least it gives you a target. If the amount you can offer is much lower than this, partnership is still a good option.

Even if you can't come close to the regular fee, it still doesn't hurt to try (remember Mark Strand). Acknowledge that the fee is low, apologize for it, and be gracious if the poet turns you down.

Work With Agents

Many well-known poets now have booking agents. You might try to bypass an agent if you or someone in your organization knows the poet and/or the poet has expressed interest in coming, but do this with care and sensitivity. Poets with agents may be under contract and legally obligated not to bypass their agencies. Beyond that, they generally have agents precisely because they are not comfortable negotiating directly and want to have someone else do it for them. Poets will not thank you for making them feel like money meanies when they are paying others to fill that role, or for getting them to agree to something they really don't want to do because they are too nice to say no. If you do approach a poet directly, be prepared to be referred to an agent. If you are, don't argue.

If a poet has an agent, there generally is a set fee, and it will be high, but this too may be negotiable. If it's out of reach for you or represents a dispro-portionate percentage of your budget, don't be afraid to ask the agent if the poet might consider either an offer that meets or nearly meets the fee but bundles several appearances or an offer that is lower but not ridiculously so. This will give the agent a chance to indicate how much wiggle room there might be. For this conversation, you should be prepared to float various scenarios. Remember, it's the agent's job both to get the poet work and also to get as much money for as little work, and as little time on the ground, as possible, so don't worry about discouraging noises as long as the agent doesn't say flat out that the offer is too low to bother the poet with. If you find out during initial queries that you aren't in or even near an acceptable range, believe it and move on. If the agent gives you a little room and this event matters to you, go ahead and try—but work hard to put together your best possible package. If you work as hard as you honorably can to come up with something good, the worst that can happen is that the agent shows the offer to the poet and the poet says no. This is disappointing but not mortifying. Mortifying is claiming you've made your best offer and then coming back shortly after being declined with a better one you could have made in the first place.

Build Package Deals

If you need to cobble together a coalition of partners, don't limit your thinking about partnerships only to literary groups. Think of every group that might have reason to be interested in this specific poet. If, for example, your poet writes about biology and the environment in a way that is credible to scientists, your university's biology department or a local environmental group might be interested in some sort of partnership. If the poet moonlights in art criticism, a museum might want to sponsor a talk. If the poet has consulted on a film or even been its subject, your local independent film theater or organization might mount a screening. If the film is about computer-generated poetry or New York painters during the 1950s—well, you get the idea. Your local library might be interested in a partnership if the poet is well known enough to draw a large audience.

Some poets are especially interested in bringing their poetry to specific kinds of groups—churches, schools, prisons, or hospitals, for example. Such groups might be able to chip in only a few hundred dollars, but the combination of a little extra money and the chance to reach out to a particular community might be persuasive. As a side note, partnerships and outreach programs, especially with and for organizations working with underserved groups such as seniors, at-risk teens, people with disabilities, and/or ethnic and religious minorities, are often persuasive to granting organizations. Some poets have already prepared specific workshops or other kinds of events that are ripe for partnerships. Nevada poet Shaun Griffin, for example, frequently works with hospital patients and has materials already prepared for that work. Ask your poets if they have specific outreach or other kinds of materials already developed and ready to go.

Whenever you get something from a partner, you will need to provide something of value in return. The best arrangements benefit all partners both in specific instances and in a larger sense. It's excellent for your program if you can broaden its reach; you may find your audience expanding beyond the usual poetry suspects. Poets, too, will be happy to reach as diverse a group as possible in as many ways as possible during the time they spend in your community. In the luckiest circumstances, your partners will think that the chance to have their names on your event is sufficient return for their investments. If this is the case, feature their names prominently on your marketing materials, and don't ever pass up a chance to thank them publicly.

Don't be stingy. The better partners' experiences with you are, the more likely they will be to work with you again—and even to be flexible in what kinds of poets and events they will consider for potential partnerships. If you can, offer partners the chance to spend less formal time with your poets in addition to putting their names on your events or holding their own. Make space for them at dinners and receptions.

Both developing and presenting proposals with many partners can be a delicate business. A poet may wish to negotiate a package that has many parts, all of which are essential to the whole. Be prepared to explain which events are connected to significant percentages of the fee you offer. If the package absolutely depends on all its elements remaining intact, make sure the poet knows that.

Until the deal is complete, make sure your partners know that it is a work in progress and may be subject to further tweaks and revisions, even to the extent of leaving entire events, and therefore partners, out. But stick as much as you can to those pieces of the package that are most appealing to the partners, and don't make changes capriciously. Let partners know you'll advocate as hard as you can for their events and participation; then follow through on the promise, working to keep the things they care most about in any final package.

We've already suggested you set the dates for your keynote or cornerstone poets first. Another good reason to do this is it will help you keep to your budget. Once you know what your big names will cost in honoraria and travel, you can make adjustments in the rest of your schedule in order to meet your budget. You may sometimes find you can add a reading; more likely, you'll have to cut back somewhere.

Checklist: Book the Talent
 A. Decide which poets you want to invite.
   1. Locate poets.
      a. Consult with experts at your local colleges and universities as well as your state and local arts agencies if you aren't sure how to find poets.

       b.   Ask friends and potential audience members who are interested in poetry whom they would like to hear.

       c.   Visit online sites such as www.youtube.com, www.poets.org, and www.poetryfoundation.org to see and hear poets reading their own poems.

  2. Develop and articulate a process for deciding which poets to invite.

       a.   Develop baseline criteria for inclusion.

       b.   Consider how you will respond to audience and community needs, ensure board and community buy-in, and enhance aesthetic, racial and ethnic, gender, and other kinds of diversity.

  3. Tell the poet what you have in mind (a reading, a conference, a statewide tour), and ask if he or she participates in such events.

B. If the poet isn't interested, thank her for her time and let her go.

C. If the poet is interested, negotiate.

  1. If he refers you to an agent, go to D.

  2. If not, and if you have no money to offer, this is the time to say so and offer any other persuasive information or incentives.

  3. If you have a set fee or an amount budgeted, say what it is.

  4. Tell the poet what will be involved. Be as specific as you can: for example, a reading, Q&A with students and community members, and dinner; morning workshops for three days, a reading, and eight manuscript consultations; readings at five venues in four towns over three days, driving across beautiful but empty and forlorn landscapes.

  5. If the poet says no and you have some wiggle room, either in the amount you're offering or in the amount of work/time on the ground you're asking for, let her know that and find out if she wants to continue to negotiate.

  6. If not, express your disappointment in positive terms (you want the poet to know she's really admired in your town, you hope you can do something another time) and graciously hang up.

D. If the poet refers you to an agent, give up on any idea that he might come for nothing or very little. If you still want to move forward, get the agent's phone number and follow up immediately, while you have momentum.

  1. Let the agent know which poet interests you.

2. Ask what the set fee is.

3. Ask if there is any wiggle room in the fee or in the structure of the event, including the number of obligations.

4. In case there's room for negotiation, be prepared to float various scenarios. Is it worth your time to make a somewhat lower offer for a very limited fly-in, fly-out event? If you can come up with the money by working with partners, would it be worth putting together a proposal for a visit that would last several days and include several appearances?

5. If either of these is the case, go back and put together the best offer you can possibly manage. You might even return to the agent with two possibilities—what you can pay for a single appearance, possibly with a Q&A and dinner afterward, and what you can manage for a fuller visit.

6. There is a good chance you will need to go back and forth with the agent a few times before you have a deal the agent can present to the poet. Remember, the poet still may not accept it.

E. Put together a package, whether to present directly or through an agent:

1. Find out if the poet already has specific outreach programs or events prepared.

2. Brainstorm possible partners, paying special attention to those whose missions intersect in some way with the poet's work.

3. Do a little research on the potential partners you come up with to make sure you know what their missions are and how your program might fit with theirs.

4. Approach your potential partners. Explain clearly and enthusiastically who the poet is and why specifically you think an organization might be interested.

5. Be clear about what you hope a partner can contribute. Be honest about the total fee you need to raise and how the partner's contribution would fit in.

6. Be clear about what you are ready to give the partner in return for the contribution you need, and give as much as you can.

7. If you already have a narrow range of dates to choose from, make sure the partner knows that.

8. Be prepared to wait. The person you speak with probably will need to check with others in the organization and look at the

budget. Clearly communicate when you need to know, and let your contact person know when you will follow up.

9. Sit down and put together your proposal. Remember to check in with each partner as you draft, confirming the dates, times, and natures of participation and what the financial contributions will be.

10. Find out what sorts of documents your partners will need. Some will have to issue their own contracts, whether with the poet or with you.

11. Before presenting the proposal, circulate a written version to all partners and ask them to sign off.

12. Present the proposal, understanding that the poet may want to negotiate further.

13. If the poet or agent wishes to negotiate further, be especially careful to ensure the poet knows which events are connected to large percentages of the fee.

14. **As soon as** you have an oral agreement, follow up by e-mail with the poet or agent, asking for confirmation that the terms in the e-mail are what everyone agreed to.

15. Once you have a confirmation, immediately follow up in writing, preferably with a contract.

16. **Do not assume the poet is booked until the signed contract arrives**.

WIND UP

So, your dates are set, partners are on board, and fees are agreed upon. Unfortunately, you don't get to kick back between now and the week before your event or events.

In the interval, communicate with your poet or poets regularly and clearly, though without making a pest of yourself over small details. Use your preparations as a way of keeping in touch, spacing out the contract and necessary requests for vitae or bios and head shots, etc. Even if your organization is as informal as they come, don't let many months go by between communications. If you don't have a contract, a poet may decide you weren't serious or that you have forgotten about her or him and make other plans.

You also want to keep in touch with the people at your venue to ensure that everything from fund-raising to marketing is happening as scheduled and planned.

Fund-raising and all the things you have to do to get ready for fund-raising are such important topics that we gave them their own section in part 2 of this Toolkit. Remember, though, that this is a bootstrap process. If you see fund-raising in your future, even in your distant future, please review that section now. It takes time to put the structures in place that will help you raise money.

PRE-EVENT PLANNING

Once you've got the space, the poet(s), and the program, the real work begins. We organized the following activities into three parts: what needs to be done to prepare for the event, what needs to be done during the event, and what needs to be done after the event. The event itself is bounded and discrete, so most of the work will be done around it, not within it. Be careful about assuming that because the event is still a long way off, you don't need to think about it yet, or that because the applause has died away, you're done. As with grant writing, this kind of thinking can lead to missed opportunities and to haphazard, seat-of-the-pants organization.

On the other hand, it's useful to remember that work can and will expand to fit the time available. There are all kinds of things that, in your perfect world, you might want to do in preparation for, or in the aftermath of, your event. But don't make yourself crazy. You need to set priorities and make choices, especially if you're doing this and also having a life, including work, family, etc. We've tried to limit our recommended actions to those that are likely to create a return on the investment of your valuable time.

Poet Wrangling

We put this section first because the way you interact with and take care of your poets is one of the most important elements of building a good program. You want poets to be happy before, during, and after your events. A poet's experience and mood affects everything else, including and especially the experience of your audience. You hope the poets you hire will be flexible and cheerful at all times, and some poets are, but it's easier for them to be flexible and cheerful when they are comfortable and treated well and when they know what to expect.

The following advice applies to your dealings with all poets, whether they are local or traveling to your event. Advice for dealing with issues specific to poets coming in from out of town appears at the end of this section.

Money

If an honorarium is involved, plan to present it no later than the time the poet actually renders service, whether the poet is local or from away. To make sure this happens, include cutting the check as part of your pre-event planning. If your program is small and the check requires only your signature, make a note to write the check and carry it with you on the date of the event. If you need a second signature, make sure you get it in advance. If you live in a larger bureaucracy, get the whole process started early. Find out well in advance how long it takes a check to move though your system (it could take up to six weeks), and add a couple of weeks to that time just in case things are running especially slowly.

Schedule

You negotiated the basic outlines of the schedule (the number of events, including meals, book signings, and social gatherings) at the time of booking. After this, you shouldn't add any responsibilities for the poet, but you may still need to fiddle with timing. If you have some flexibility, consult with the poet about when he wants meals or downtime or whether he prefers to do manuscript consultations in the morning or in the afternoon. Once you've settled the timing of events, present the poet with a formal written schedule. This can be e-mailed in advance, but you should also present (or have your representative present) a hard copy at your organization's first in-person contact with the poet. The schedule should include the date and time of each event, a short description if you are asking for something specific, and, if you're providing transportation, the name and cell phone number of each driver. Make sure to feature the name and cell phone number of the person overseeing arrangements prominently at the top of the schedule. Even if you don't think your program is complex enough to require a schedule (say, a single reading by a local poet), send an e-mail a few days in advance with thorough information about the event's time and place, and make sure you exchange cell phone numbers with the poet in case of emergency. If your poet has a flat tire or some other mishap on the way to the reading, you want to be reachable.

Meals and Social Events

All scheduled meals and social events should be on the formal schedule. If your program includes events involving food, whether receptions, banquets, or more intimate meals with a few people, check with the poet in advance about dietary restrictions and preferred mealtimes. Whatever your event and whatever the poet's dietary restrictions, make sure there's at least one reasonable main course—preferably more than one if you're dining at a restaurant—and a selection of side dishes to choose from. (We are reminded of one keynote speaker we know, a vegetarian, who was presented with two large onions, partly cooked, at the dinner in his honor. This was in Sweden, but still.) You might think a poet is being finicky and unreasonable in her limitations—and perhaps she is—but the goal is to keep her happy and healthy under your care.

Downtime

Also important to a successful program, especially one with multiple events, is downtime for the poet. Poets spend substantial time alone, cultivating their inner lives. Though some are gregarious and engaged when they're out, others, if they spend too much time in company without breaks, can go a little crazy. Even the gregarious ones may like to choose how and when to be gregarious at least some of the time they're with you. Therefore, though you may be tempted to schedule every minute of the time you have with a poet, it's actually in your best interests not to. Like good food, downtime will increase the chances that your poet is rested, prepared, cheerful, and engaged. Good times for scheduled breaks are first thing in the morning, just before or after lunch, and in the late afternoon before dinner. If you have flexibility in scheduling a poet's downtime, check with him. Blocks of two hours or more will allow him to exercise or nap in addition to freshening up. Make sure that your final printed schedule blocks this time out clearly, and help your poet preserve it. If the poet wants to take a walk or run, he might ask you or someone else to come along as a guide and companion. If you're not fit, don't accept the invitation even if you want to. If you're up to the task, though, this can be a great time to deepen your relationship with him. Still, it's probably best not to offer this service in any more than the most general way unless you're asked, lest the poet should experience your offer as a kind of pressure. Do offer maps, route advice, or inside knowledge if you have it. If you don't, someone else will.

Packets

Packets containing detailed information about the event schedule, locations, and contact information relieve your poets of the need to wonder and worry about where they have to be next and free them to attend to what you've asked them to do. The contents of the packets will vary depending on your event; see the checklist for more details. Poets should receive event packets at first contact (at the airport, hotel, or registration desk, as the case may be); e-mailing a schedule in advance is also a good idea. If two or more poets are presenting together and have books, giving them copies of one another's books is a very nice courtesy, if you have the money. Otherwise, copies of individual poems will do. It's also a nice touch to include copies of the series or event poster for the poets to take home. Many of us remember the old days of AWP, when the conference was still so small that the names of all the presenters could fit on a T-shirt. Each presenter received a shirt in the registration packets; many of us still treasure these, as battered as they may be by now. Finally, if poets need to return receipts for anything, include a stamped envelope addressed to the person responsible for reimbursement. The commonsense rule for packets and schedules is to give as much information as you can, in as clear a format as you can, about what visitors really need on a minute-by-minute basis (phone numbers, reservation numbers, times, places) together at the top of the schedule.

Transportation

If you're transporting a poet to an event, whether from home, a hotel, or a pre-event reception, arrive a few minutes (perhaps five) before the scheduled pickup time. In the latter case, let the poet know five or ten minutes before you need to depart. Because not all poets are precisely punctual, allow plenty of time to get from the pickup site to the event. When the poet is ready to go, ask if she has books, reading copies, exercises, speech— whatever will be needed at the event. Even with clear schedules, people who are nervous, perhaps far from home, and in a rush can be confused or forgetful. On the way to the event, go over what the poet can expect. Will there be a Q&A? Will she be expected to sign books after the event? When will there be food?

Correspondence

Of course, you will keep all financial records, receipts, and copies of all agreements and contracts on file. But there is a good reason for keeping all your correspondence with poets: it can provide a good part of what will eventually become the rich and lively history of your organization. Poets who are not well known now may become famous in the future. When your organization celebrates its tenth anniversary or twentieth or hundredth, those who come after you will appreciate that you preserved such documents.

Planning and Reimbursement for Traveling Poets

Please remember that poets as a rule earn very little. Young poets in particular may not have extra cash on hand to pay for their travel, but heavy out-of-pocket expenses can be a problem for a poet at any career stage. If you are covering expenses, be prepared to book and pay for plane tickets and hotel rooms up front. If you can, estimate and pay for other expenses up front as well. One of our Toolkit members, Orlando White, invites poets to remote areas on the Navajo reservation. Often, poets must drive their own cars to get there or rent cars and drive in from the nearest airport. He has arranged with his institution to figure mileage or rental fees and send checks in advance of readings so poets have travel money when they are on the road and need it.

Travel Arrangements

If poets prefer to make their own arrangements and be reimbursed for expenses after they are incurred, make sure to let them know any limitations (no first-class or upgradable fares, for example). In addition, it's fine to ask poets to check with you before finalizing tickets, etc., to avoid expensive surprises. Still, be as flexible as you can in accommodating poets' desires. Don't make them suffer multiple flights and long layovers to save only a few dollars. If your bureaucracy requires expenses to be incurred before reimbursement checks can be issued, cut and send checks immediately upon receiving receipts. Make sure to know, so you can let poets know, how long it usually takes your system to cut and send checks. Follow up to make sure that checks reach the poets.

Whether you are making arrangements or a poet is, act on them, or remind the poet to do so, well in advance. This will increase your chances of having a choice of reasonably priced flights, rooms, rental cars, and whatever else you need. When the University of Utah Guest Writers Series (GWS) schedules a reading during the Sundance Film Festival, it lines up rooms months ahead of time—a year in advance, if possible—because the GWS knows that many regular festival attendees book rooms for the following year immediately after the current year's festival. Airline seats also fill up fast during festival weeks, and they may cost a little more than at other times. The same is true for any big event. If your small town holds a classic car show every year and draws lots of out-of-towners, you'll want to be aware and act accordingly.

Even under ordinary circumstances, mark your calendar at least two months out from every reading and start on arrangements then. This allows you to watch airline prices for a few weeks if they seem high. Again, if your poet is booking her own ticket, gently nudge her as the date approaches, with assurances that you'll have your reimbursement forms filled out and ready to put through the minute she e-mails you her receipts.

Communicate often with your poets as your event approaches, continuing to be as clear as possible about what they can expect. This includes providing advance information not only about events and transportation but also about housing and meals. If you want to house poets in private homes rather than in hotels or motels, make sure the poets are aware and agreeable. If you expect poets to share space (whether a room, a bathroom, a condo, or a house), please let them know in advance.

Airport to Hotel

Schedule a poet's incoming flight, train, or bus in such a way that she, if all goes well, can go to the hotel, check in, and change clothes before the event. It is a lovely courtesy to send actual people—staff, board members, or volunteers—to transport poets from the airport or depot to the hotel instead of directing them to take taxis or shuttles. If you don't already know a poet and aren't sure she will recognize you, a nice touch is to wait at the security exit or baggage claim (a place clearly designated on the schedule) holding a copy of her latest collection either in addition to or instead of a sign. If you absolutely can't provide personal transportation for the poet, give clear instructions about taxis and shuttles.

When you arrive at the hotel or destination, don't just drop the poet off; go inside and make sure everything is as expected. Before you depart, hand the poet his packet, including a fresh copy of the schedule, and let him know when the next pickup is and by whom. For a traveling poet staying in a hotel, the packet should include the hotel phone, address, and reservation number; a map of the hotel area; and a list of nearby attractions, restaurants, bookstores, etc.

Checklist: Wrangle the Poet

A. All poets
1. Money
   a. Know your system for getting checks cut, including how long it takes, who needs to sign, etc.
   b. Put a reminder on your calendar that leaves plenty of time for things to go wrong.
   c. Follow up in person if necessary.
   d. Hand the honorarium check to the poet before or at the event.
2. Schedule
   a. Write down everything the poet agreed to do, including formal and informal presentations, consultations, and social events.
   b. Begin with those things that are firm in the schedule—readings, workshops, receptions, etc. Block those in.
   c. Create a separate list for more flexible activities: downtime, individual manuscript consultations, lunch with the head of your organization, what have you. If you can, consult with the poet about preferred time frames for these activities.
   d. Leave as much play in the schedule as you can.
   e. For each entry, include the date and time of the event, a short description, names of crucial people (introducer, etc.), name and cell phone number of the poet's escort or ride, and any other crucial information.
   f. At the top of the schedule, include your own phone numbers and the numbers for the person in charge of hosting this poet's visit.
   g. Run a draft of the schedule by the poet before setting it in stone.
3. Packets
   a. Provide a cover sheet with contact information, hotel reservation number, etc.

      b. Include the final schedule, including pickup times and names and phone numbers of people providing transportation.

      c. Supply a map of the area where the event is taking place and/or the area around the poet's hotel.

      d. If possible, provide books by other poets involved or copies of individual poems.

      e. Include a copy of the series or event poster for the poet.

      f. Supply a stamped envelope addressed to the person responsible for reimbursement.

4. Transportation

      a. Assign transportation for every poet to every event.

      b. Make sure that drivers and escorts know event times AND the expected pickup times, which should have leeway built in.

      c. Make sure drivers and escorts know what their events are, who else is involved, and other basics in case the poets have questions.

      d. Circulate the list, with phone numbers, to everyone involved in transportation. Keep a master list for yourself and other organizers.

      e. Double-check to make sure every poet has transportation to every event.

5. Correspondence

      a. Develop a plan for storing correspondence, including any significant e-mails.

      b. Make sure someone else in the organization knows where it is stored.

B. Traveling poets

1. Reimbursement

      a. If possible, estimate and pay travel costs up front.

      b. If not, pay for as much as you can (plane tickets, hotel rooms, etc.) yourself rather than asking the poet to do it and get reimbursed.

      c. If the poet is making arrangements, ask her to check with you before finalizing tickets.

      d. Don't make a poet suffer multiple flights and long layovers to save only a few dollars.

     e. Cut and send checks immediately upon receiving receipts.

     f. Let the poet know how long it usually takes checks to arrive.

     g. Check with the poet to make sure the check arrived.

2. Arrangements

     a. Check to see if major events are occurring around the time of your event, and book ahead accordingly.

     b. Otherwise, start on arrangements two months in advance.

     c. Communicate with your poets often about events, transportation, housing, and meals.

     d. Schedule the incoming flight, train, or bus so the poet has time on the ground before the event.

     e. If possible, have a person pick the poet up instead of directing him to take a taxi or shuttle.

     f. Designate a meeting place and a way for the poet to recognize you.

     g. If you can't provide personal transportation, give clear instructions about taxis and shuttles.

     h. At your destination, take the poet inside and make sure everything is as expected.

     i. Hand the poet her packet.

     j. Let the poet know when the next pickup is and by whom.

Wrangling Everything and Everyone Else

As your event approaches, stay in close touch not only with your poets but also with your board and staff members and with the people at your venues. Remember the "many hands" rule, and learn to organize and delegate.

If you want people, especially volunteers, to sign up for tasks, you need to help them become invested in the program. That means involving them in the planning and giving them some choice as to their roles. Make decisions based on preference and know-how (**don't** save all the plummy assignments for yourself), and try not to give assignments to people who are fundamentally ill suited for them. For example, don't put your shyest board member in charge of planning and hosting social events or introducing the Nobel laureate. At your planning meeting, make a list of the various activities that together make up your overall event: for example, an evening reading followed immediately by a reception and the next day by a brown-bag, lunchtime Q&A. Next, break these activities down into the steps you need to accomplish to make each one happen. This list will vary depending on the type, size, and duration of the program you're mounting, but it will generally include certain basic elements:

1. arrange for space, and keep in touch with the people who run your venue(s)
2. arrange and follow up on advertising and publicity for all public elements of the event
3. consider other audience-building measures, such as working with teachers to provide credit for attendance or working with the appropriate departments at your local schools and colleges for poets who write out of disciplines such as science, visual art, etc.
4. arrange invitations to smaller activities, such as private receptions and dinners
5. make reservations for dinners and arrange for reception food and drink
6. keep the website up-to-date
7. arrange for book sales and signings
8. see to details such as room setup, audio, etc.
9. prepare introductions
10. plan for and follow through on evaluation.

Depending on the kind of event you're mounting, you may also have to do some of the following:

1. book travel and housing for poets
2. run registration/preregistration
3. arrange and inform registrants about practical matters, including start times, parking, housing, program schedules, etc.
4. plan for the transportation and entertainment of poets
5. put out contest announcements and rules; hire judges and screeners; receive and code manuscripts; inform entrants, including both winners and nonwinners, of the results; announce the winners publicly
6. design and order T-shirts, tote bags, and other gear

7. design programs and arrange for their production
8. identify and hire additional people (poets, editors, etc.) as needed beyond your featured poets to sit on panels, consult on manuscripts, give craft talks, etc.
9. arrange group outings such as hikes, museum visits, etc.

Once you have your lists together, consult with your board and staff about dividing and sharing the responsibilities. If you have enough people and a complex set of tasks, form committees to be responsible for categories of related duties, such as communicating with and taking care of poets on the one hand or handling publicity, media, print materials, and websites on the other. Try to have people work at least in pairs so somebody will be aware if something is slipping through the cracks. Identify which responsibilities your partners might be willing or expecting to take on, and check with them to make sure you're all on the same page. Presumably, if one of your partners is a bookstore, the store will arrange for book sales at the event. The group that runs your space may take responsibility for setup and cleanup, water for presenters, sound, etc. If so, help keep track of all the small details, such as putting the bookstore people in touch with the space people to make sure the needed book tables are part of the setup.

Checklist: Wrangle Everyone and Everything Else

A. Help board and staff become and remain invested in the event.
1. Involve them in the planning, and hold regular meetings as the event approaches.
   a. Make lists of all the various activities making up your overall event.
   b. Break these activities down into the steps you need to accomplish to make each one happen.
2. Give people some choice about their roles.
   a. Make decisions based on preference, suitability, and know-how.
   b. Make desirable assignments available to everyone.
3. If you have enough people, form appropriate committees; at least try to have people work in pairs.
4. Check with your partners about which responsibilities they will take on.

5. Check in regularly with all of the above to stay aware of what is happening and what still needs to be done.

Media and Public Relations

Like the care and treatment of poets, this is an area we single out because it deserves special consideration. Getting attention for events can be difficult, especially at first and especially if you are not headlining famous poets—if you are headlining famous poets, you want to make sure they get the press and the audiences they deserve. Publicizing a series of events can help you; your targeted media have dates in advance and can see that you have specific events coming up that are especially exciting.

These days, it's impossible to overestimate the importance of a good website. Both audience members and members of the media may want to Google your program for more information. If people can get information online, they won't have to track down a person—you—to answer trivial questions. Avoid at all costs turning the design and maintenance of your site over to a well-meaning but inexperienced volunteer; you should make the initial investment to hire a professional or try to enlist a professional to donate web work. The look of the site matters; navigability matters even more. A professional will know how to create an easy, positive online experience and will know when you need permission to use the designs, photos, words, and materials of others and how to get those permissions. If one of your primary partnership groups has a well-developed website, the people there might be willing to add and maintain a page for you. If they are generous enough to do this, make sure you are meticulous about sending them updated information regularly as your program develops—and make sure to thank them often!

Even if you send out a schedule and post one online, however, don't count on reporters to keep track of you or even to follow up. Because they are busy and receive lots of press releases about lots of different events, make a plan to put and keep your events on their radar. After you send out an initial release announcing your series and your first event, schedule a release for each subsequent event as well. The initial release should go out well in advance—up to a month—so an interested reporter will have time to plan a feature story instead of just a simple announcement. Follow-up announcements should go out at least two or three weeks in advance.

Target your releases broadly but also as thoughtfully as possible. Because you're a member of your own audience and so represent part of your target demographic, start with places where you get your news and information. Pay particular attention to them in the months preceding your event to find out which reporters are on the arts and literary beats so you can target them by name. But don't stop with your own familiar news outlets, unless you're trying to reach only a very narrow audience of people just like you. Whether you read the local newspaper and listen to NPR or get your news from websites, local entertainment or alternative weeklies, or alternative radio stations, cover outlets used by literary types of various ages and sensibilities. Don't scorn TV, either—some PBS affiliates and even local commercial stations do segments featuring events in the community. Look at what is offered at free newsstands in local coffee shops and music venues—while you're at it, put up posters on their bulletin boards and place flyers on their counters if they'll let you. Don't forget Facebook and Twitter—more and more arts organizations are using them to get out their news.

When your releases have gone out, don't sit back and wait for media responses to pour in. Follow up on your releases a few days after they go out, paying particular attention to those outlets and journalists you think reach your audience. If your event really is newsworthy and falls within the beat of the reporter in question, he or she will probably be grateful that you followed up—or at least not be too irritated. The follow-up call also gives you a second opportunity to make a pitch and convince the reporter that this really is newsworthy. If, as is likely, the reporter hasn't seen (or has forgotten about) the release, offer to send it again. Even if you think the reporter has ignored you, be polite.

Once you have a relationship with a particular reporter, you can send out more casual heads-ups further in advance—for example, an e-mail as soon as you've solidified the schedule, with an offer to help set up interviews. Make sure the reporter still gets all the regular releases when they go out, with follow-up calls or e-mails from you.

It's always good news when a reporter wants to interview you about your events. Whether the interview is with a print reporter or a local radio host or for a TV program, be well prepared. During the interview, make sure you have a full schedule in front of you, as well as a program description, very brief bios of the poets involved, and lists of their publications so you will have something to say even if your memory goes blank. If you are being interviewed for radio or television—whether the interview is taped or live—take a few poems to read if you're asked and maybe even a few quotes from critics about the work of the poets you're featuring. If you're nervous about your ability to think on your feet—and who isn't, especially at first—jot down some notes that will help you recall your own thoughts about the poets and about the program. If you are prepared and interesting, the interviewer will be more likely to invite you back in the future.

Radio interviews require only that you dress neatly and reasonably professionally to help the interviewer take you seriously—unless you're doing the interview by phone, in which case nobody can see that you're still in your pajamas. (According to one school of thought, you'll always be too lackadaisical during a phone interview if you're in your pajamas, but we think this is very person dependent. Some are lackadaisical no matter what they have on; others are energetic even in their jammies.)

If you're asked to do an interview for television, consider carefully what to wear. Some arts lovers think this sort of concern is beneath them, but the attention of the interviewer and the viewer should be on your program or event, not on your clothes. Your outfit should be becoming according to your own lights, and it absolutely should reflect who you are. You don't need to wear a suit if you wouldn't in "real life," but your clothing should reflect the best, most public version of who you are, as if, for example, you were interviewing for your dream job, presumably with like-minded people you want to impress.

Too much skin, whether you are a woman or a man, is distracting, as is underwear that shows, even if in a hip and trendy way. If you're not sure you can walk confidently, perhaps even up and down a few flights of stairs, in whatever shoes and skirt or pants you plan to wear, test drive them in advance. If you plan to wear a skirt, put it on beforehand and sit down on chairs of several heights in front of a mirror, looking at views from the side and the front to make sure you won't reveal more than you mean to if there's no table between you and the camera. The same goes for low-cut shirts and pants that ride low. You don't want to spend the whole interview tugging at your clothing—or, worse, see the segment later and discover you were overexposed. If you wear makeup, a light touch is best.

Finally, practice talking in front of a few friends who can tell you about any physical and verbal tics that might be annoying on camera—slouching, shrugging, scratching, biting your nails or chewing your hair, saying "you know" a lot, whatever. You want to be, and look, alert, composed, and interested in what is happening. Ask only people you trust to be honest and kind—and if you do ask for advice, listen to what your advisors say, even (or especially) if they're your friends. Don't get defensive or upset.

Checklist: Arrange Media and Public Relations

A. Publish a multi-event schedule as far in advance as possible.
B. Obtain bios, head shots, and perhaps short poems or quotes from your poets, making sure to get credit information for the head shots and permission to use both the photographs and the words.
C. Get your website up and running with the help of a professional.
   1. Try to find a professional designer or website company to donate time or to join your board with the primary task of building a website.
   2. If this doesn't pan out, see whether one of your primary part-nership groups is willing to add and maintain a page for you.
   3. Be meticulous about updating information.
D. Create a schedule for press releases.
   1. Target your releases broadly but thoughtfully to the following:
      a. Key reporters at outlets where you get news and information
      b. Local daily papers
      c. Local news, arts, and alternative weeklies and monthlies
      d. Local NPR and PBS affiliates
      e. Alternative radio and TV stations.
   2. Send out a release or packet when the series is announced (a month or so before the first event). This should include the following:
      a. The schedule
      b. A program description
      c. Very brief bios of participating poets.
   3. After a week or ten days, follow up by phone with reporters you think will be most interested. Be prepared to pitch your program: why does it deserve attention? Don't assume the reporter knows who the poets are; indicate which of them you think might be of most interest, including those who have received prizes the reporter may have heard of. If there is a local link to a poet, let the reporter know.
   4. Continue with a release for each individual event, two weeks in advance.
   5. Follow up with selected reporters a few days after the release goes out.
   6. If possible, develop relationships with selected reporters.

E. Go high tech—use Facebook and Twitter.

F. Go low tech—use bulletin boards and flyer cubbies at local coffee shops and music stores, grocery stores, and colleges and universities.

G. Use your networks of college and high school teachers.

H. Give interviews when asked.

    1. Be well prepared.

    2. Take a schedule, a program description, bios of the poets and lists of their publications, copies of a few poems, and notes, and be prepared to leave these with the reporter or interviewer.

    3. For in-person interviews, dress neatly.

    4. For television interviews, dress carefully, as yourself, with these provisos:

        a. Avoid showing too much skin.

        b. Make sure you can walk, stand, and sit comfortably without revealing more than you mean to.

        c. Use a light touch with makeup.

        d. Remember, the focus is the program, not you.

    5. If you're inexperienced, get friends to do practice interviews with you. Trust them.

THE THING ITSELF

Now that negotiations and scheduling are out of the way, you will begin planning the actual logistics of the event. Toolkit member Elizabeth Allen rightly points out that by this time, if you've done your planning well, all you need to do is show up and open the door.

She's kidding, of course. You also want to be a competent, friendly, and charming host. And you will need to troubleshoot, constantly.

Arrival

When you arrive at the venue, check in with your hosts so they know you're there and ready to help if needed. If the poet arrives with you—or whenever he does arrive—introduce him to key people (another good reason to leave a little slack in the schedule). These would include your generous hosts, whoever is introducing the poet if this person isn't you, key people from your organization, your bookseller, anyone from cosponsoring or supporting organizations, and, if there's still time and you're dining after the event, the people with whom the poet will be eating. Make sure there is water at the podium or table, that there are enough chairs, and that the sound system, if you have one, works.

Introductions

Introductions are important in setting the mood for the evening and in helping poets feel welcome and appreciated. Begin by introducing yourself—name and affiliation only. Thank your sponsors and supporters, the people who run your venue, and anyone else who contributed significantly to the event. Let everyone know when and where the next event will be. Remind audience members to turn off their cell phones. If there will be a signing after the presentation, announce it. Finally, introduce your poet or poets.

Ideally, the introduction of a poet should include mention of her major awards and recent books and communicate something interesting about her work. This last bit should be smart above all and respectful but not fawning. You can be witty but not at the poet's expense (being witty at your own expense is fine, as long as you don't overdo it—the introduction should be about the poet, not about you). Whoever introduces the poet **must** read her work before she arrives—as much of it as possible. If that person is you, there are advantages beyond helping you make a good introduction; for one thing, it gives you something to talk with the poet about over dinner or during car trips. It also, as we said, helps the poet feel welcome and appreciated. As we already know, an appreciated poet is likely to be a happy, pleasant poet.

An introduction needs to do a lot of things in a short time. Because your audience is there to hear the poet or poets, not the introducer, no introduction should ever go longer than five minutes (three is better) or, at the very most, 10 percent of the allotted presentation time, which is usually forty-five to fifty minutes for a single presenter. If you are introducing multiple poets, adjust accordingly; for a large panel, it may be best simply to say the poets' names and refer the audience to the program or bio sheet. After you compose your remarks, read them aloud before the event to make sure they come in under time.

When you take your seat, your job during a reading, talk, panel, class, or other kind of presentation is to be the best listener in the house. You may be busy and preoccupied with logistics, but take this time to give yourself over to the pleasures of poetry and the intellectual life you helped create. This is what you have been working for all these weeks or months. Don't check your e-mail or make lists. Just participate.

The Book Signing

During the signing, you have three parties to worry about: the poet, the book buyers, and the bookseller. You made all your arrangements and agreements with the bookseller before the reading, and you accounted for the signing in the poet's schedule, so the timeline shouldn't be an issue at this point. But actually confining the signing to its allotted time can be difficult, especially if the event itself was a great success. If the poet is especially famous or popular, it might be difficult to get him out of the building at a reasonable time. Don't count on the poet to hurry things along—it's his job to be as charming as possible to the book buyers. If you need to end the signing by a certain time, especially if the poet has somewhere to be after the signing—another event, a late dinner—stand by—or have your most courteous board member stand by—and help keep things moving. If a fan takes up more than a reasonable amount of time, help out by gently saying that the poet hasn't eaten yet or that it's getting late and a lot of people are waiting. If you are kind and courteous, most fans will understand.

After the Formal Events

If you're dining late or having a late reception after an event, please consider that your poet is likely to be tired. Don't rush a poet who is having a good time, but don't indulge your own impulse to linger, especially if she is relying on you for transportation, without offering her a way out (read: an immediate ride to wherever she needs to go) regularly through the evening. Whatever your post-event plans are, be sure to feed and water your poet.

Checklist: Manage the Thing Itself

  A. Arrival
1. Check in with your hosts.
2. Introduce the poet to hosts, the introducer if it's not you, key people from your organization, your bookseller, people from cosponsoring or supporting organizations, and the people with whom the poet will be eating.
3. Check water, chairs, and sound system.

B. Introductions
1. Introduce yourself—name and affiliation only.
2. Thank sponsors and supporters, people who run your venue, and anyone else who contributed significantly to the event.
3. Announce the time and place of the next event.
4. Remind audience members to turn off their cell phones.
5. If there will be a signing after the presentation, announce it.
6. Introduce your poet or poets.
   a. Mention major awards and recent books.
   b. Say something interesting about the poet's work.
   c. Stay under 10 percent of the allotted presentation time per presenter.
C. Book signing
1. Keep an eye on the allotted time, and politely keep the line moving.
2. Offer to help the bookseller if necessary.
D. After the Formal Events
1. If there is a reception or dinner, make sure the poet gets food and drink. If no reception or dinner was planned, make sure the poet gets food and drink.
2. Make sure the poet has the option to leave after a reasonable time.

FINISHING TOUCHES

Farewells

Make sure your poet is taken care of to the best of your ability, not just from the beginning of the event until its end but, if he's come in from elsewhere, also from the beginning to the end of the entire visit. "The visit" for all intents and purposes may end when the poet is delivered back to the hotel after the event ends, especially if he is staying on in town to visit friends or vacation. In such a case, you should provide a phone number in case he needs your help and then bow out.

Otherwise, make good arrangements for the poet to get to the airport or train station, even if the flight or train is the day after the event finishes and you're anxious to turn your attention elsewhere. There is no single ideal way to do this. Though it is generous and good to offer a ride to the airport (and to follow through if the offer is accepted), the poet may be worn out and looking for some anonymous time to herself. In this case, she might actually prefer to take a shuttle or taxi, so you should also offer that as an option. Likewise, if you're transporting the poet and the flight is in the late morning or early afternoon, it is nice to offer to take the poet to breakfast or lunch. Accompany any such offer with an easy way out, saying, for example, "I know you're probably tired and would just as soon get room service, but if you'd rather have company for breakfast"—you get the idea.

These days, it's tempting to do all the follow up by e-mail, and you should send out an e-mail thanking poets immediately after all events. However, it's even nicer to follow e-mails with old-fashioned notes on paper.

If there is outstanding business—a poet needs to send you receipts for reimbursement, or, horror of horrors, the honorarium check wasn't ready, follow up about these matters immediately. Your thank-you e-mail should include the name and address of the person to whom receipts should be sent (even if a stamped, addressed envelope was included in the materials the poet received on arrival) and a date by which the poet should expect any checks to arrive.

On that date, send an e-mail to make sure the poet received the checks. If not, immediately trace all payments to find out where they are in your system.

Final Reports

Your last task is to write thank-you notes to and final reports for partners and funders. Everyone who helped you should get at least an e-mail and preferably a note. If a partner was especially helpful, treating him or her to lunch or a refreshing beverage wouldn't be out of line.

All your major funders, whether they require final reports or not, should get letters telling them what you did with their money and thanking them for their support.

Granting organizations generally require you to fill out forms. These forms tend to follow the structures of the grant proposals, asking you to compare what you said you would do to what you actually did. As a rule, nobody expects proposals and final reports to match exactly, but if you did something much different from what you promised, you should talk about why your plans changed and how you compensated for anything you said you would do and didn't. This time, your budget will reflect not what you hoped or planned to do but what you actually did. Thus, it must be based on actual expenditures and receipts. **This is important. Granting agencies have to report to auditors, and they may ask to audit you.** If they do ask for an audit, you will need to show that you kept good and accurate records and reported your expenditures honestly. Again, the income line and the expenditures line should be the same—in other words, your budget should balance. If you came in under budget, there may be a place to report cash on hand.

Checklist: Make Farewells and Write Final Reports

A. Make sure your poet has transportation to the airport or train station, whether he is leaving right after the event or several days later.

B. Send an e-mail thanking your poet immediately after the event.
   1. Include a reference and timeline for anything you need to get to the poet (honorarium, etc.).
   2. If there are receipts outstanding, include a reminder.
   3. Include the name and address of the person to whom the receipts should go.

C. Follow the e-mail with an old-fashioned note on paper.

D. Follow up with an e-mail to make sure all checks arrived; trace anything that is outstanding.

E. Write thank-you notes to individual donors and foundations not requiring formal reports.

F. Complete final reports for funders who require them. Be meticulous.

G. Arrange thank-you events (such as lunches and drinks or even a big barbecue) for the very helpful.

PART 4

BENT NAILS
AND SHORT BOARDS

When Something Goes Wrong—And It Will

Of course, you want everything to go smoothly and well. But things do go wrong. Both the important news and the good news is that an arts organization is not a hospital. For us, a crisis involving injury or any kind of life-threatening event is rare, though of course such an event can happen at a poetry reading as easily as it can anywhere.

To handle a crisis at any level of importance, you need the ability to make good judgment calls, which requires a level head. When you're just learning about a problem or already in the middle of one, your adrenalin is high. Make the time to pause for a moment, take a deep breath, and calm yourself. If you know you aren't the calm person in your organization, immediately call the person who is. It doesn't hurt to designate an organizational emergency point person in advance.

Consider first what category your emergency falls into: major or minor. Does it require instant action, or do you have a bit of time for consideration. Major problems that require instant action include fire, even a small one; learning that one of your visiting "stars" has a stalker and the stalker has just arrived at the venue; or an injury or other medical problem that might require medical care. In such cases, get the experts involved immediately. Unless you are trained and certified for emergencies, there is nothing else for you to do. Whoever is needed—fire department, police, EMTs—make the call as soon as you know there's a problem.

Other kinds of crises involve issues that are important to you but not immediately threatening to life, limb, or the organization. In such a case, you almost certainly have the time and the space to treat your crisis in a level-headed and measured way, if only you can stand back and get perspective.

So, the checks aren't ready on time. The newspaper prints the wrong day or time for an event (worse, it's your fault). A poet cancels at the last minute, your venue is flooded, a board member passes away unexpectedly (though not, thank goodness, at your event), or any number of like things go awry.

Small things—even a flooded venue—can usually be dealt with in the moment. Chances are, another venue can be found. Yes, it's probably a lesser one, and then you have to get the word out as far as possible and put a flyer on the door and probably leave a person there too, in the damp and cold, to tell people where to go. You have to start late to give people a chance to get there, your audience is affected and possibly even disgruntled, and everyone will remember this particular event and its mayhem. This may be a good thing. When people arrive safely and see that you waited for them, and the poet, fueled by more adrenalin than usual, gives a bang-up reading in spite of less-than-perfect conditions, the audience members who took the trouble to come will be glad they were intrepid. They will bond with other intrepid souls and may even be committed to your events in a new way.

If your poet calls to tell you he has a flat tire and no spare, you can send someone out to fetch him—and keep your audience apprised of the progress of his approach and/or repairs. People will remember, and, if you handled things well, their memories will be fond. Don't forget to help the poet get home afterward.

Crises like these are more anxiety-provoking than finding that the sound system doesn't work (the poet, alas, will probably have to bellow) or there's no bottled water and no cup (someone might have something in the car) or the bookseller didn't show up (make phone calls and even offer to send a board member out for the books if someone can unlock the shop).

Remember, you should try to fix even small, headachy kinds of problems instead of letting them slide, especially if they affect the poet and her experience directly. She should at least feel you did your best. Whether you succeed or not, the first rule is to keep both your head and your sense of humor. Remember, if something goes wrong and you handle it well, people will remember that event in particular with fondness and even pleasure.

MAJOR PROBLEMS

Below are just five examples of the kinds of more serious problems you can expect to face at one time or another.

Loss of Venue

We've already dealt with the one-time, last-minute catastrophe. But it's worse when you lose your venue in a bigger way—say, for most or all of your season and/or permanently.

In the best-case scenario, you will have plenty of notice and plenty of time to find a new place. It helps if you can look at this as an opportunity as well as a problem (which, let's face it, any big inconvenience always seems to be at the time). The truth is, groups outgrow venues or, having settled into them, don't always realize that new and even better places may have come along. We don't think City Art regrets having moved from the basement of the Lutheran church, however nostalgically we all look back at it, to fancy, modern new digs at the library, even though the iconic hat didn't fit in and had to retire. Writers at Work found a new kind of mood and spirit when it was forced by skyrocketing resort costs (the Olympic Games were coming) to move, with much trepidation, from Park City, Utah, to a wooded college campus in Salt Lake City. Though it lost an element of hip, it gained a new constituency, which followed it when it moved back into the mountains a few years later. On the other hand, Poets House, in New York City, and the University of Arizona Poetry Center both had the excitement and very hard work of designing their own spaces and, in the process, of reaffirming and reimagining who they were. In all such cases, board and staff members have to work very hard not only to rebrand the organization but also to communicate clearly and joyously what the move is and what it means.

It's harder when you have the rug pulled out from under you at the last minute, especially if you get the news that you're losing your venue late and even more especially if it comes after publicity materials naming the old venue already have been widely distributed. In such a case, you will be seeking a new venue on short notice, which is problematic because you may end up in a place that isn't a perfect fit and then have to move again the next year (you should avoid this—work as hard as you can to get a good venue from the beginning). You also will be trying to get word out to your constituents that things are different now, and they are different than you said they would be.

You can (and must) ask all your usual media outlets to print or read announcements as prominently as possible, but these simply will not reach everyone. Even if you manage to take down and replace every single poster you hung in public, which is probably impossible, there still will be posters and flyers hanging from magnets on innumerable refrigerators. And even if the change will take effect after your first event or two and you know enough in advance to announce the change at these early events, well, face it, some audience members attend only a few readings in a series, and they may never hear these announcements; others don't listen or simply forget. People—for the first few readings, maybe lots of people and probably some for every event of the season—are simply going to go to the wrong place. And you have to figure out what to do about it!

In such a case, for every reading of the season, someone from your board or staff must, with the permission of the hosts at your old venue, post a notice on the door. For at least the first few readings, you will probably also need to post a person at the old venue to direct audience members, reassure them that the reading will start a few minutes late to give people time to get there, and urge them to take the extra trip. If the problem is that the venue is actually no longer there—it was torn down, maybe, which means there's no longer a door to hang a notice from—you'll have to post a living person for every event for the rest of the season. This is a huge pain in the neck, but there's not much you can do about it.

Cancellation

First, remember that almost every organization has had to replace a poet at one time or another. Life is complicated, and things come up. Second, remember that most poets do not cancel events capriciously or because some better offer has come along or even because they suddenly develop a fear of flying. If a poet cancels, chances are she has a good reason. In the moment, be as gracious as you hope she would be if you lost your funding and had to back out of a commitment. Express your disappointment, of course, but in a way that is sympathetic to and focused on the poet and whatever crisis she faces, be it illness, family issues, or something else (even the fear-of-flying thing, which is, for those who have it, a very serious matter). Whatever is keeping her away, chances are it's not about you. If the event is still a few weeks or more away, ask whether she is willing to reschedule, assuming you have another date available.

If rescheduling isn't practical, you need to decide whether you want to cancel the event altogether or find a substitute for the poet, basing your decision on the needs of your organization and its audience. Of course, finding an acceptable substitute will take time and effort and may be impossible for either a solo appearance or a group presentation if the poet who needs to be replaced is very well known and is the focus of the event. If you can't find someone who at least approaches the original poet's reputation—or, alternatively, someone who is beloved in your community—canceling might be the way to go.

If the poet is more or less equal among several presenters or faculty, you will need to decide whether the remaining presenters can fill in; whether you have time to replace the poet with someone equally well regarded, or nearly so; or whether to cancel the part of the event involving that poet.

If you find out later that the poet's cancellation was capricious, there's no need to have a confrontation. You've learned your lesson. Don't invite him again.

Loss of Funding

Perhaps the biggest issue can be a catastrophic drop in funding from one or more than one source. This is something many organizations—even venerable and respected ones—have experienced during recent economic downturns. If this happens to you, first look hard at your budget and see where you can trim. If you're paying for receptions, for example, cancel them, institute a brown-bag policy, or see if you can find local eateries to donate food. If you're spending a lot on dinners out, get board members to host potluck events at their homes. In the worst case—and of course this will be a last resort—you may have to cut salaries or staff, perhaps even return to an all-volunteer effort until you weather the crisis. Think hard about what you are losing and whether you have the volunteer commitment to pull the work off before you take this route. Consult with your staff members before making a decision because they may have ideas about how to weather the storm.

You may not be able to cover all your losses even by pulling your belt in tightly, so you should simultaneously beat the bushes for new sources of funding—both emergency grants and additional regular funding lines. The likeliest sources for emergency grants are individuals who are already committed to your organization; individuals can be nimble and responsive in a way that granting organizations aren't. If you have a little lead time, you may find foundations that give one-time mini grants in moments of opportunity or crisis. Meanwhile, cast your net outside your usual list of foundations and groups for partnerships. Are there new groups coming along whose missions and values are similar to yours?

Of course, if you lose a major source of funding and you simply can't replace it before your event or series, you may need to cut back on the number of poets—or the number of high-priced poets—you are bringing in. If you have already made agreements, this is a touchy business, especially if agents are involved. If you have unpleasant news to deliver, do it immediately and with due apologies and contrition. Fortunately, your contract probably includes an escape clause; it might also include a kill fee, which is some percentage of the poet's fee you have agreed to pay if you have to cancel her appearance. A generous and kindly poet may waive the kill fee if your organization is in trouble, but she is not obligated to do so. If she doesn't, pay it if you can.

The worst-case scenario is that your organization is in a financial crisis because of financial mismanagement or, worse (but fortunately also rarer), some sort of criminal activity. It's worth mentioning here that members of nonprofit boards are responsible for the financial well-being of their organizations, even if their organizations also have directors and/or CFOs. However, if no actual malfeasance is involved, this responsibility is mitigated if the organization was properly incorporated. To avoid malfeasance, board members need to know what kind of money their organization is taking in and how much it's spending and on what. If you are a board member, you should see a financial report every quarter and a complete report annually. If it looks to you as if the finances are getting away from the director or CFO, it is your job to interfere—don't refrain out of misplaced courtesy. If you are the director or CFO and the organization is getting into trouble, communicate with and rally your board sooner rather than later. If you suspect that someone has a hand in the till, you need to make your suspicions known to staff and board members and, ultimately, if you don't receive a satisfactory accounting, to the authorities.

If things have become very bad financially, your organization may have to reorganize in a major way, which could mean canceling an event or a set of events while you raise money and otherwise regroup. During its own recent reorganization, Writers at Work canceled its annual summer conference but still held a competition and mounted mini workshops in the fall and spring. These brought in money and kept regular supporters and participants involved. If you have to regroup, don't vanish from your supporters' radar screens. Chances are, they will be looking for ways to help you out. You might be surprised to find little checks coming in and nice turnouts for your fund-raising events.

Serious Injury or Death

First, we are sorry. This is what we all most fear. Fortunately, this kind of catastrophe is truly rare at poetry events, which, perhaps strangely, tend to be relatively safe places to be in this day and age. Nonetheless, as artists and art lovers know better than most, mortality catches up with us all.

In this case, there are two possibilities: the first, which we dealt with above, is that a serious injury or even a death occurs at your event. You, as instructed, immediately call the proper authorities. If there is an injury or some sort of removal must occur, someone connected closely to the organization—probably not the leader but someone high in leadership—should either travel with the injured person and/or family members who are present or go to the hospital or other destination. Another board or staff member should be in charge of finding and notifying family members if none are present.

This is obviously a somewhat more harrowing case than if the tragic event occurs offstage. However, once the ambulance, police officers, and designated board member are gone, the leadership members remaining behind face the same question you will face if a board member, an organizational leader, a participating poet, or someone else especially close to your community has a crisis or dies quite close to your event: do you continue? If you do, how do you do so sensitively and in a way that honors the loss?

The truth is, unless the tragedy is unusually horrific or has befallen someone so central to your event that it absolutely can't continue, you will probably decide to go on. For one thing, if the person is or was really close to the organization, he or she would probably want this. (Don't say this, though, if you don't think it's true.) For another thing, people often want to be in company after a catastrophic event, and poetry is uniquely suited to helping people process strong human emotion. Something like a poetry reading might be precisely what your community requires.

However, you don't want to make this decision hastily or automatically; take into account the feelings of everyone involved, including poets, participants, constituents, audience members, and your board and staff. When the immediate drama is over, check with your poet or poets; if they are game to do something, circulate quietly among the audience and participants. If people are simply in the mood to leave, they will begin to do so—and there is your answer. But if they seem to want to stay behind and be together, you can proceed with your event, though gently and probably differently, in a way that acknowledges and even incorporates what has happened. If your event is a reading, your poet will probably give a different reading than she had originally planned. If it's a workshop, she may switch lesson plans, perhaps working explicitly with elegy or catastrophe.

If there's a little time between your community's tragedy and your event, you might incorporate a reading or other kind of brief celebration into the event in honor of the person. If he is or was a poet whose work received a lot of critical attention, it might even be appropriate to incorporate some sort of panel about the work. But don't be overly self-indulgent as an organization. Be loving but dignified and restrained.

Fire, Gas Leak, or Similar Problem During the Event

This is simple but not easy. If you experience a fire, smell gas or chemicals, or have any similar kind of problem, evacuate immediately. Again, it's probably a good idea to designate in advance your calmest board or staff member to be in charge of this while your next calmest person calls the fire department or emergency services. The point person should very calmly make a general announcement about the problem and give instructions about how to proceed. Your staff and board members should then circulate among your participants, making sure that everyone is heading steadily and calmly to the exits. You are responsible for making sure everyone gets out and for checking the restrooms and other anterooms before you leave yourself.

If the fire department comes, takes care of the problem, and clears the venue for use, you may proceed with the event if your poet(s) and participants are still willing.

Responsibility

It is important to remember that you are in charge and therefore responsible if something does go awry. One thing to consider: if your organization has grown to the point that it has a major budget and/or if it offers multiday events, especially if there is any programming at all for kids under eighteen, your board might consider getting director's insurance. Of course, this doesn't obviate the need for you to behave with care, but it may protect you as individuals if something unforeseen goes wrong and the organization is sued as a result.

Every crisis provides you with an opportunity to remind yourself of your mission and values and to check in with and listen to your audience. It never hurts to keep asking, even during good times, what you're doing that is most important to your core mission and what is nice but inessential. Then, when something bad happens, you already have an idea of what you need to save from the flames or rising waters and what, with a sigh, you can let go.

Checklist: Cope With Catastrophe

A. When bad news of any kind comes in, stop for a moment to take stock.
   1. Are you sure you correctly interpreted the news you have? If you're looking at a financial statement, take out your calculator. If someone brings you news of an accident, take the time to listen and ask questions.
   2. When you are sure there is a problem, ask yourself who needs to know about it. Who are the best people to consider what actions to take?
   3. Consider which people are in the best position to take action. These may not be the same people who make the initial decisions.
   4. If these people are professionals, contact them immediately and give them all the information you have about the problem—do not hide details out of embarrassment or for any other reason.

5. If you don't need to bring in professionals, contact the people on your staff or board who can help. Again, make sure they know everything about the problem.

B. Consider what kinds of announcements you need to make, first to your inner circle, then to wider staff and board circles, and finally to your supporters and audience members. This may be a matter of stepping almost immediately (or, in the case of evacuation, immediately) in front of a microphone, or it may involve long-term press strategies. Either way, think about what you're doing before you do it.

1. If you need to manage an in-event crisis as it unfolds, designate a spokesperson.
2. If you need to evacuate, do so immediately.
3. If you have the time, spend a few moments developing a strategy and a message. Don't take a long time—make sure the group is getting accurate news from a calm spokesperson rather than relying on rumor.
4. If your announcements involve schedule changes, personnel changes, or other changes affecting public events, consider how to get the word out more widely, whether through media announcements, announcements at events, public notices, posters, or other means, and assign someone to do so.
5. Regardless of the kind of announcement you need to make, seriously consider wording and tone. If you have to evacuate, give instructions clearly and calmly. If a poet cancels, let people know in a way that is kind toward the poet. If you need to announce a budget shortfall, be as straightforward as possible about the problem and let people know you are working toward a resolution. If an injury or worse occurs at your event, be sensitive and sympathetic but calm.

C. In the case of a crisis that unfolds over time—such as a funding or budget crisis or a loss of space—work as quickly as is practical with your group's leaders to develop a long-term strategy to address the crisis.

1. Remind yourselves of your core values and mission. What can you let go of? What is essential to who you are and what you do?
2. If possible, cut back your programming rather than suspending it altogether. If you must suspend a major event, consider

whether you can support a couple of mini events. It's hard to start up again from nothing, especially if your supporters have stopped thinking about you.

3. Make sure your plan is something you are happy to share with your board members and supporters. Be honest with them and yourself: Is this right? Will it work?

4. With this in mind, develop a communication plan for the long term so you can continue to get news of your progress and events to your supporters.

D. As your crisis passes and you ratchet up your programs, make sure to continue to check in with your values and increase your communications, in both directions.

E. Don't forget to remember why you do this. Don't give up!

THE GOOD NEWS IN THE BAD NEWS

Even with all this in mind, please don't forget the huge rewards involved in this work—they more than outweigh all the little things that will constantly go wrong and the big things that may, very occasionally, go wrong. Nobody ever built a house without hitting her thumb with a hammer from time to time. When this happens, put your thumb in your mouth until the sting goes away and keep going—as have all of our essayists, members of our Toolkit team, and many of you.

Look at what we have all built together so far. Think about what is still out there to build. Houses and neighborhoods, cities and states, and countries and continents full of poetry. Communities of all sizes and constructions, alive in the word and so in the world.

PART 5

NUTS, BOLTS, AND WIDGETS

Tools for Tinkering[1]

ADDITIONAL READING: BOOKS AND JOURNALS

Borrup, Tom. *The Creative Community Builder's Handbook: How to Transform Communities Using Local Assets, Arts, and Culture.* St. Paul, MN: Fieldstone Alliance, 2006.

Bray, Ilona. *Effective Fundraising for Nonprofits: Real-World Strategies That Work.* 3rd ed. Berkeley, CA: Nolo, 2010.

Burnett, Ken. *The Zen of Fundraising: 89 Timeless Ideas to Strengthen and Develop Your Donor Relationships.* San Francisco: Jossey-Bass, 2006.

Connolly, Paul, and Marcelle Hinand Cady. *Increasing Cultural Participation: An Audience Development Planning Handbook for Presenters, Producers and Their Collaborators.* New York, NY: The Wallace Foundation, 2001. http://www.wallacefoundation.org/KnowledgeCenter/Knowledge

Topics/CurrentAreasofFocus/ArtsParticipation/Pages/IncreasingCulturalParticipation.aspx. (Home page: http://www.wallacefoundation.org/Pages/default.aspx.)

Cryer, Shelly. *The Nonprofit Career Guide: How to Land a Job That Makes a Difference.* Saint Paul, MN: Fieldstone Alliance, 2008.

Dropkin, Murray, Jim Halpin, and Bill La Touche. *The Budget-Building Book for Nonprofits: A Step-by-Step Guide for Managers and Boards.* 2nd ed. San Francisco: Jossey-Bass, 2007.

Drucker, Peter F. *Managing the Nonprofit Organization: Principles and Practices.* New York: HarperCollins, 1990.

Elizabeth, Lynne, and Suzanne Young, eds. *Works of Heart: Building Village Through the Arts*, Oakland, CA: New Village Press, 2005.

Ewell, Maryo Gard, and Michael F. Warlum, *The Arts in the Small Community.* Robert E. Gard Wisconsin Idea Foundation and the University of Wisconsin–Madison, 2006. http://www.gardfoundation.org/index.html

Frazier, Chapman Hood. "Building Community through Poetry: A Role for Imagination in the Classroom." *English Journal* 92, no. 5 (May 2003): 65–70.

Gard, Robert. *Prairie Visions: A Personal Search for the Springs of Regional Arts and Folklife.* Minocqua, WI: Heartland Press, 1987.

Graves, James Bau. *Cultural Democracy: The Arts, Community, and the Public Purpose.* Champaign: University of Illinois Press, 2005.

International Journal of Arts Management (IJAM). http://www.gestiondesarts.com/index.php?id=720.

Karsh, Ellen, and Arlen Sue Fox. *The Only Grant Writing Book You'll Ever Need: Top Grant Writers and Grant Givers Share Their Secrets,* 3rd ed. New York: Basic Books, 2009.

Klein, Kim. *Fundraising for Social Change,* 5th ed. San Francisco: Jossey-Bass, 2007.

Korza, Pam, Maren Brown, and Craig Dreeszen, eds. *Fundamentals of Arts Management,* 5th ed. Amherst, MA: Arts Extension Service, University of Massachusetts, 2007.

Lansana, Quraysh Ali, and Toni Asante Lightfoot, eds. *Dream of a Word: The Tia Chucha Press Poetry Anthology.* Foreword by Luis J. Rodriguez. Chicago: Tia Chucha Press, 2005.

La Piana, David, *The Nonprofit Strategy Revolution: Real-Time Strategic Planning in a Rapid-Response World*. Saint Paul, MN: Fieldstone Alliance, 2008.

La Piana, David. *Play to Win: The Nonprofit Guide to Competitive Strategy*. San Francisco: Jossey-Bass, 2010.

Letts, Christine W., William P. Ryan, and Allen Grossman. *High Performance Nonprofit Organizations: Managing Upstream for Greater Impact*. New York: John Wiley & Sons, 1998.

Mattessich, Paul W. *Manager's Guide to Program Evaluation: Planning, Contracting, and Managing for Useful Results*. St. Paul, MN: Amherst H. Wilder Foundation, 2003.

Mattessich, Paul W., Marta Murray-Close, Barbara R. Monsey, and Wilder Research Center. *Collaboration: What Makes It Work*. 2nd ed. St. Paul, MN: Amherst H. Wilder Foundation, 2001.

Michael, Pamela, ed. *River of Words: Images and Poems in Praise of Water*. Introduction by Robert Hass. Berkeley, CA: Heyday Press, 2003

Michael, Pamela, ed. *River of Words: Young Poets and Artists on the Nature of Things*. Introduction by Robert Hass. Minneapolis, MN: Milkweed Editions, 2008.

Ong, Walter. *Orality and Literacy: The Technologizing of the Word*. London: Routledge, 1982.

Poets House. *The Poetry in The Branches Source Book: A Guide to Creating a Complete Poetry Environment in Diverse Library Settings*. Rev. ed. New York: Poets House, 2009.

Reich, Brian, and Dan Solomon. *Media Rules!: Mastering Today's Technology to Connect With and Keep Your Audience*. Hoboken, NJ: John Wiley & Sons, 2007.

Rodriguez, Luis J., Michael Warr, and Julie Parson-Nesbitt, eds. *Power Lines: A Decade of Poetry from Chicago's Guild Complex*. Chicago: Tia Chucha Press, 1999.

Simon, Judith Sharken, and J. Terence Donovan. *The Five Life Stages of Nonprofit Organizations: Where You Are, Where You're Going, and What to Expect When You Get There*. Saint Paul, MN: Fieldstone Alliance, 2001.

Smith, Marc Kelly. *Crowdpleaser*. Chicago: Collage Press, 1996.

Smith, Marc Kelly, and Joe Kraynak. *The Complete Idiot's Guide to Slam Poetry*. New York: Alpha Books, 2006.

————. *Stage a Poetry Slam: Creating Performance Poetry Events—Insider Tips, Backstage Advice, and Lots of Examples.* Naperville, IL: Sourcebooks MediaFusion, 2009.

Stone, Michael K., and Zenobia Barlow, eds. *Ecological Literacy: Educating Our Children for a Sustainable World.* Preface by Fritof Capra. San Francisco: Sierra Club Books, 2005.

Tempel, Eugene R., Timothy L. Seiler, and Eva E. Aldrich, eds. *Achieving Excellence in Fundraising.* 3rd ed. San Francisco: Jossey-Bass, 2010.

Warwick, Mal, Ted Hart, and Nick Allen, eds. *Fundraising on the Internet: The ePhilanthropyFoundation.org's Guide to Success Online.* 2nd ed. San Francisco: Jossey-Bass, 2002.

Wolfred, Tim. *Managing Executive Transitions: A Guide for Nonprofits.* Saint Paul, MN: Fieldstone Alliance, 2009.

ORGANIZATIONS

Academy of American Poets.
  http://www.poets.org/.
Americans for the Arts.
  http://www.artsusa.org/.
Anna Deavere Smith Works, Inc.
  http://www.annadeaveresmithworks.org/.
Arts Education Partnership.
  http://aep-arts.org/.
Association of Arts Administration Educators (AAAE).
  http://www.artsadministration.org/explore.
Association of Writers & Writing Programs (AWP).
  http://www.awpwriter.org/.
BoardSource.
  http://www.boardsource.org/.
Cave Canem.
  http://cavecanempoets.org/.
Center for Arts and Cultural Policy Studies, Princeton University.
  http://www.princeton.edu/~artspol/workpap.html.
Curb Center for Art, Enterprise & Public Policy, Vanderbilt University.
  http://www.vanderbilt.edu/curbcenter/.
Foundation Center.
  http://foundationcenter.org/.

Idealware.
 http://www.idealware.org/.
Lannan Foundation.
 http://www.lannan.org/.
National Assembly of State Arts Agencies.
 http://www.nasaa-arts.org/.
National Council of Nonprofits.
 http://www.councilofnonprofits.org/.
National Endowment for the Arts.
 http://nea.gov/.
Nonprofit Academic Centers Council.
 http://www.naccouncil.org/default.asp.
Nonprofit Finance Fund.
 http://nonprofitfinancefund.org/.
Nonprofits Assistance Fund.
 http://www.nonprofitsassistancefund.org/.
Pen American Center.
 http://www.pen.org/.
Poetry at Tech.
 http://www.poetry.gatech.edu/poetryhome.php.
Poetry Foundation.
 http://www.poetryfoundation.org/.
Poetry International.
 http://www.poetry.nl/read/english/.
Poetry Society of America.
 http://www.poetrysociety.org/psa/.
Poets & Writers.
 http://www.pw.org/.
Poets House.
 http://www.poetshouse.org/.
River of Words.
 http://www.riverofwords.org/.
Society for Nonprofit Organizations.
 http://www.snpo.org/.
Teachers & Writers Collaborative.
 http://twc.org/.
Techsoup.
 http://home.techsoup.org/pages/about.aspx.

Tia Chucha's Centro Cultural & Bookstore.
  http://www.tiachucha.com/.
Tucson Indian Center: American Indian Association of Tucson, Inc.
  http://ticenter.org/default.aspx.
University of Arizona Poetry Center.
  http://poetry.arizona.edu/.
The University of Iowa International Writing Program.
  http://iwp.uiowa.edu/.
Urban Institute.
  http://www.urban.org/nonprofits/index.cfm.
VSA: The International Organization on Arts and Disability.
  http://www.vsarts.org/.
W3C Web Accessibility Initiative.
  http://www.w3.org/WAI/.
Writers in the Schools (WITS).
  http://www.witshouston.org/.

WEB-BASED MATERIALS

Artists' Health Insurance Resource Center.
  http://www.ahirc.org/.
Arts & Business Council of Americans for the Arts. "National Arts Mar-
  keting Project."
  http://www.artsmarketing.org/about.
ArtsJournal.
  http://www.artsjournal.com/.
Barry's Blog: News, Advice, and Opinion for the Arts Administrator. Western
  States Arts Federation.
  http://blog.westaf.org/2006_04_01_archive.html.
BoardSource. *Principles Workbook: Steering Your Board Toward Good Gover-
  nance and Ethical Practice.*
  http://www.boardsource.org/Bookstore.asp?Item=1099
Chronicle of Philanthropy.
  http://philanthropy.com/section/Home/172.
Colorado Nonprofit Association. "Working with the Media: Nonprofit
  Toolkit."
  http://www.coloradononprofits.org/media%20toolkit.pdf.

Community Arts Network.
http://wayback.archive-it.org/2077/20100906194747/
http://www.communityarts.net/
Council of Literary Magazines and Presses. "Creating a Code of Ethics for Competitions."
http://www.clmp.org/about/nonmembersform.html.
Cultural Policy and the Arts National Archive, Princeton University
http://www.cpanda.org/cpanda/.
E-poets.net. "An Incomplete History of Slam."
http://www.e-poets.net/library/slam/converge.html.
Favorite Poem Project.
http://www.favoritepoem.org/.
Free Management Library C/O Authenticity Consulting, LLC. "Free Complete Toolkit for Boards."
http://www.managementhelp.org/boards/boards.htm.
Grantsmakers in the Arts. *GIA New's Blog.*
http://www.giarts.org/blogs/gia-news.
Grantsmakers in the Arts. *Janet's Blog.*
http://www.giarts.org/blogs/janet.
Impact Arts: Evaluating the Social Impact of the Arts. Americans for the Arts, Animating Democracy.
http://impact.animatingdemocracy.org/.
Independent Sector. "Resources."
http://www.independentsector.org/resources.
IRS.gov. "Charities & Other Non-Profits."
http://www.irs.gov/charities/index.html.
Journal of Arts Management, Law, and Society.
http://heldref.metapress.com/app/home/journal.asp?referrer=parent&backto=linkingpublicationresults,1:119929,1&linkin=634263836403376250. (Home page: http://heldref.metapress.com/app/home/browse-publications.asp.)
Kennedy Center. "ArtsEdge."
http://artsedge.kennedy-center.org/educators.aspx.
Library of Congress. "Poetry."
http://www.loc.gov/poetry/.
Library of Congress, U.S. Copyright Office. "Copyright."
http://www.copyright.gov/.

Litline. "Organizations." Illinois State University.
  http://www.litline.org/links/organizations.html.
Marrero, Erica. "Former Gang Member Says Art Is an Antidote to Vio-
  lence: Author and Activist Luis J. Rodriguez Helps Troubled Youth in
  Mexico." August 10, 2010. America.gov, U.S. Department of State.
  http://www.america.gov/st/peopleplace-english/2010/May/20100504
  105000MEorerraM0.1975977.html.
McCarthy, Kevin F., Elizabeth Heneghan Ondaatje, and Laura Zakaras.
  Guide to the Literature on Participation in the Arts. Rand Corporation,
  2001. Last modified December 7, 2007.
  http://www.rand.org/pubs/drafts/DRU2308/.
National Endowment for the Arts. "Lessons Learned: A Planning Toolsite."
  http://arts.endow.gov/resources/Lessons/index.html.
National Endowment for the Arts. "Literature Resources."
  http://arts.endow.gov/resources/disciplines/lit/resources.html.
National Endowment for the Arts. "Poetry Out Loud: National Recitation
  Contest."
  http://www.nea.gov/national/poetry/index.html.
National Endowment for the Arts. "NEA Office for AccessAbility."
  http://arts.endow.gov/resources/Accessibility/index.html.
National Endowment for the Arts. "State & Regional Partners."
  http://www.arts.gov/partner/state/SAA_RAO_list.html.
Nonprofit Quarterly.
  http://www.nonprofitquarterly.org/.
Panel on the Nonprofit Sector. *Principles for Good Governance and Ethical
  Practices: A Guide for Charities and Foundations.* Panel on the Nonprofit
  Sector, 2007.
  http://www.nonprofitpanel.org/Report/index.html.
Panel on the Nonprofit Sector. *Strengthening Transparency, Governance,
  Accountability of Charitable Organizations: A Final Report to Congress and
  the Nonprofit Sector.* Panel on the Nonprofit Sector, 2005.
  http://www.nonprofitpanel.org/Report/index.html.
Panel on the Nonprofit Sector. *Strengthening Transparency, Governance,
  Accountability of Charitable Organizations: A Supplement to the Final Report
  to Congress and the Nonprofit Sector.* Panel on the Nonprofit Sector, 2006.
  http://www.nonprofitpanel.org/Report/index.html.
Poetry Out Loud.
  http://www.poetryoutloud.org/.

Poets House. Directory of American Poetry Books Database.
　http://www.poetshouse.org/directory.htm.
Taylor, Andrew. *The Artful Manager: On the Business of Arts & Culture* (blog).
　ArtsJournal.
　http://www.artsjournal.com/artfulmanager/.
USA.gov. "USA.gov for Nonprofits."
　http://www.usa.gov/Business/Nonprofit.shtml.
The Wallace Foundation. "Arts Participation & Arts Education Research."
　http://www.wallacefoundation.org/KnowledgeCenter/Knowledge
　Topics/CurrentAreasofFocus/ArtsParticipation/Pages/default.aspx.
W. K. Kellogg Foundation. *W.K. Kellogg Foundation Evaluation Handbook.*
　http://www.wkkf.org/knowledge-center/resources/2010/
　W-K-Kellogg-Foundation-Evaluation-Handbook.aspx.

NOTE

1. This information is provided as possible resources to use when thinking about creating community around poetry, but inclusion is not intended as an endorsement of a particular way of doing something or of specific content. These are the resources and organizations we came across during our research and as a result of requests we put out to people in the poetry community. It is not meant to be an exhaustive list. This information is generalized and does not address any reader's specific situation. Readers of these materials should seek their own answers and individual legal counsel to address their own specific circumstances, wishes, needs, and relevant laws.

CONTRIBUTORS

ESSAYISTS

ELIZABETH ALEXANDER is a poet, essayist, playwright, teacher, and current chair of the African American Studies Department at Yale University. She has served on the faculty and as a board member and is now honorary director of Cave Canem, an organization dedicated to the development and endurance of African American poetic voices. Her poetry collection *American Sublime* was a finalist for the Pulitzer Prize, and her sixth book of poems is *Crave Radiance: New and Selected Poems, 1990–2010*. Alexander was selected to compose and read a poem at the presidential inauguration of Barack Obama in 2009.

SHERWIN BITSUI is the author of two poetry books, *Shapeshift* and *Flood Song*. His honors include a Whiting Writers Award, a 2010 PEN Open Book Award, and an American Book Award. Bitsui is originally from Baa'oogeedí (White Cone, Arizona) on the Navajo Nation. Currently, he lives in Tucson. He is Diné of the Todich'íi'nii (Bitter Water Clan), born for the Tł'ízíłání (Many Goats Clan).

LEE BRICCETTI is a poet and the executive director of Poets House, a national poetry library and literary center for poets and the public, which documents the wealth and diversity of modern poetry and stimulates public dialogue on issues of poetry in culture. The author of *Day Mark,* she has received a New York Foundation for the Arts Award for Poetry and has been a poetry fellow at the Fine Arts Work Center in Provincetown.

ALISON HAWTHORNE DEMING is a poet, essayist, and professor in creative writing at the University of Arizona. From 1990 until 2000, she served as director of the University of Arizona Poetry Center, an internationally renowned poetry library, where she continues to serve as a member of the Development Board. In addition to her works of nonfiction and essays, she is the author of four collections of poetry, including *Science and Other Poems* and, most recently, *Rope.*

DANA GIOIA is a poet, critic, and current director of the Aspen Institute's Harman-Eisner Program in the Arts. Under his former leadership as chairman, the National Endowment for the Arts reached millions of Americans through grants and arts programs such as Poetry Out Loud, a poetry recitation contest offered in partnership with the Poetry Foundation that has, in the past five years, involved over three-quarters of a million high school students. His most recent book of poems, *Interrogations at Noon,* won the American Book Award. His critical collection, *Can Poetry Matter?,* was a finalist for the National Book Critics Circle award.

ROBERT HASS served as poet laureate of the United States from 1995 to 1997 and was awarded the 2007 National Book Award and the 2008 Pulitzer Prize for *Time and Materials: Poems 1997–2005.* In addition to being a professor of English at the University of California, Berkeley, he is the cofounder of River of Words, an organization that champions environmental and arts education, where he continues to serve as a judge, advisor, and co-chairman of the board. His most recent book is *The Apple Trees at Olema: New and Selected Poems.*

BAS KWAKMAN is the managing director of Poetry International Rotterdam (the Netherlands), a literary organization working to promote international exchange among poets, poetry translators, poetry connoisseurs, and poetry lovers. Poetry International's projects include its online poetry magazine, www.poetryinternational.org, which has over twenty international partners, and the annual Rotterdam Poetry International Festival. Prior to joining Poetry International, Kwakman was a founder and an editor of *Tortuca*, a magazine for art and literature, and worked as an independent visual artist and a poet.

THOMAS LUX is a poet who currently holds the Bourne Chair in Poetry at the Georgia Institute of Technology, where he also runs the Poetry at Tech program, one of the premier showcases of poetry in the Southeast, and serves as director of the McEver Visiting Writers program. The author of eleven poetry collections, most recently *God Particles,* and a recipient of the Kingsley Tufts Poetry Award, he is also on the MFA faculties of Sarah Lawrence College and Warren Wilson College.

CHRISTOPHER MERRILL has published four collections of poetry, including *Watch Fire*, for which he received the Peter I. B. Lavan Younger Poets Award from the Academy of American Poets; translations of Aleš Debeljak's *Anxious Moments* and *The City and the Child*; several edited volumes; and four books of nonfiction. His work has been translated into twenty-five languages, his journalism appears widely, and for ten years he was the book critic for the daily radio news program *The World*. He has held the William H. Jenks Chair in Contemporary Letters at the College of the Holy Cross and now directs the International Writing Program at the University of Iowa.

LUIS RODRIGUEZ is a poet, journalist, fiction writer, children's book author, critic, and author of the memoir *Always Running: La Vida Loca, Gang Days in L.A.* He has founded or cofounded numerous community organizations, including Chicago's Guild Complex, Youth Struggling for Survival, Tia Chucha Press, and Tia Chucha's Centro Cultural & Bookstore, which provides a bookstore, performance space, and workshop center for its inner city neighborhood and sponsors Celebrating Words: Written, Performed & Sung, a literacy and performing arts festival.

ANNA DEAVERE SMITH is an actress, playwright, author, and professor at New York University. Her work exploring American character and national identity has earned her many awards, including a MacArthur Fellowship, two Obie Awards, and two Tony nominations. Her play *Fires in the Mirror* was a finalist for the Pulitzer Prize. She is founding director of Anna Deavere Smith Works, Inc., a center that convenes artists whose work addresses the world's most pressing problems.

PATRICIA SMITH is an author, performer, playwright, teacher, and four-time National Poetry Slam champion, the most successful competitor in slam history. Her fifth book of poetry, *Blood Dazzler*, was a finalist for the 2008 National Book Award. In addition to being published in numerous journals and anthologies, her work can be found in stage productions, on CD, in an award-winning short film, and in HBO's *Def Poetry Jam*. She is a professor of creative writing at the City University of New York/College of Staten Island and a faculty member at both Cave Canem and the Stonecoast MFA Program at the University of Southern Maine.

TOOLKIT COLLABORATORS

SUSAN BOSKOFF is executive director of the Nevada Arts Council, a division of the Department of Cultural Affairs. In partnership with arts organizations, schools, and communities, the Arts Council actively works to bring artists, a diversity of art forms, and audiences together in Nevada's metropolitan centers and isolated rural towns. Its public programs include the Nevada Circuit Riders, Nevada Folklife Archives, and the Nevada Touring Initiative, which includes the Tumblewords Literary Program. The Council also partners with the National Endowment for the Arts and the Poetry Foundation on the annual Poetry Out Loud recitation competition.

KATHARINE COLES is the inaugural director of the Harriet Monroe Poetry Institute at the Poetry Foundation. Her most recent collection of poems, *Fault*, came out in 2008; she has also published novels and essays and has collaborated with various visual artists on projects resulting in both temporary and permanent installations. She is a professor at the University of Utah, where she founded and co-directs the Utah Symposium in Science and Literature. In 2006, she was named to a five-year term as poet laureate of Utah.

TREE SWENSON is the executive director of the Academy of American Poets, a nonprofit organization dedicated to supporting American poets and fostering appreciation of contemporary poetry through programs such as Poets.org, National Poetry Month, the Poetry Audio Archive, and the literary journal *American Poet,* as well as through its numerous awards and prizes for poets. Prior to joining the Academy, Swenson served as director of programs for the Massachusetts Cultural Council and was the cofounder, publisher, and executive director of Copper Canyon Press.

ORLANDO WHITE is from Tólikan, Arizona. He is Diné of the Naa-neesht'ézhi Tábaahí and born for the Naakai Diné'e. He holds a BFA from the Institute of American Indian Arts and an MFA from Brown University. White is the author of *Bone Light* and he teaches at Diné College and lives in Tsaile, Arizona.

ELIZABETH ALLEN is the project manager for the Harriet Monroe Poetry Institute and has been with the Poetry Foundation since 2004. She holds an MA in cultural and educational leadership and policy studies from Loyola University. Before joining the Poetry Foundation, she served as executive assistant to Stanley Fish at the College of Liberal Arts and Sciences at the University of Illinois at Chicago and coordinated the Field Museum of Natural History's lecture series.